PHYSICS of the SOUL

PHYSICS of the SOUL

THE QUANTUM
BOOK OF
LIVING, DYING,
REINCARNATION,
AND IMMORTALITY

AMIT GOSWAMI, PH.D.

 HAMPTON ROADS
PUBLISHING COMPANY, INC.

Cover design by Bookwrights Design
Cover photo by Corbis Images
Illustrations by Ruth Leahman
For information write:

Hampton Roads Publishing Company, Inc.
1125 Stoney Ridge Road
Charlottesville, VA 22902

434-296-2772
fax: 434-296-5096
e-mail: hrpc@hrpub.com
www.hrpub.com

If you are unable to order this book from your local
bookseller, you may order directly from the publisher.
Call 1-800-766-8009, toll-free.
Library of Congress Catalog Card Number: 2001091199
ISBN 1-57174-332-4
10 9 8 7 6 5 4 3 2 1
Printed on acid-free paper in Canada

To my friend Hugh Harrison,
who was instrumental in beginning
the research that led to this book,

and to my wife, Uma,
without whose wisdom and insights this book
could not have achieved its current fulfillment.

TABLE OF CONTENTS

PREFACE

The difficult problem about the idea of reincarnation is solved. Are you interested?

Philosophers have always stumbled over the reincarnation hypothesis because they cannot see how to answer the critical question: What is it that transmigrates from one incarnate body to another so that these bodies can be said to form a continuity, and how does it happen? The popular answer of a transmigrating soul is not philosophically astute because of the implied dualism: how does the nonmaterial soul interact with the physical body?

The answer given in this book to these questions—one based on quantum physics—is both scientific and philosophically satisfying. Can reincarnation truly be scientific, you may wonder. Yes, as I will demonstrate in this book. With a reincarnational schema in place within our science of ourselves, we can also deal intelligently with the important quest for immortality that excites most humans. Even the phenomenon of UFOs begins to make some scientific sense. You will see.

Conventional science is grounded in the idea that matter is the building block of all things. Life, mind, and consciousness, accordingly, are held to be mere epiphenomena (secondary phenomena) of matter. In such a view, death ends all epiphenomena that somehow manifest in living beings. (Tellingly, however, materialist models have been singularly unsuccessful in developing satisfactory models for the emergence of life, let alone of mind and consciousness, in matter.) The reincarnational question obviously makes no sense in this view.

Yet, half the world's population believes in religions that support reincarnation. More compellingly, very good scientific data in several different areas now seem to support the reincarnational models of these religions. In many cultures, there are books of the dead describing the after-death journey of the soul. Among such books of the dead, a famous one is from the Tibetan culture called the Tibetan Book of the Dead. People brought back from the threshold of death describe their near-death experiences in terms strikingly similar to those in the Tibetan Book of the Dead. There is also much data, and with a lot of corroboration, validating reincarnational-memory recall. The popular, but controversial, phenomenon of channeling has received considerable scientific support. The phenomenon of spirit guides and angels experienced by many people even in this scientific culture has been the subject of both successful books and television shows.

Although conventional scientists dismiss most of this new data as subjective or even fraudulent, in truth, it represents real anomalies for the materialist paradigm because if these things are true then the materialist contention that "there is nothing but matter" is directly falsified. In fact, reincarnation and near-death experiences are not the only anomalous phenomena for materialist science. Its limits are being challenged on a number of fronts. There are problems of "punctuation marks" in biological evolution, which Steven Gould has popularized; there are problems of biological morphogenesis that Rupert Sheldrake has brought to our attention; there are problems of mind-body healing on which such luminaries as Deepak Chopra and Larry Dossey have written extensively. There are anomalies of extrasensory perception, and even of normal perception. Our creativity and spirituality must be regarded as anomalous phenomena for the materialist paradigm. Most notably, anomalies and paradoxes in physics itself, in quantum physics, have been the subject of many recent books.

The new science of reincarnation is an outgrowth of a new paradigm of science within the primacy of consciousness that has been developing for some time. My recent book, *The Self-Aware Universe: How Consciousness Creates the Material*

World, delineates how all the paradoxes and anomalies of quantum physics can be resolved if we base science on the metaphysical assumption that consciousness, not matter, is the ground of all being. In a subsequent book, *The Physicist's View of Nature, Vol. II: The Quantum Revolution*, I have shown how the new paradigm of science (which I call science within consciousness, or idealist science) can be extended to explain not only the anomalies of psychology—normal and paranormal—but also those of biology, cognitive science, and mind-body medicine. This new paradigm also integrates science with spirituality, which is the subject of my book *The Visionary Window: A Quantum Physicist's Guide to Enlightenment*. In the present book, I further explore and extend the new science to incorporate survival after death, reincarnation, and immortality.

In truth, I began research on *Physics of the Soul* almost immediately after *The Self-Aware Universe* was published, and all the wonderful things reported in my subsequent books mentioned above really grew out of this research. This book was almost published in a premature form in 1997, but I am glad, in retrospect, that the deal fell through. Subsequently, what held back the publication of *Physics of the Soul* is the intriguing question of resurrection and immortality. Only after the insight about the physics of immortality came to me was I prepared to publish the book you are holding now. Anyway, I will share with you all the stories leading to my various insights.

Is there a soul that survives death and transmigrates from one body to another? I will show that when quantum ideas are included in our model of consciousness in the context of idealist science, there is a soul-like entity—I call it the *quantum monad*—that mediates reincarnation. If reincarnation is scientific, how should we live and die? I examine the consequences of the new science of reincarnation on our worldview, on how we die and how we live, and how we should view our quest for immortality. Can we ever develop a physics of immortality? Yes, we can, although aspects of such a physics will perhaps take decades, maybe even centuries, to experimentally verify and evolutionarily manifest. And yet, I suggest we may take heart for such a venture from some controversial data that have been with us for many decades—the UFO data.

I have been writing this book since 1994. Many people contributed to the development of this book. The many discussions with my Theosophical friend Hugh Harrison were instrumental, as were those with philosophers Robert Tompkins and Kirsten Larsen. For a while, Hugh, Kirsten, Robert, and I had a discussion group for these issues that helped considerably. Of great value, too, were discussions with such luminaries in the field as Stan Grof, Satwant Pasricha, and Kenneth Ring. More recently, I have benefited from long discussions with the psychiatrist Uma Goswami and the mystic/philosopher Swami Swaroopananda. I thank you all.

I also thank the Infinity Foundation and Rajiv Malhotra, and Barbara Stewart for support during part of the period of writing of this book. Finally, I would like to thank the editorial staff at Hampton Roads for taking good care of all the details of the actual publication.

1.

FROM DEATH TO IMMORTALITY

What is death? This seems easy to answer. Death is when life ends; it is the cessation of life. But do we know what life is? Do we know what its cessation means? Those questions are not so easy to answer, at least not in science.

Most people are little interested in scientific definitions of life and death. In 1993, after my book came out proposing a new scientific paradigm for the nature of reality, a science based on the primacy of consciousness, I was on a call-in radio show. The first question was not on the nature of reality or consciousness. It was, is there life after death? At first, I was surprised; then I realized that this is the ultimate question about reality for many people.

Even children want to know. In a letter to God, a child wrote, "Dear God, what happens when we die? I don't want to do it. I just want to know what it is like."

What happens after death? In the past, this was a question you would take to your local priest or minister or guru or mullah or rabbi or Zen master or shaman. This was not regarded as a question of science at all. Science in those days dealt with mundane aspects of the world; religion was the source of answers to questions that mattered more intimately to people: how to live life, what happens after death, how to know God, and such.

Not that one always got answers. A Zen aspirant went to a Zen master and asked, "What happens after death?" The Zen master replied, "I don't know." The practitioner was surprised.

1

"But you are a master!" he protested. "But I am not a dead master," came the answer.

However, many gurus of various religions were often less hesitant to provide answers. And the answers, for the most part, were simple (at least, those from organized religions). God is the ultimate emperor of the world, which is divided into good and evil. If you belong to the good, you end up after death in Heaven, a very desirable place of peace and joy. If, however, you follow evil, death thrusts you into Hell, engulfing you in fire and brimstone and suffering. The message of religion was "be good." And if being good is not rewarded here on Earth, it will be rewarded after death. Alas! In this sophisticated scientific age, this kind of answer does not satisfy.

So are you going to get sophisticated and satisfying answers in this book? I hope so. The answers are based on a new physics called quantum physics, which when grounded in the philosophy of primacy of consciousness, gives us a visionary window through which flow gale winds of new answers to age-old questions. The questions and answers regarding what happens after death are only the latest of the discoveries of this new science. Read on.

What Survives?

Who are you after death? Clearly, the after-death you could not be a physical or corporeal entity. So the idea of an incorporeal soul is popular. It is your soul that survives the death of your body, you are told. And after death, the soul goes either to Heaven or to Hell, depending on how you fare on judgment day.

The pictures that many people make of what they expect Heaven to be like suggest that even in Heaven they very much expect to have their egos intact, as in Hollywood movies. To them, the ego is the soul. However, objections can be raised against such a belief.

How do we get our ego-identity? Clearly, our experiences as we grow up shape the ego. Memories of these experiences most probably are preserved in the physical brain. Moreover, experiences alone (nurture) are not the whole of ego-development; it seems logical that our genetic endowment (nature) also plays a role. But both genetic and brain memories are physical. With the demise of the body and the consequent decay of these physical memories, can the ego function?

Another argument against the soul as ego has been raised by the psychologist Charles Tart. Tart (1990) points out that the body and the brain are stabilizing influences for our identity. In dreaming, for example, we lose awareness of our physical body, and look what happens. Our identity can shift from one dream-body to another many times during the dream; there just isn't much stability in who we identify with. Similar things happen with sensory deprivation and psychedelic drugs. The normal, stable ego-identity that we experience in our waking awareness disappears in these altered states of consciousness. Tart thinks that this may indicate what the altered state of consciousness that we attain after death is like, unless there are other kinds of stabilization processes that we don't know about.

So the nature of the soul, the nature of what survives at death, is a difficult and controversial question. It gets even more controversial, even more puzzling, when we ponder the continuum pictures—life and death as a continuum—of many cultures. Not only does something survive death, but that something returns in another body in another birth, and on and on the process goes.

Reincarnation

The picture of a soul surviving in either Heaven or Hell after death is more or less the picture in popular Judeo-Christian cultures. Other cultures have it somewhat differently. Sometimes—for example, in Islam—the differences are minor. But sometimes the differences in the view of after-death reality are quite radical. Hindus in India, Buddhists in Tibet and elsewhere (although in Buddhism the concept of soul is very subtle), and many people of Chinese and Japanese ancestry even outside Buddhism believe in the soul and in Heaven

3

and Hell, but for them a sojourn in Heaven or Hell is only the beginning of the journey. Heaven and Hell, in these cultures, are temporary residences, after which the soul must once again return to Earth. How long you stay in your temporary Heaven or Hell depends on your karma, a concept of cause and effect that comprises a ledger of good and evil but with one major difference.

Doing good accrues you good karma, and bad deeds increase bad karma in your karmic ledger—just as in Christianity. Bad karma is unwelcome, of course; for example, many Chinese fear that if their earthly deeds are really bad, they will be born as rats or even as worms in the next life. But even good karma does not stop the wheel from turning. However much good karma you accrue, you cannot stay in heavenly perfection forever; you always come back to earthly imperfection. Thus enters the subtle idea that even good karma is not good enough. Even then you remain tied to the wheel of karma, the cycle of recurring reincarnation. And the karmic wheel is seen as propelling the vehicle of suffering.

What can be better than accruing good karma, doing good in all your earthside actions and experiences? The Hindu and Buddhist idea is that there is an ultimate, perfected way of living, the discovery of which gets you off the wheel of karma. Hindus call this *moksha*, literally meaning liberation; and Buddhists call it *nirvana*, literally translated as extinction of the flame of desire.

We can use philosophy to explain these differences between the Judeo-Christian and Hindu/Buddhist views in what happens after death. In one philosophy, the specific model of after-death reality that a culture develops depends on whether the culture is materially rich or poor. The purpose of religion is to entice people to live in the good rather than in the evil. If the culture is materially poor, people live in hope of enjoying the good life after death. If they knew about reincarnation, they would not hesitate to be bad once in a while and to take the risk of temporary hell. There is always the next life for being good. So the idea of eternal hell is important to keep them in line; they already know hell, they don't want an eternity of it. In affluent societies, on the other hand, the idea of reincarnation can be told.

In affluent societies, people live in a class system in which most people are middle class. If you are middle class, then the worst thing that can happen to you is to become poor. Then the threat of reincarnation works since bad karma not only begets hell, it also begets a lesser life form (a lower class, for example) in the next incarnation. Such was the case with the Hindu caste system in affluent ancient India, where the idea of reincarnation flourished. This is now changing in India; most people are now poor there and the idea of reincarnation is no longer all that popular. On the other hand, today's Western societies with increased affluence have increasingly become class systems. And no wonder the idea of reincarnation is now taking hold in these societies.

It makes sense. In After Death 100, you learn the basic concepts, God, good and evil, soul, heaven and hell. In After Death 300, you get the idea of reincarnation, the wheel of karma. There you ask questions that you couldn't think of in the one-hundred-level course. If there is life after death, why not life before life? Why do bad things happen to good people? And the best one, how can a truly just and benevolent God not give everyone the good life of Heaven?

Compared to these courses, the idea of liberation is a five-hundred-level graduate course. You enter it only after you have indulged in a lot of "karma-cola." You enter it when you ask questions about the very nature of reality and about your connection to it, when you intuit that you, the world, and God are not separate and independent from one another. You enter it when the whole world of sentient beings becomes your family, and you want to serve your family in a new way.

The philosopher Michael Grosso has called the recent revival of interest in reincarnation in America "the spontaneous formation of a myth of reincarnation," but it is more than the formation of a myth. I think we have graduated en masse from After Death 100 to the three-hundred-level course. And some of us already ponder taking the graduate course.

When does the transition to the next-level course take place? The philosopher Alan Watts explained it pretty well. To Watts (1962), the wheel of karma is much like being at a carnival. Initially, as a soul, you are less adventurous. You hold on to the good life when you reincarnate. Only later do you realize that there is a greater learning opportunity in taking the more risky rides—being born as poor (but virtuous) or living a bumpy but creative life. But, even then, the ultimate suffering of boredom catches up with you; the idea of eternal attachment to the karmic wheel will seem dreadful to all of us sooner or later. The filmmaker Woody Allen in *Hannah and Her Sisters* captures this sentiment perfectly:

> . . . Nietzsche with his theory of eternal recurrence. He said that the life we live, we're gonna live over and over again the exact same way as eternity. Great. This means I'll have to sit through the Ice Capades again. It's not worth it
> (Quoted in Fischer 1993).

When we feel this way, then we can turn to the idea of liberation.

Notice that both the Christian idea of eternity in heaven and the Eastern idea of liberation, in essence, refer to a stage that we truly can call immortality of the soul—no more birth, no more death. The former (heaven) is only a somewhat simplified version of how we get there—it omits the intermediate steps.

So don't think that ideas of reincarnation are entirely Eastern, only recently imported to the West. Reincarnation was an accepted part of the Judaism into which Jesus was born. It is held by many scholars that before 553 A.D., Christianity also accepted the idea of reincarnation. In that year, it is said that a decree was passed by the fifth Ecumenical Council against the idea that souls reincarnate, although other scholars think that the council never officially made such a decree. (For a good discussion, see Bache 1991 and MacGregor 1978.)

Many scholars also think that the division about reincarnation in the West is not a division between West and East but a division between the esoteric and exoteric threads of Western religions. Reincarnation is embraced by Sufis, the esoteric branch of Islam. Hasidic Judaism supports reincarnation, as do the gnostic and other mystical traditions in Christianity (Bache 1991; Cranston and Williams 1984).

The idea of reincarnation occurs frequently in Western thought outside of any religious context. Beginning with Pythagoras and Plato, people such as David Hume, Ralph Waldo Emerson, Henry Thoreau, Benjamin Franklin, J. W. von Goethe all believed in reincarnation. Goethe wrote:

The soul of man is like to water;
From Heaven it cometh
To Heaven it riseth
And then returneth to Earth,
Forever alternating
> (From *Song of the Spirits over the Waters,*
> as quoted in Viney 1993).

And Franklin wrote for his own epitaph when he was only twenty-two:

The Body of B. Franklin
Printer,
Like the Cover of an Old Book,
Its Contents Torn Out
And
Stripped of its Lettering and Guilding,
Lies Here
Food for Worms,
But the Work shall not be Lost,
For it Will as He Believed
Appear Once More
In a New and More Elegant Edition
Revised and Corrected
By the Author (Quoted in Cranston and Williams 1984).

7

The Theosophy movement, in which reincarnation is a basic doctrine, rapidly took hold in the West in the nineteenth century because the seed for accepting reincarnation was already there. More recently, public opinion polls indicate that a substantial number of Westerners, perhaps as large as 25 percent, believe in reincarnation (Gallup 1982). The philosopher C. J. Ducass maintained that "the belief in the continuity in life originates [in children] altogether spontaneously." The data we have of reincarnational-memory recall shows that there are now many such cases in the Western world (Stevenson 1974). If reincarnation is not a culture-bound theme, if it is universal, then it is natural to ask if the idea is scientific.

Are Survival and Reincarnation Ideas Scientific?

Does any of this discussion make sense under the scientific scrutiny of our age? Several decades ago the answer would necessarily have been a resounding no, but not anymore. A primary reason is good data. I referred above to the data concerning reincarnational-memory recall. Much of this data, aspects of which have been verified, is about children recalling their past lives. Much more data has been obtained from what is called past-life regressions: people seem to remember past-life incidents under hypnosis, trauma, drugs, or other special techniques. (For a review, see Cranston and Williams 1984.) And much of the recalled memory has been corroborated. In many cases the possibility of fraud has been eliminated.

Most importantly, reincarnational-memory recall is not the only data. Near-death experiences—experiences of people who are brought back from clinical death states—corroborate very well the descriptions of after-death reality, at least some phases of it, found in "books of the dead" of ancient cultures. (For a review of books of the dead, see Grof 1994.) Near-death experiencers describe being out of their bodies, going through a tunnel into another world, seeing long-dead relatives, spiritual beings of light, and so forth.

In the past few decades, science has also begun a timely but unexpected reevaluation of ancient wisdom. Whereas the general trend of science since the seventeenth century has been to evolve toward a material focus, science in the closing decades of the twentieth century began to explore the previously marginalized spiritual arena. In this book I will demonstrate that the aborning new paradigm of science is quite consonant with ideas such as God, soul, heaven, hell, karma, reincarnation—the whole gamut.

Such ideas are extremely subtle when properly formulated and understood. Our conditioned tendency is to think about them in a crude, materialist manner.[1] For example, most people think of heaven as a place patterned after Earth (witness some of Hollywood's movie depictions). Popular religions often portray it that way, and we fall prey to that mode of thinking from childhood. But clearly, the "other world," if it exists, must be radically different from this one.

Modern science has pretty compelling support for a monist world—the idea that there is only one substance that makes up reality. If there were a dual world of soul substance, how could such a world interact with the material one? What can mediate such interaction? Clearly, neither soul substance nor material substance can act as the mediator. Also, would not such interaction involve the exchange of energy between the two worlds? If so, the energy ledger of the material world would show occasional excess or deficit, but the truth is, it doesn't. That the energy of the material world is a constant is a physical law—the law of energy conservation. Therefore, the scientific wisdom, rightly, is to avoid interaction dualism (a legacy of the philosopher René Descartes) in our thinking about reality; dualism and science are like oil and water: they don't gel.

So the old science of the past three centuries taught us that all phenomena are phenomena of things that are made of

---

[1] I use the word "materialist" to denote people who believe in the primacy of matter—that only matter is real; such people are also called material realists.

matter. It is a monism based on the idea that matter is the ground of all being. The new paradigm posits instead a monism based on the primacy of consciousness—that consciousness (variously called Spirit, God, Godhead, Ain Sof, Tao, Brahman, etc., in popular and spiritual traditions), not matter, is the ground of all being; it is a monism based on a consciousness that is unitive and transcendent but one that becomes many in sentient beings such as us. We are that consciousness. All the world of experience, including matter, is the material manifestation of transcendent forms of consciousness.

The allegory of Plato's cave makes the situation clear. Plato imagined human experience to be a shadow show: We are in a cave strapped into chairs so that we always face the wall on which a light from outside projects the shadows of ideal archetypal forms. We take the shadows as reality, but their source is behind us in the archetypes. And ultimately, light is the only reality, for light is all we see. In monism based on the primacy of consciousness, consciousness is the light in Plato's cave, the archetypes make up the transcendent reality, and the shadow show is the immanent reality.

Such a monistic view of reality, which I call monistic idealism, is very old and constitutes the basis of all the world's great spiritual traditions, which is why it is sometimes called the perennial philosophy. In esoteric Christianity, the ground of being is called the Godhead, the transcendent archetypal world is heaven, and the world of experience is Earth. In the past, the scientific acceptance of this view was limited because idealists could not explain concepts such as transcendence and self-reference (how the one divides into a subject/self that can refer to itself and object(s) that are separate from itself) in scientifically accessible terms. The new paradigm of a science within consciousness, sometimes called idealist science, began when these concepts gained scientific credibility. This has been the subject of several recent books, including my own (Goswami 1993; Herbert 1993).

This is genuine progress. Materialism is pure metaphysics; there is no way to verify objectively that everything, including mind and consciousness, arises from matter. The perennial philosophy of old was what we may call experiential metaphysics because great spiritual teachers from all traditions have always claimed to have directly seen that being is grounded in a limitless, transcendent, and unitive consciousness. In contrast, monistic idealism—perennial philosophy in the new context of the science within consciousness—is not only experiential but also experimental metaphysics since, at least in part, its metaphysical ideas are verifiable not only by private individual experiences but also by experiments in the public arena.[2]

If you grew up in the West's still very materialist culture, your worldview very likely is a strange and confused amalgam of materialism (the supremacy of matter) and Cartesian interaction dualism (the spirit world exists as a separate and independent world made of a nonmaterial substance that somehow interacts with the material world). Not so long ago, people tried to prove the existence of soul by attempting (unconvincingly) to show that a body loses weight upon death in violation of the principle of conservation of energy.

Even avowed monistic idealists often fall prey to dualistic soul-talk a la Descartes when discussing death and reincarnation. They talk of establishing the validity of ghosts, apparitions, as objects of the same shared physical reality as a chair or a tree. I see a chair because it reflects light to my eyes. Can a ghost, if it is an other-worldly nonmaterial being, emit a signal or reflect light for my senses to pick up? Obviously not. A most important challenge to our science within consciousness is to recast the discussion of the phenomena related to death and reincarnation from the monistic perspective. This is the challenge I take up in this book. If dualist concepts have to be used, we must find explanations that do not violate the laws of science; we must reconcile these concepts within an overall monistic view. This is what I have been able to accomplish.

---

[2]The phrase "experimental metaphysics" was coined by the philosopher Abner Shimony.

The Soul and the Quantum

What survives? Does what survives reincarnate in some way that we may call a true continuum—birth-death-rebirth, on and on? During an intense period of research that lasted about a year, I found my answer. There is a "soul" that survives the death of the physical body, and it does reincarnate in another body to form a continuum. Yes, such soul-talk makes sense in a science based on consciousness, but only when we think of the soul in terms of the "quantum."

The situation is similar to what happened toward the end of the nineteenth century. Physicists found that thinking of matter and light in the old Newtonian way—namely, matter is always localized, traveling in well-defined trajectories, and light is always wavelike, dispersed, capable of being at more than one place at the same time—gave them anomalies and paradoxes. They discovered a new way of thinking—the quantum way.

The word quantum means "a discrete quantity." For example, a quantum of light, called a photon, is a discrete, indivisible amount of energy, a localized energy bundle. Recognizing that light has a localized particle nature in addition to its more familiar wave nature and that matter has a wave nature in addition to its more familiar localized particle nature eliminated the anomalies and paradoxes referred to above.

Thus, the significance of the word quantum goes well beyond discreteness. Quantum dynamics gives unexpected, almost magical, potency to objects of the submicroscopic domain.

- What does it mean to say that matter is wave-like and thereby it can be at more than one place at once? If this sounds paradoxical, the paradox is resolved by realizing that the waves of matter are waves of possibility (technically represented by mathematical functions called wave functions); they are at two (or more) places at once only in possibility, only as the superposition of the two (or more) possibilities.

- Quantum objects exist as a superposition of possibilities until our observation brings about actuality from potentiality, one actual, localized event from the many potential events. If a particular possibility has a great probability to actualize, upon observation, there the possibility wave is correspondingly strong; where the wave is weak, the probability is small for its corresponding possibility to actualize.

  An example will clarify the situation. Suppose we release an electron in a room. In a matter of moments, the electron wave spreads all over the room. And now suppose we set up a grid of electron detectors, called Geiger counters, in the room. Do all the counters go ticking? No. Only one of the Geiger counters ticks. Conclusion? Before observation, the electron does spread all over space, but only as a wave of possibility. And observation brings about the collapse of the possibility wave into an actual event.

- Quantum mechanics is a probability calculus that enables us to calculate the probability of each possibility that is allowed in every dynamical situation. Probability begets uncertainty. We no longer can know an object's whereabouts with certainty. The movement of quantum objects is always shrouded with some uncertainty.

- Before quantum physics was properly understood, a materialist metaphysics prevailed in science—elementary particles make atoms, atoms make molecules, molecules make cells including neurons, neurons make the brain, and brain makes consciousness. This theory of causation is called the theory of upward causation: cause moves up from the micro elementary particles all the way to the macro brain and consciousness. There is no causal power in any entity of the world but in the interactions between elementary particles.

  But if we ourselves are nothing but material possibilities, how can our observation collapse waves of possibility? The interaction of possibility with possibility only begets more complex possibility, never actuality. So if there were only upward causation in the world, quantum collapse would be a paradox. In the correct paradox-free interpretation of quantum physics, upward causation is only capable of producing material waves of possibility for (nonmaterial) consciousness to choose from, and consciousness has the ultimate power, called downward causation, to create manifest reality by freely choosing among the possibilities offered. Consciousness no longer is seen as brain epiphenomenon but as the ground of being, in which all material possibilities, including the brain, are embedded.

- Quantum objects can take a discontinuous leap—now it's here, and then it's there; such a leap is called a quantum leap. An atom emits light when an electron takes a quantum leap from a higher energy atomic state to a lower one. You can appreciate the radicalness of this quantum leap when you visualize it as the electron jumping from a higher orbit around the atomic nucleus to a lower one without traveling through the space between the orbits.

  In the same vein, downward causation is discontinuous in every which way: causally (we cannot assign a precise cause for it), mechanically (we cannot make a mechanical model for it), algorithmically (there is no mathematics for it), and logically (its logic is circular: the observer is essential for collapse to occur, but the observer is only possibility before collapse has taken place).[3]

- Quantum objects, when suitably correlated, are experimentally found to influence one another nonlocally, that is, without signals through space and without taking a finite time. Thus, correlated quantum objects must be interconnected in

---

[3]If you have trouble visualizing a wave in the brain, albeit a wave of possibility, "because waves travel," realize that waves in a confined space are standing waves; they "wave" while standing at the same place, as in a musical instrument.

a domain that transcends space and time. Nonlocality implies transcendence. It follows that all quantum waves of possibility reside in a domain that transcends space and time; we will call it the domain of transcendent potentia (meaning potentiality), to use Aristotle's term adapted by Werner Heisenberg.

And don't think that possibility is less real than actuality; it may be the other way around. What is potential may be more real than what is manifest because potentia exists in a timeless domain whereas any actuality is merely ephemeral: it exists in time. This is the way Easterners think, how mystics all over the world think, and how physicists who heed the message of quantum physics think.

Does the quantum "magic"—being in two places at once, downward causation, quantum leaps, and nonlocal connections—which is so potent and clear in the submicroscopic realm, extend to the macroworld of our experience? The breakthrough idea of recent times is that our brain involves quantum processing in every case of observation which is a quantum measurement. The brain responds to a stimulus by presenting a pool of macroscopically distinguishable quantum possibilities (a possibility wave), one of which precipitates as the experienced event when consciousness so chooses.[4]

You may already see part of the right metaphor here for the quantum physics of the soul. While the physical body, when alive, represents possibilities which always must manifest as a localized structure that has a finite beginning and a finite end, the soul represents possibilities, potentia without localized structure in manifestation. As transcendent potentia without the fixation of local manifestation in time and space, it

---

[4]The quantum in the brain has been investigated by many authors, among them, Walker (1970); Bass (1975); Stuart, Takahashy, and Umezawa (1978); Stapp (1982, 1993); Wolf (1984); Goswami (1989, 1990, 1993); Herbert (1993); Eccles (1994).

transmigrates (that is, is nonlocally experienced) from one incarnation in one locality and time to another in a different point of space and time.

The concept of soul sheds its Cartesian, dualist paradoxes when we imbue it with quantum dynamics and downward causation, as you will see; and quantum dynamics also gives it an unexpected potency that enables us to see validity in esoteric teachings and to explain anomalous data. There is, of course, the important question of how the soul looked upon as structureless quantum possibilities remembers each of its individualized incarnate life experiences cumulatively, but not to worry. This is the question I have been able to solve and the answer constitutes an important part of this book.

In the Bhagavad Gita, Krishna says to Arjuna, "Both you and I have been reincarnated many times before. I remember, you don't." In India, the wise say that liberation brings back the memory of past incarnations and banishes the fear of death. But this way of dealing with the fear of death is arduous, available to only a few people in a given era.

My vision is that a science of reincarnation, firmly in place and grounded in ideas of a transmigrating soul within a new quantum dynamics that is convincing and satisfying (you will see!), will lessen our fear of death. Death will then be accepted as part of life, and we won't frantically try to deny it. The discovery of deep meaning in the phenomenon of death will also bring meaningfulness in our exploration of life. As we are able to live fully, we will see death as a frame for a creative opportunity, a necessary step to a renewal of life.

Creativity in the Life-Death-Rebirth Cycle

What happens after death? The Chinese philosopher Confucius said:

You want to know of Death?
Well, I shall save my breath.
When you know Life, why then,
We'll talk of Death again.

Confucius is right about one thing. Until we die, we have virtually no chance of empirically verifying what happens after death. Today, people report near-death experiences in situations where they "die" briefly in some sense but are revived by restoring the heartbeat or some such thing. Yet these much-touted experiences are, strictly speaking, not experiences of the after-death state.

But do we have to depend on strict empiricism to build a science? Clearly, any conclusions we reach about survival after death and reincarnation will have to depend largely on theory, on intuition or experiential glimpses, and on our own creativity; the help from empirical data will be, at best, secondary. But it will still be science if we can experimentally verify some of its important hypotheses and if it is useful, if it can be used to lay out a procedure for the art of discovering the nature of death and what happens at death.

Is there an art of dying that can be investigated with a science? It sure seems so. The Tibetan spiritual teacher Sogyal Rinpoche (1993) recalls a childhood anecdote. During a journey, a lama was dying. As was customary, an associate wanted to call the Rinpoche, the spiritual guru of the lama. But the lama said that there was no need, he knew what to do. And with that he closed his eyes and died. The associate did, however, fetch the Rinpoche anyway. The Rinpoche took one look at the "dead" lama and said affectionately, "Old lama, don't stay in that state . . . sometimes obstacles can arise." Then, before the eyes of an amazed Sogyal, the lama came back to life. The Rinpoche then guided the lama through the process of conscious dying.

The well-known Tibetan Book of the Dead is a book precisely designed for the guidance of a dying person.[5] Can we develop a science to understand it? No other than the current Dalai Lama himself wrote, "Death and dying provide a meeting

---

[5]All references to the Tibetan Book of the Dead are for the Evans-Wentz 1960 translation.

point between the Tibetan Buddhist and modern scientific traditions. I believe both have a great deal to contribute to each other on the level of understanding and of practical benefit." I concur. This book is an integration of age-old art and modern science, specifically, of the ideas in the Tibetan Book of the Dead and quantum physics.

The approach to death involves both science and art, but neither is completely objective. The literature and what data we have can give you ideas of where to begin your thinking, but you are the boss here. The real significance of this inquiry is to enable you to discover the truth about death yourself.

If so many people's intuition (and yours, too, perhaps, since you are reading this book) is correct and we do reincarnate, then death is the greatest rite of passage that we ever face. This is why some people go so far as to say that our whole life is a preparation for death. "The answer to human life is not to be found within the limits of [one] human life," said the psychologist Carl Jung. When we comprehend this in our hearts, we see that death is part of an ultimate creative process.

The creative process has four general stages: preparation, incubation, insight, and manifestation. Preparation is reviewing the known and preparing the groundwork for creative insight. Incubation is unconscious processing—processing without awareness. Whereas preparation is striving, unconscious processing is processing without conscious striving, but it is not sleep either. These two stages are intermingled as alternate striving and relaxing—alternate doing and nondoing, if you will. Insight is the dawning of the new idea, the shift of context. It is a quantum leap of thought—a discontinuous transition in thought without going through the intermediate steps (Goswami 1996, 1999). Manifestation is bringing about the transformation demanded by the insight.

Is life a preparation for death? It would be more correct to say that our whole life comprises the first two stages—preparation and incubation—of the creative discovery of the nature of after-death reality. The moment of death holds the possibility of insight about reality as well as manifestation of the insight. Consider the possibility that with this insight, depending on the depth of the insight, I (you) can choose what happens after my (your) death—the manifestation of our insight. And if we miss our insight this time, then more unconscious processing, more preparation, until . . .

So by choosing how we die, we decide individually, case by case, what happens after death. Such a scenario changes our entire orientation toward death, doesn't it?

People say, with some justification, that death is like sleep, that it is a great sleep. I contend that there is also a greater possibility. Some people of advanced spirituality experience sleeplike states called *nirvikalpa samadhi*, in which, although like sleep, there is no subject-object split experience; there is unconscious processing that gives rise to creative insights upon "waking" up. So it is your choice. Do you want to die to enter a great sleep so when you "wake" up in the next incarnation you are virtually the same as before? Or can you die to enter a great *samadhi* so that when you find yourself in the next incarnation, there is a new you—the result of a creative insight?

From Death to Immortality

People often wonder about the meaning of life, especially about the meaning of their own life. In the reincarnational schema, we begin to get a glimpse of the answers to the questions of meaning. These questions are about ourselves, our self-nature, and, generally speaking, about the nature of our consciousness. First we explore these questions in the outer arena; this constitutes our materialist phase. Upon many incarnations, when answers don't come that way, we turn inward. In the beginning, the inward journey is very tentative and much tainted by the habit patterns we acquire from the outer journey. But gradually, understanding begins to dawn. And then suddenly the final understanding, we have no more questions, and we are liberated. Now we are outside the birth-death-rebirth cycle; we are immortal. If the final understanding happens during our life, when we die this time, we won't come back. If the understanding happens at the moment of death, then also we won't come back; it will be our final death.

In one of the *Upanishads* of India, there is a hymn:

Take me from the unreal to the real
Take me from darkness to the light
Take me from death to immortality.

Liberation is the immortality referred to in this hymn. In developing a scientific theory of reincarnation, this is one kind of immortality that we must explore.

But many people, today and in the past, think of immortality in an altogether different vein—immortality in the physical body, acquiring a physical body that never dies. There is also one of the foundational features of Christianity—Jesus' resurrection. How do we interpret resurrection? Obviously, the most straightforward interpretation would be resurrection in a (immortal?) physical body. Can the idea of physical immortality or resurrection after death in an immortal physical body be supported by science? Can this kind of question even be entertained by science?

The answer from this author is, yes, although the reasoning will border on speculation. But imagine the distance we have come in science. Not so long ago, even consciousness was considered the "hard" question of science. But when we do science within the primacy of consciousness, science finds new clarity and power (the power of downward causation), and with this added power, new answers can be sought and found. You will see.

2.

THE TIBETAN BOOK OF
THE DEAD IS CORRECT—
IT'S OUR JOB TO PROVE IT!

Of all the books of the dead, the Tibetan Book of the Dead is remarkable as a picture of human life and death forming a continuum of learning experiences. In this picture, there are passageways which the Tibetans call *bardos* that take one to states of living while others correspond to doorways of states after death; this model looks at life and death as one continuous series of transitions ("death is in life, life is in death"). There was a comic strip in the newspaper, called *B.C.*, in which a palmist, while looking at a client's palm, exclaims, "This is amazing! I have never seen a lifeline that formed a complete circle." To which the client replies, "I'm into reincarnation." He could also have said, "I'm into the Tibetan Book of the Dead."

Before we go into a description of the bardos, a short discussion of Buddhist metaphysics is useful. Actually, the metaphysics is the same as that of monistic idealism, which we have already examined, but different names are used. Thus, consciousness as the ground of being is called *Dharmakaya* in Buddhism. The transcendent realm of archetypes is called *Sambhogakaya*. And finally, the manifest realm of experience is called *Nirmanakaya*.

The first bardo is birth; the second is one's lifetime from childhood through adulthood to the moment before death, which is the third bardo. The fourth bardo begins the journey in death; it is the beginning of a series of opportunities for the soul (the surviving "self") that is departing the body.[6] In the fourth bardo, the clear light of pure consciousness (Dharmakaya) appears. If the soul recognizes the clear light, it becomes free of the karmic wheel and needs no longer reincarnate. The fifth bardo in death parallels the second bardo in life; the soul here encounters first the peaceful gods and next the wrathful gods—the demons or *asuras*—the forms of the archetypal world (Sambhogakaya). The clear light is now seen as dull light, and recognition leads no longer to total freedom from the karmic wheel of *samsara* (the manifest world) but to a nirvanic path leading to liberation in the (nonmaterial) form of Sambhogakaya; failure to recognize the light leads to the sixth bardo, the samsaric path.

The sixth bardo is the bardo of reincarnation; the spirit has missed the opportunities afforded it to identify with pure consciousness or the archetypal transcendent world of Sambhogakaya. All that is left for it is the worldly path of rebirth. Depending on the karma, it is now reborn in one of six *lokas* (places) that include Heaven and Hell as well as Earth, until the karmic debt is paid or credit accrued. After the sixth bardo, the soul must be incarnated in physical form (Nirmanakaya) where only new karma can accrue.

Incidentally, the description of the after-death transition of the last two bardos is very similar in Hinduism, in which the two possibilities in the fifth bardo are referred to as *devayana*, the path to the gods (depicted as a path going up to the sky), and *pitriyana*, the path to the father (depicted as a path that turns like a bow toward the Earth).

---

[6]There is a problem here. The Tibetan Book of the Dead is written in the second person; it is addressed to the person who is dying. Thus, strictly speaking, there is no reference to a soul. However, the context makes it clear that in a third-person translation of the message of the book, the use of the imagery of the soul (for the surviving self) is appropriate.

I have, of course, grown up with these ideas, albeit in the Hindu context, although I encountered the Tibetan Book of the Dead much later in my life. These very picturesque descriptions always provoked a negative reaction in my rational scientific self, even in young adulthood. The very dualistic picture of a soul without a body roaming (where?) various paths of nowhere did not make sense to me. The fact that nobody could verify that there were such experiences if nobody could come back to life from death produced further discomfort.

It is interesting that modern science has a concept called the black hole—the state of a massive star that has collapsed under its own gravity, leaving a singular hole in space—which has a "horizon" beyond which everything can fall in and nothing can escape. Thus, nobody can come back from a black hole to tell us how it is in there, either, and yet it is not true that we cannot know what happens to something inside the horizon. We know because we have a very reliable theory, Einstein's general theory of relativity, to inform us.

I mention this because the power of theory is often underestimated in our culture, but in modern physics theoretical "things" that we cannot directly verify give us dependable predictions upon which successful technologies are built. (You can see this in the case of quantum mechanics; the theoretical idea of transcendent possibility waves in potentia led to the technology of transistors.) We also give these theories credibility because they are discovered through our creativity.

Returning to my prejudice against books of the dead, my uneasiness continued until May of 1994, more than a year after my friend Hugh Harrison came to study the new physics with me. I knew that Hugh and his late wife, Ruth, in the early 1980s, had built an exhibit named the Continuum Center in Bandon, Oregon, which basically promulgated the idea of death and life as a continuous journey. Occasionally, Hugh talked about it and about ideas of reincarnation; he contended that if there is life after death, as in Christianity, then, by symmetry, there must be life before life. Hugh was a sympathizer of the Theosophy movement in the West that Madame Helena

Blavatsky started more than a hundred and twenty-five years ago. Theosophists consider reincarnation among the basic principles of reality (Blavatsky 1968; Judge 1973). Yet I was very noncommittal about those ideas.

In the first week of May 1994, however, something unexpected took place, unexpected and unforgettable. I was swamped with work that consisted mostly of polishing up old ideas for publication, writing rebuttals, etc. Creativity was not active in my life, and life seemed to have lost its rudder once again. This put me in a state of rare heaviness one night. I watched the TV show *Picket Fences*, an episode that focused on some of the ethical problems of death. I went to sleep with a heaviness of heart that I had almost forgotten, but in the morning, in a reverie state of half-dream/half-wakefulness, I felt very light, and the first inkling that the Tibetan Book of the Dead was correct and useful began to form in my dreamy mind's sky. Actually, it was more than an inkling; it was an admonition that I clearly heard: "The Tibetan Book of the Dead is correct; it's your job to prove it." Since it was a Saturday, I was able to stay in a creative haze most of the day, during which time some new ideas about death and reincarnation as a theory of science began to take shape. What provided the light with which to look were the ideas of quantum physics. The fundamental idea that turned me on the most was quantum nonlocality.

Quantum Possibilities and Their Measurement

Objects, according to quantum physics, are possibility waves, technically called wave functions. If you insert a two-slitted screen in the path of the electron, as in the famous double-slit experiment (fig. 2.1), which slit will the electron pass through? Both slits simultaneously. Do you have trouble visualizing this? Relax. This happens pre-actuality, in possibility only. The electron passes simultaneously 50 percent through one slit and 50 percent through the other, but in possibility.

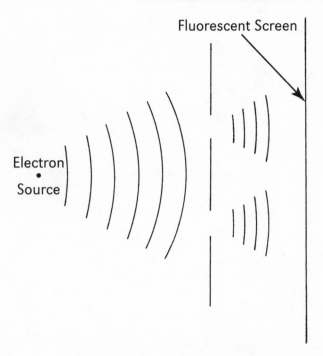

Fig. 2.1. The double-slit experiment.

How do we know this? Because the two possibility waves from the two slits spread and interfere with one another. They add to one another in such a way as to reinforce the wave in some places and to destroy it in between those places (fig. 2.2). In effect, this allows the electrons to arrive at many places beyond the two-slitted screen where they could not have gone had they traveled via a single slit as marbles do. If you shoot marbles through a two-slitted screen, marbles will land only behind the slits. But when a beam of electrons passes through a double-slitted screen before falling on a fluorescent plate, it forms a pattern of light and dark bands (fig. 2.3), not just two blobs behind the two slits. The light bands are the places where the wave is reinforced, that is, where the probability for the electrons to arrive is high. In between the light bands, the probability of arrival is low, and we get no electrons; hence the dark band.

Constructive Interference: Reinforcement

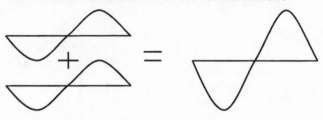

Destructive Interference: Cancellation

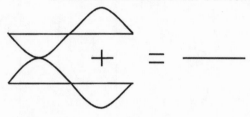

Fig. 2.2. Waves arriving at the fluorescent screen in phase reinforce each other (constructive interference); waves arriving at a point out of phase cancel each other out.

Interference pattern of flashes on screen

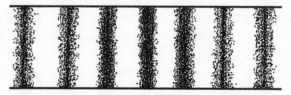

Fig. 2.3. The resulting interference pattern of alternate bright and dark fringes.

But then, if electrons travel as possibility waves, what brings actuality out of the possibilities? Undeniably, whenever we observe, whenever we measure, we see a unique actuality. After all, when we look at the fluorescent plate in the above double-slit experiment, each electron arrives at a single spot, not spread out all over. The succinct answer that has surfaced in recent years is that an observer's looking creates a unique actuality from the sprawling possibility wave—that is, conscious looking manifests the actual event from all the possible ones.[7]

A comedian in Calcutta once went to a sweet shop. He saw some *rasagullas* (balls of milk curd and sugar) in the showcase and wanted some. But when the shopkeeper began to bring out the rasagullas from the showcase, the comedian objected. "I don't want those. Bring me some from your reserves." The shopkeeper was surprised. "But these are from the same fresh batch I made this morning," he protested. "But people have been looking at the ones in the showcase," objected the comedian.

It is debatable whether looking changes things in a showcase, but the effect of looking in the world of quantum physics is undeniable and drastic—it collapses possibility into actuality. Note the special use of the word "collapse." Physicists are attached to this word to denote quantum measurement because of the image of spread-out waves suddenly collapsing to a localized particle, which is the appropriate image when we are measuring electrons (fig. 2.4). Accordingly, we will use this word even when we speak of quantum possibilities in the brain out of which consciousness chooses the actuality that we experience.

Eye of the Observer

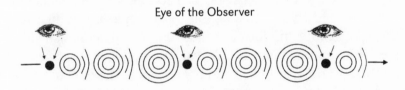

Fig. 2.4. When we look, we collapse the electron's wave to localize at one place. But between our observations, an electron spreads out as a wave of possibility in transcendent potentia.

Note, however, that the waves of possibility do not travel in space and time, because if they did, the waves could not have

---

[7]Strictly speaking, this is a matter of interpretation. However, as shown in Goswami 1993, this is the only paradox-free interpretation.

collapsed instantly to a particle. (In space and time, all things take a finite speed to move. The maximum speed limit was discovered by Einstein; it is the speed of light.) Quantum waves are possibility waves in transcendent potentia, and it takes consciousness to collapse possibility into actuality, which it does by exercising its freedom of choice, the previously mentioned power of downward causation.

Quantum Measurements and the Nature of Consciousness

But this solution of quantum collapse by consciousness, originally suggested by the mathematician John von Neumann (1955), is rejected by many quantum scientists, because they picture consciousness as a dual separate world interacting with this material world in the fashion that Descartes asserted long ago, and that picture is laden with difficult questions. What would mediate the interaction of consciousness with the material world? How would consciousness interact with the material world without violating the law of physics that energy is conserved for the physical world?

In order to make sense of consciousness collapsing quantum possibility into actuality, this Cartesian legacy of dualistic thinking about consciousness must give way to a monistic idealist thinking. In monistic idealist thinking, consciousness is all there is; it is the one ground of all being, the only ultimate reality. Consciousness can collapse material possibilities because it transcends the material universe; it is beyond the jurisdiction of quantum mechanics. All possibilities are within consciousness. When it chooses, it simply recognizes one of the possibilities, and no mediation by a third substance, no dualistic energy exchange is involved.

Study the gestalt picture (fig. 2.5) in which the same lines represent two superimposed pictures, one of a young woman, the other of an old woman. The artist called the picture "My Wife and My Mother-in-Law." When we perceive the young woman (or the old), we are not *doing* anything to the picture. We are just recognizing and choosing among the possibilities that are already present. The process of conscious collapse is like this.

Fig. 2.5. A gestalt picture, "My Wife and My Mother-in-Law," by W. E. Hill. If you are seeing the mother-in-law, in order to see the wife you don't do anything to the picture; all you do is change your perspective of looking. The possibilities of both wife and the mother-in-law are within your consciousness; all you do is recognize one possibility or the other.

Conventionalists also object against consciousness converting the quantum possibilities into certain actuality on the ground that people may choose differently from their individual consciousness. What if two people are simultaneously choosing the same event—what then? If they choose different, contradictory actualities, would that not generate pandemonium? If only one choice prevails, then whose choice? For example, suppose you and I arrive from perpendicular directions at a streetlight operated by a quantum device and we both want a green light. Who gets to go first, whose choice counts? The monistic idealist answer is, there is only one chooser, consciousness is one. You and I have individual thoughts, feelings, dreams, etc., but we don't *have* consciousness, let alone separate ones; we *are* consciousness. And it is the same consciousness for all of us (Goswami 1993). (See also Blood 1993.)[8]

So we choose, but in the nonordinary state of consciousness in which you and I are one, our choices don't conflict. The monistic idealist interpretation of quantum measurement has another important facet (Goswami 1993). Consciousness is the ground of being; we cannot turn it off. So does consciousness choose always whenever an ambiguity arises? But then there would be no double-slit interference pattern because consciousness would already have chosen which slit the electron would pass through before the electron has a chance to interfere with its alter ego.

The answer to this puzzle is to realize that every quantum measurement needs a sentient observer. Note also that when we observe an external object, in response to the stimulus, our brain produces a number of macroscopically distinguishable possibilities; this is the brain's possibility wave. Therefore, in an act of observation, a quantum measurement, consciousness not only collapses the possibility wave of the object, but also the possibility wave of the brain. The quantum measurement in our brains sets up our self-reference—a cognitive distinction between us, subjects, and the field of awareness of objects we experience (fig. 2.6). Think of a rose-patterned carpet which you see as a single object lying on the floor. Now imagine that you see the roses and the background pattern of leaves as separate objects. But this is an appearance; there is only the fabric, and the roses and the leaves have no separate existence apart from the fabric. Similarly, the distinction of self and object, upon quantum measurement, is only appearance.

What makes the brain so special that self-reference, the ability to refer to itself, happens? Consider the circular logic inherent here:

---

[8]The Australian physicist Ludwig Bass (1971) had independently arrived at the same conclusion much earlier.

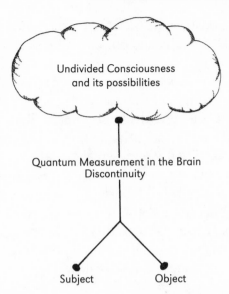

Fig. 2.6. Collapse of the quantum possibility wave in the observer's brain leads to self-reference—a split of consciousness into subject and object(s).

There is no collapse without the brain; but there is no brain, only possibilities, unless there is collapse.

Such circular logic (a familiar example is the chicken or the egg—which comes first?) is called a tangled hierarchy. The quantum measurement in the brain is a tangled hierarchy, and this gives rise to our self-reference—the apparent subject-object split nature of experience. (See chapter 7 for further details.)

There is a price for experience. Experiences produce memories which condition our self-referential system—our brain. The influence of conditioning on quantum measurement is what gives the appearance that our actions arise from an ego/I acting on the basis of its past experiences, its character. But it is an assumed identity that the free-willing consciousness dons in the interest of having a reference point. Our ordinary states of consciousness are clouded by this ego-identity. (More on this in chapter 7.)

So, to summarize, what does it take for us to recognize our power of downward causation? It takes the nonordinary

31

state of consciousness in which we experience our oneness beyond our individuality and our cocreatorship of the subject-object split world.

All this I knew from my previous work (Goswami 1993). I also knew that in spite of the ego-development, all is not lost. Some experiences involve the kind of nonordinary state of consciousness referred to above that helps us penetrate this cloud of conditioning. When we are creative, when we experience ESP, when we love, in those moments we rise above the conditioning, and we act in full knowledge of our oneness and our co-creatorship, as we collapse the available possibilities with full freedom of choice. Perhaps this also happens when we die. In the moments preceding death, we become privy to one consciousness, and through it, nonlocality.

Quantum Nonlocality and How It Applies to the Human Brain: An Example of Experimental Metaphysics

For materialists, there is only the material world, only things moving in time and space; there is no conceptual base for another world. When you think questions like, What happens to me after death? you think dualistically. You think that the surviving part of you, your soul, goes to another world, a dual world. But the logic of the scientist thwarts you. How does the dual world interact with this space-time one? And if it doesn't, there is no sense worrying about it, because you aren't going to know. Quantum physics gives us an alternative—consciousness can mediate the interaction between two disparate bodies. Let me elaborate.

In quantum mechanics, we can correlate objects so that they remain interconnected (phase entangled) even when separated by vast distances (fig. 2.7). When we observe, the correlated quantum objects collapse into actualities, into separateness, but the entangled nature of their collapse shows without doubt that they were correlated. How was the correlation preserved over a long distance, and manifested taking no time, without an exchange of signals? Clearly, the correlation and its collapse are nonlocal, involving a domain of intercon-nectedness that transcends the immanent space-time domain of reality where things are seen as independent and separate.

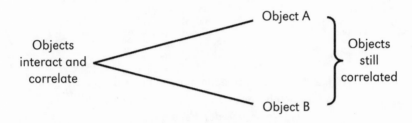

Fig. 2.7. Once two quantum objects are correlated via interaction, the correlation remains even if the objects are separated by vast distances.

Our understanding and acceptance of a transcendent realm of interconnectedness has taken a quantum leap as a result of an experiment in quantum physics conducted in 1982 by a group of French physicists led by Alain Aspect (Aspect, Dalibard, and Roger 1982). This is an experiment in which two correlated photons influence one another at a distance without exchanging signals. It's as if you are dancing in Los Angeles and your partner is dancing in New York but you are both coordinated in the same dance steps without the aid of televi-sion or any other signal processing device.

A little detail will help to clarify further the nonlocality of the quantum measurement process. Recall that in quantum physics, objects are waves of possibilities before we observe them. Thus, a quantum of light (photon) has no attribute until a measurement is done on it. Aspect's experiment concen-trated on a two-valued attribute of the photon called polariza-tion along or perpendicular to some axis (something that a Polaroid sunglass measures; the two-valuedness is clear when you realize that no light photon can pass through two perpendicularly crossed Polaroids, one with axis vertical, the other horizontal; see figure 2.8).

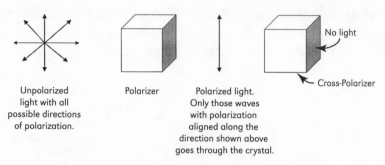

Unpolarized light with all possible directions of polarization.

Polarizer

Polarized light. Only those waves with polarization aligned along the direction shown above goes through the crystal.

No light

Cross-Polarizer

Fig. 2.8. The two-valuedness of light's polarization is revealed by looking at light through crossed Polaroids; you don't see anything.

In Aspect's experiment, an atom emits a pair of photons so correlated that if one is polarized along a certain axis, the other should be polarized along the same axis. But quantum objects are only possibilities, so photons do not start with any set polarization axis; only our observation can fix a polarization axis for them. And if we observe one correlated photon, thereby giving it a designated polarization, the other photon's polarization is also immediately designated, no matter how far it is from the first photon. If the two photons are so far apart that when we measure one that not even light (which travels with the fastest speed in nature) can mediate its influence on the other, we must conclude that the influence is nonlocal, taking place without the intermediary of local signals. This is what Aspect and his collaborators found experimentally.

How are the two photons connected, if not through signals going through space taking time? They are connected through a nonlocal domain of consciousness that transcends space and time. It also follows that consciousness, acting nonlocally, simultaneously collapses the states of two correlated quantum objects.

Translated in terms of people, if two people are correlated and then move to opposite ends of the Earth, if one of them sees a light flash, the other one may see the flash as well even without an actual stimulus (fig. 2.9). Does this sound preposterous? In truth, such nonlocal mutual influence and communication between humans has been known for millennia in the domain of mental thought. It's called telepathy.

Origin of Correlation

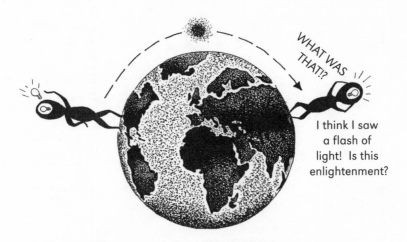

Fig. 2.9. The miracle of nonlocal correlations. Once correlated at some origin, if one subject sees a light flash, the other sees it, too. Is this just a metaphor?

Recently, telepathy has been demonstrated in scientifically controlled experiments. In experiments called distant or remote viewing, one psychic views an object selected arbitrarily by a computer while his partner in the lab draws a picture of the object viewed under the supervision of the experimenter. The picture is then matched by computer with the original object viewed (Jahn 1982).

In another kind of experiment showing nonlocal interconnectedness, a subject is watched from a remote distance via closed circuit television without her knowledge. Even so, her behavior is affected by being watched (Andrews 1990, 1994).

The experiment by the University of Mexico neurophysiologist Jacobo Grinberg-Zylberbaum and his collaborators (1994) supports the idea of nonlocality in human brains even more objectively—this experiment for brains is the equivalent of the objective Aspect experiment for photons. Two subjects are

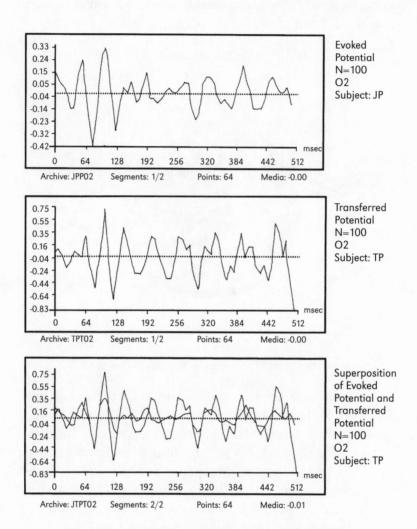

Fig. 2.10. In Grinberg-Zylberbaum's experiment, if two subjects are correlated and one of them is shown a light flash that produces a distinct evoked potential in the EEG attached to his scalp, a transferred potential of comparable strength and phase (70% overlap) appears in the nonstimulated partner's EEG. Note the difference of scale of the ordinate in the two figures.
(Courtesy Jacobo Grinberg-Zylberbaum)

instructed to meditate together for a period of twenty minutes in order to establish a "direct communication"; then they enter separate faraday chambers (metallic enclosures that block all electromagnetic signals) while maintaining their direct communication for the duration of the experiment. One of the subjects is now shown a series of light flashes that produce an evoked potential, a unique electrophysiological response of the brain to a sensory stimulus, which is measured by an EEG machine (fig. 2.10, upper).

Amazingly, in about one in four cases, the unstimulated brain also shows an electrical activity, a "transferred" potential quite similar in shape and strength to the evoked potential (fig. 2.10, middle and bottom). Control subjects who are not correlated and experimental subjects who, by their own reports, do not achieve or maintain direct communication never show any transferred potential (fig. 2.11). The straightforward explanation is quantum nonlocality—the two brains act as a nonlocally correlated quantum system. In response to a stimulus to only one of the correlated brains, consciousness collapses similar states in the two brains, hence the similarity of the brain potentials. Grinberg-Zylberbaum's experimental results and conclusions have now been replicated (for auditory stimuli) in London by the neuropsychiatrist Peter Fenwick (1999).

Admittedly, in these experiments, the correlated unstimulated subject does not actually experience the stimulus experienced by his or her partner; that will probably take another leap in the purity of intention. Nevertheless, that one subject's brain waves can be communicated to another subject without local signal transfer is truly remarkable.

The striking similarity between the correlated brains and the correlated photons is clear, but there is also a striking difference. The similarity is that in both cases the initial correlation is produced by some "interaction." In the case of the photons, the interaction is purely physical. But in the case of the correlated brains, consciousness is involved. For correlated photons, as soon as the possibility wave of one is collapsed by measurement, the objects become uncorrelated. But in the case of correlated

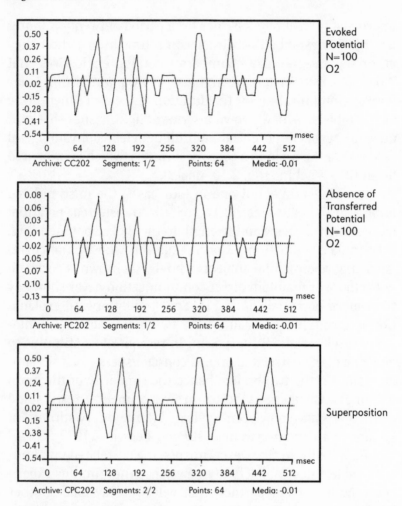

Fig. 2.11. A control subject without correlation, even when there is a distinct evoked potential in the stimulated subject's EEG, shows no transferred potential. Note scale. (Courtesy Jacobo Grinberg-Zylberbaum)

brains, consciousness not only establishes correlation initially, but also maintains the correlation over the duration of the experiment through intentionality.

To get a clear evoked potential, experimenters typically use an averaging procedure over one-hundred or so light flashes in order to eliminate the "noise." But the brains do not become uncorrelated as soon as one observer sees a light flash. The only conclusion is that consciousness reestablishes the correlation every time it is broken. This is why it is crucial that the subjects maintain their meditative intention of direct communication throughout the entire duration of the experiment.

This difference between nonlocally connected correlated photons and correlated brains is highly significant. The nonlocality of correlated photons, although striking in terms of demonstrating the radicalness of quantum physics, cannot be used to transfer information, according to a theorem attributed to physicist Philippe Eberhard. But in the case of the correlated brains, since consciousness is involved in establishing and maintaining the correlation, Eberhard's theorem does not apply, and message transfer is not forbidden. When one subject sees a light flash, consciousness collapses a similar event out of the possibilities in the other subject's brain (fig. 2.12).

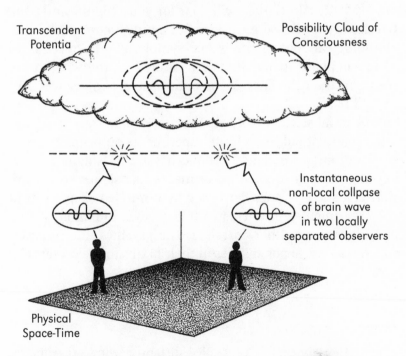

Transcendent Potentia

Possibility Cloud of Consciousness

Instantaneous non-local collpase of brain wave in two locally separated observers

Physical Space-Time

Fig. 2.12. Consciousness mediates the transfer of electric potential from one correlated brain to another.

It was this last realization that led me to think that perhaps one can make a realistic model of reincarnation, and yes, even of the Tibetan Book of the Dead. What is one of the most striking piece of datum in reincarnation studies? A child recalling past-life memory triggered by seeing his or her house (or some such thing) in a previous life. Suppose the memory was caused via the nonlocal transfer of the relevant information from the child's previous incarnation! This is further elaborated in the following two chapters.

One more comment: The conscious intention and the agreement of the two subjects are crucial for the success of any telepathic communication. However, the intention is not an egoic one; simple thinking and willing will not do. Instead, it is a letting go to a state of consciousness beyond ego, where the two are one. Jesus knew about this since he said, "If two of you agree down here on Earth concerning anything you ask for, My Father in Heaven will do it for you." Significantly, the Greek word for the verb "to agree" is *symphonein*, which is the etymological root of the word "symphony." To agree is to vibrate in phase, in quantum correlation. Isn't this what we are seeing in the coherence of the brainwave data of figures 2.10 and 2.11?

Materialist scientists sometimes complain that they more often than not fail to replicate experiments on telepathy, even with well-known psychics. I think they are missing one of the key ingredients in such experiments: conscious intention. Consciousness is one. Perhaps closed-minded skepticism of the experimenter interferes with conscious intention so that consciousness neither correlates the psychics nor collapses (nearly) identical possibilities in their brains in the presence of such hostility.[9]

---

[9]One of the pioneers of controlled distant-viewing experiments, physicist Russell Targ, with whom I have had many discussions on the subject, feels the same way as I do.

The Delayed-Choice Experiment

What is interesting is that quantum nonlocality extends not only over space but also over time. Are you sufficiently intrigued to consider the delayed-choice experiment, which leads to this conclusion (Wheeler 1983)?

A light beam is split into two beams of equal intensity by using a half-silvered mirror M_1; these two beams are then reflected by two regular mirrors A and B to a crossing point P on the right (figure 2.13, where we may or may not put another half-silvered mirror). Originally, the experiment was designed to demonstrate wave-particle complementarity: in

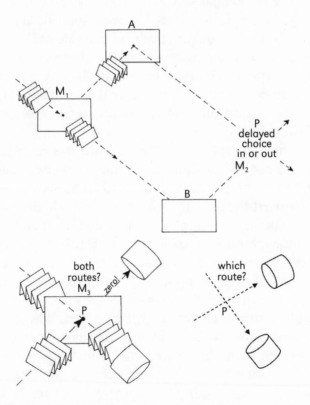

Fig. 2.13. The delayed-choice experiment. The arrangements for seeing the wave nature (interference, the signal is cancelled out at one of the detectors) and the particle nature (no interference, both detectors tick) of light is shown in the lower left and the lower right figures, respectively.

one experimental setting a quantum object shows as wavelike, being two places at the same time (the double-slit arrangement considered earlier is also such an arrangement); in another setting, we detect the particle, localized at one place at a time (as when we detect a radioactive emanation with a Geiger counter). If we choose to detect the particle mode of light, we put detectors or counters past the point of crossing P, as shown in the lower right in figure 2.13. One or the other counter will tick, defining the localized path of the object, to show its particle aspect.

To detect the wave aspect of the object we take advantage of the phenomenon of wave addition, as in the double-slit case, by putting a second half-silvered mirror M_2 at P (fig. 2.13, bottom left). The two waves created by beam splitting at M_1 will be forced by M_2 to add constructively on one side of P, where the counter ticks, and destructively on the other side, where now the counter never ticks. But notice that when we are detecting the wave mode of light, we must agree that each light quantum is traveling by both routes A and B; otherwise, how can there be addition of waves?

But the subtlest aspect of the experiment is yet to come. In the delayed-choice experiment, the experimenter decides at the very last moment, in the very last pico (10^{-12}) second, whether or not to insert the half-silvered mirror at P, whether or not to measure the wave aspect (the decision is manifested by mechanical means, of course). In effect, this means that the light quanta have already traveled past the point of splitting M_1 if you think of them as ordinary Newtonian objects. Even so, inserting the mirror at P always shows the wave aspect and not inserting the mirror shows the particle aspect. Was each quantum of light moving in one path or two? The light quanta seem to respond to even our delayed choice instantly and retroactively. (Incidentally, this shows that the photon itself cannot collapse its own possibility wave, if you have wondered about that, for how else would it respond to our delayed choice?)

A quantum object travels one path or both paths, exactly in harmony with our choice. How is this possible? Because the paths of the objects are only *possible* paths, the objects are only waves of possibilities before we manifest them by observation. No path is laid out in concrete; possibility becomes actuality in what seems a retroactive manner, in what seems to be backward causation.

One aside: There is no manifest quantum object until we *see* it, even if the object is the entire cosmos. There is no manifest cosmos—only possibilities—until the first sentient being (presumably, the first living cell) observes the universe. The observation collapses the universe, along with the entire causal pathway that led to that first sentience, retroactively. And the observation is self-referential—the sentience of the first living cell is co-created along with the universe.

So if we have objects correlated not only across space but also across time, conscious choice and collapse of the causal pathway at any point of time will precipitate the entire pathway. The point to realize is that in quantum physics there is neither space nor time *until* consciousness has chosen to collapse an event. Conventional thinking about time has to accommodate this quantum weirdness.

An incident happening now may be correlated with an incident then (or in the future), which can account for all kinds of events that Carl Jung called examples of synchronicity—acausal but meaningful coincidences (Jung and Pauli 1955). One of my first attempts at understanding reincarnation was through the use of the concept of quantum nonlocality in time (see chapters 3 and 4).

Incidentally, the delayed-choice experiment was verified in the laboratory in the mid-1980s (Hellmuth, Zajonc, and Walther 1986). It even made the pages of *Newsweek* in its June 19, 1995, issue.

Possibility Waves Do Not Collapse until We Observe

However counterintuitive it may seem to you, quantum possibilities do not become actuality until we, sentient beings, look at them and choose—this is the message of the delayed-choice experiment. A recent experiment by parapsychologist Helmut Schimdt has further confirmed this message.

Schmidt has done pioneering research on psychokinesis for many years. In his experiments, psychics try to move a physical object or try to influence a physical outcome via conscious intention as opposed to mental telepathy in which the outcome of influence involves internal thoughts only.

In one series of experiments, psychics try to influence random-number generation, sequences of positive and negative random numbers. Psychics try to bias the random-number generator in favor of positive numbers, for example.

In a typical experiment, the random number generator produces a sequence of one hundred binary events (with outcome 0 or 1) that are displayed as a sequence of 100 red (for a 0-bit) and green (for a 1-bit) light flashes, and the psychic is instructed to mentally enforce more red than green (or vice versa). The sequence of red and green flashes is recorded and printed at the end of the run.

A radioactive sample giving out its decay products, such as electrons, is a very good random-number generator since radioactive decay, being a quantum process, being probabilistic, is entirely random for a large number of events. Yet, Schmidt's subjects have been known to influence random radioactive decay by a small but statistically significant amount, signifying the effectiveness of psychokinesis (Schmidt 1976).

But Schmidt's 1993 experiment is a milestone (subject to replication by other experimenters, of course) because here he has introduced a new element in the experiment. The experiment still uses radioactive random-number generators, except that the radioactive decay, the detection of the product by electronic counters, the recording of the information on floppy disks, the computer generation of random number sequence, are all carried out days, even months, ahead of time without anyone seeing the information at any time. The computer even makes a printout of the scores and, with utmost care that nobody sees them, the printout is sealed and sent to independent observers.

The independent observer, in turn, leaves the seals intact

and randomly specifies whether the psychic subject should go for more red or more green. In the subsequent session, the psychic follows the independent observer's randomly chosen assignment and does his or her intentional influencing of more red (or green) as he or she looks at the data stored in the computer. The independent observer now opens the sealed printout and directly verifies if there is a deviation of the printouts in his/her own chosen direction. And indeed, a statistically significant effect is found—the odds would be 8000 to 1 against such an outcome (Schmidt 1993).

How should we interpret the experiment? The straightforward interpretation is that the radioactive decay, the detection of the product, the computer record and printout, all remained in potentia as possibilities until an observation was made (by the psychic). Because they were only possibilities when the psychic was looking at the data, he/she was able to influence the outcome with his/her intention. Nothing became actuality until conscious observation was made.

If this interpretation is correct, then preinspection of the data should inhibit subsequent effort at psychokinesis. This is indeed found to be the case if the preinspection is thorough (Schmidt 1993).

Schmidt has repeated his measurement several times with different independent observers. Although individual experiments have not always produced an unambiguous conclusion, his experiments show (with the assurance of three standard deviations, which, though not outstanding using standards of physics experiments, are certainly compatible with that achieved in psychological experiments) that psychics are able to influence random radioactive events even when looking at the data on a delayed basis, and, therefore, that possibility waves do not collapse until a sentient observer looks.

Let's go back again to the question of why we don't seem to be cognizant that we are creating our own reality. In truth, we rarely are in the state of consciousness that chooses freely. It happens when we are creative, for example, when we experience deep compassion for another being, when we get moral insights, or when we are in communion with nature. Spiritual traditions call such exalted self-experiences by names like Atman (in Hinduism), the Holy Spirit (in Christianity), and so forth. I call it the quantum self because of its connection with complete freedom of choice in quantum measurement. The self in these experiences is universal, transpersonal, unitive. In contrast, our ordinary experiences are dominated by our egos, very personal and conditioned (hardly any creativity there), in which quantum freedom gives way to almost 100 percent conditioning via many reflections in the mirror of memory of past experiences (Mitchell and Goswami 1992). Indeed, neurophysiologists find that there is a time lag of half a second between a subject's receiving a stimulus and verbally reporting the experience (Libet et al. 1979). The half-second is the time we use for multiple reflection of the stimulus in the mirror of memory. As a result, the primary experience or even secondary experiences with some freedom of choice becomes preconscious when we identify with our memory, our ego.

But whenever we escape the ego-identity, whenever we are able to delve into the preconscious, the possibility of freedom appears. I am convinced that there is a stage in the dying process at which the ego-identity fades substantially. Thus, death affords all of us, if we can remain conscious in dying, the opportunity to see ourselves as the creator of the world—as God.

The Changing View of God

I was talking to a class of high school students about science and ethics in Deary, Idaho, and, naturally, the question of God came up. Now I am quite aware of the fact that you cannot talk about God in the classroom—this is such a taboo that even *The Wall Street Journal* did an article on it. (In my university class on the philosophy of physics, we referred to God as the G-word.) When I asked how many students believed in the existence of God, only a handful of students raised their hands. But when I asked how many believed that there may be an organizing principle, a causally potent creative principle beyond matter, almost all the students raised their hands.

So this is one of the ways our thinking about God is changing. Although the traditional image of God is that of an emperor sitting on a throne in the sky and dishing out reward and punishment for our good and bad deeds, this is now minority thinking since hierarchies have been under attack by the advance of democracy, movements for racial equality, gender equality, and so forth. In general, at least, most of us think of God as the creative principle behind the world, and it is this idea that science within consciousness upholds.

But there are some subtleties. For example, take consciousness. Is consciousness synonymous with God? No, consciousness is the ground of being; it's what is called the Godhead in Christianity and Yahweh (YHWH) in Judaism, and the ineffable, absolute Tao in Taoism. God comes into the picture when consciousness creates the manifest world via quantum measurement. Think of God as the creative principle, the chooser of actuality from quantum possibility in all creative acts of manifestation.

In every creative act that we participate in, we encounter the God within that is us. In this limited sense we are God. But we as individuals cannot fathom the movement of consciousness that is engaged in all creation via all sentient beings. In that sense we are not God. So it boils down to a paradox—we are both God and not God. As a quantum connoisseur, that does not surprise you, does it?

One way to resolve the paradox is to say that in a creative act we become the quantum self, that we recognize our God-potency through the universal, quantum self-identity. The creative and spiritual journeys of humans can be looked upon as, in the philosopher Martin Buber's words, I-thou relationships (I prefer the word "encounter" instead of relationship) immortalized by Michelangelo's mural, on the ceiling of the Sistine Chapel, of Adam and God reaching out to each other.

The materialist deification of matter partly grew out of the reaction to the Old Testament God as the emperor of Heaven. That God indeed is not needed in our science. But God is needed in science as a creative principle not only to resolve the quantum measurement paradox, but also as the explanatory principle for creativity in biological evolution (Goswami 1997), in mind-body healing (Chopra 1989), and so forth. Thus, the new view of God is the way out of both dogmas, religious and scientific.

The Definitions of Life and Death

Does collapse of quantum possibilities occur only in conjunction with the human brain? How about animals with brains, or even without brains? It seems reasonable to postulate that self-referential quantum measurement begins with and defines life in a single living cell. A living cell is autonomous and has self-integrity; it perceives itself as distinct and separate from its environment. It makes sense to say that quantum measurements inside the living cell create the distinction of life from its environment (fig. 2.14). Before quantum measurement, there is only consciousness and its possibilities; afterwards there is separation—life and environment.

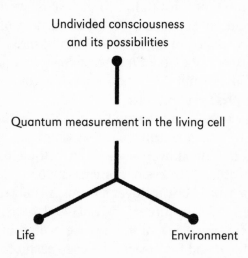

Undivided consciousness
and its possibilities

Quantum measurement in the living cell

Life   Environment

Fig. 2.14. Self-reference arising from quantum measurement in the living cell leads to the living cell's cognitive distinction between life and environment.

This division of one consciousness into two separate beings becomes more and more sophisticated as cells make conglomerates. Eventually, with the development of the brain, we see the world as mental subjects separate from meaningful objects.

A science based on consciousness thus gives us a clear definition of life. Surely, you see the possibility that such a science can resolve some of the recalcitrant problems of materialist models that cannot answer the simple question "what is life?"[10] By defining life, the science within consciousness gives a clear definition of death also; death occurs when consciousness withdraws its self-referential supervention (transcendent intervention) from living matter.

---

[10]With one exception. The biologist Humberto Maturana has defined life as the ability to cognize (as in subject-object split), but this is far from being the consensus among biologists.

3.

NONLOCALITY AND REINCARNATION: A CAVALIER CONVERSATION WITH MY WIFE

When I told my wife that I was thinking about whether a scientific theory of the meaning of death and of ideas such as reincarnation can be built, she was nonenthusiastic. A conversation ensued, nevertheless, and slowly she warmed up.

"Haven't you had enough of theorizing for now?" she teased. She was referring to the fact that I had recently published a book on the nature of reality.

"Not when it's so much fun!" I laughed. "And after all, I'd be in stimulating company. Alan Watts (1962) speculated about the meaning of reincarnation. He said that we choose the scenarios of our lives before we come Earthside. And Carl Sagan (1973) used to say that CETI would fulfill the meaning of life— that's Communication with Extraterrestrial Intelligence, you know."

My wife shook her head in amusement. "You're picking some far-out examples of questions of meaning. Is that a portent of what's coming?"

"That's what makes it fun. Anyhow, here's my idea. Fred Alan Wolf (1984) says that creativity is nonlocal in time. What is a creative idea today is commonplace tomorrow. Doesn't this mean that we borrow ideas from the future in a creative experience?

50

"Nonlocality, you remember, is one of those quantum phenomena that play a central role in our new paradigm of reality. It means communication or influence without exchanging signals through space-time—in other words, it is an out-of-this-world connection."

"Right," my better half interrupted. "I don't find that idea particularly startling."

"But now, brace yourself," I went on, pausing significantly (I never lose a chance to impress her). "Suppose we can borrow also from the past. What would that be?"

"Learning from history. We humans have been trying to do that ever since we could reflect on our experience, although we seem to be slow learners as far as the big lessons like war are concerned."

Her answer was predictable (which pleased me). I said with not a little fanfare, "No, that's not what I mean. Suppose there are patterns of being from which the themes of becoming are borrowed. When we borrow an unfamiliar theme, we say it is creative, but of course the unfamiliar today is familiar tomorrow, so nothing is unfamiliar from a timeless perspective."

I added, now rushing a little, "You see, the themes themselves reside in the nonlocal domain, right? Where there is no time and where the past, present, and future coexist. So, just as we can borrow a theme (it would probably be more appropriate to say that a theme borrows us) ahead of its time in creativity, why shouldn't we be able to borrow themes from the past that are also in the nonlocal domain? The concept of karma—"

"Aha!" exclaimed my wife. "The scientist finally acknowledges the limits of his science and returns to the esoteric cosmology for the meaning of death. Classic! Who needs physics for that? And watch it! Many people know more about esoteric theories of karma and reincarnation than you," she said with not a little scorn.

"Hold it, you're bringing in a classical, competitive framework. Hear me out," I said. "Science likes symmetry, especially time symmetry. If time is nonlinear in the nonlocal domain and things can come to us without signals from the future, then they can also come to us nonlocally from the past."

"I can't find fault with your logic, speculative though it is," she bantered, backing off. "So how does this benefit us?"

Pleased with her attentiveness and the use of "us," I went on. "Let me give you an example I once heard about. A woman had a pain in her neck for which doctors could find no physical cause, and psychiatrists had also given her a clean bill of mental health. Then a past-life therapist hypnotically regressed her to her previous lives. So she was tripping down the memory lane of the centuries when, all of a sudden, she felt a choking pain in her neck and experienced the end of a lifetime in which she died on the gallows. After she came back from the hypnotic trance, the pain in her neck was gone, and it never came back."

My woman was laughing. "What a difference two decades make! Are you forgetting your own experience with past-life regression?"

She was referring to an incident in the mid-1970s that I shared with her. I had left the field of nuclear physics and was groping for a new interest in another area of physics when a self-avowed past-life regression therapist approached me. I was persuaded to do a regression with this person and one of the episodes I recalled was about some great, juicy, sexy escapades from my allegedly twelfth-century past. Unfortunately, I also had the distinct feeling that I was unconsciously concocting the entire scene, that it was a fantasy. This colored my view of the rest of my experience which made psychological sense, so it was useful.

"That was twenty-five years ago," I said. "The data of regression therapy is much better now. Also we have a new worldview and a new science to explore it."

"I know, I know," said my wife, continuing to smile.

"And also, don't forget, the Tibetan Book of the Dead is correct—"

"And it's your job to prove it," my wife finished the sentence, still chuckling. "I'm sorry," she laughed, "but I have this image of you as the lone scientist galloping to the rescue of reincarnation, and I'm your faithful sidekick riding scout at your side."

I grinned. "It's a funny image, all right. But if we remember that reincarnation is an attempt to explain real experiences that people have, we at least have to respect the intent. I have a friend, let's call him Paul, a very intelligent, hardheaded, high-powered professor with all the credentials—a Ph.D., directorship of an institute, and all that. He always shared my opinion that reincarnation is absurd. But then he had a series of "past-life" experiences in which a couple of Buddhist monks, one from the eleventh century and one from the thirteenth, urged him to develop his spiritual life. What's a poor academic to make of such an experience? There are just too many people throughout history who have reported such experiences to discount them all as deluded, and many of them—like my friend—have been respected, feet-on-the-ground types. It's a puzzle that keeps pestering me off and on.

"And then I intuited: what if we cast off some of the peripheral beliefs in souls and the like and recast reincarnational experiences in terms of nonlocal themes from the past that we are sharing today with somebody in the past—like Aspect's photons, only across time? What then?" I was referring to the French physicist Alain Aspect's classic experiment in which he demonstrated that correlated grains of light called photons indeed influence one another across space without exchanging signals.

"What then, indeed?" my sweetheart replied. "I'll play devil's advocate for science. What's your evidence?"

"As a theorist, I don't prove things empirically myself, but I can cite evidence collected by others. Dr. Ian Stevenson of the University of Virginia Medical Center is a serious and respected researcher of reincarnation. Actually, he has some very intriguing data about children who remember their past lives that is very resistant to any explanation other than reincarnation. Then there is data on near-death experiences that also suggest quantum nonlocality."

"I suppose so, but frankly, I'm having a little trouble with this."

"Well, I'm just intuiting, but it makes sense that if creativity is remembering an idea from the nonlocal theme park before its time, then there can also be karma, or causes that haunt us from the past via the same nonlocal theme-sharing."

"Amit, it seems to me that you're digging your own grave. You've worked so hard to refute determinism, and now you seem to be saying that past karma determines our lives. That's worse than hidden-variables determinism. It's not only old wine in a new bottle, but it's rotten wine."

My wife was referring to scientific attempts to explain away quantum nonlocality by postulating that hidden (unknown) variables are "really" responsible for quantum weirdness. The existence of such variables, which would save materialist beliefs, have been ruled out by Aspect's and others' experiments.

"But you're forgetting, sweetheart, I am not necessarily buying the popular interpretation of karma. The stuff of the nonlocal theme park is like H. G. Wells's invisible man. It has no manifest form until we give it form by living it. It's the experiencer who puts clothes on the invisible man."

"So why don't you put some clothes on your friend's experiences as Buddhist monks?"

"OK," I said with relish. "Let's go shopping at the nonlocal theme park clothing store. Say there were two Zen aspirants in the past whose unfinished business in their spiritual work was a theme in the nonlocal theme park; their business was unfinished because they didn't bring about a satisfactory manifestation of the theme."

"Well," my loved one sighed in mock admiration, "you have a fantastic imagination."

Bowing my appreciation, I continued. "Now suppose those guys were having a nonlocally correlated precognitive experience with my friend. Those guys of the past nonlocally influenced Paul's spiritual destiny. When consciousness was collapsing possibilities of the correlated event in those guys of long ago, the experience of my friend in the future was also locked in, except it would be in limbo for a few centuries."

"I don't understand," said my wife, frowning.

"Remember Aspect's experiment?" I asked. When she nodded her affirmative, I continued. "If two photons are correlated and the wave function of one is collapsed, the other's wave function is also collapsed; its possibility becomes a certainty, irrespective of when an experimenter actually observes the second photon's state. See?"

"Okay, I see it now. So when your friend had his experience, he was spontaneously experiencing predestined events."

"Exactly. Of course, my friend's case is unusual. What I think is more common is for dying people nonlocally to share their life story as it flashes by their mind's sky with their subsequent incarnations as they are being born. This is more likely because death and birth are special egoless times. Conscious intentions that produce nonlocal correlations between people are strong then. The psychiatrist Stan Grof has found much evidence for the recall of such reincarnational memories by using techniques that he calls holotropic breathing. How is your strangeness level, Mrs. devil's advocate? Have I crossed your strangeness threshold yet?"

"No, I'm getting into the spirit of the thing. I haven't enjoyed such a tall tale since I sat at my grandfather's knee."

I grinned. "Well, in that case, let me tell you something else. I said earlier that these other guys from Paul's past were influencing Paul's life. But we really can't tell that it was not Paul who initiated the whole mutual influencing."

Now my wife seemed intrigued. I went on. "A philosopher named Brier concocted an interesting story: Suppose somebody conspires to kill a friend of yours by planting a time bomb in his desk drawer while he is at lunch. You happen to walk into your friend's office after the bomber leaves to borrow a pencil; you open the drawer and see the bomb set to go off in one hour, but suddenly you are called away for an emergency. Of course, you intend to call your friend at lunch to warn him about the bomb, and to call the bomb squad. Unfortunately, absorbed in your own predicament, you forget to call until much later. Now, of course, you hope that your friend did not return to his office after lunch and is still alive; but chances are that he did, and he died. Can you do anything?

"If you know about quantum nonlocality and backward causation, then yes! You cry out in your mind the needed warning to your friend and hope that he picked it up—'heard' your warning—in time to save himself from the bomb. But he could pick it up only creatively or precognitively, for which there is a small but finite chance. It's far more likely, of course, that your warning came too late, and your friend was blown to smithereens. So, although it is far more likely that those Zen aspirants of the past centuries initiated the whole series of experiences that Paul had, we cannot rule out that Paul may have been the one who called out to the past, to his past lives."

"Are you saying that the future can change the past? Tell me, my impetuous frontiersman, aren't you making a shambles of Einstein's relativity? Have you no respect?"

"Of course, I have. Einstein is practically the physicist's archetype of God. You probably don't know this, but Einstein had very similar ideas about existence as I am proposing."

"Really? You never cease to amaze me," said the woman I love. I could not tell if she was faking her admiration or not.

"Really. Einstein had an interesting perspective on death. He maintained that past, present, and future all exist, at some level, simultaneously, although time-traveling to the past is forbidden for people of one time frame to another. When his dear friend Michelangelo Besso died, Einstein consoled Besso's wife saying exactly that, 'For we convinced physicists, the distinction between past, present, and future is only an illusion, however persistent.' Perhaps Einstein intuited that people do live on in their respective time frames; I am only giving more scientific savvy to that intuition. People do live on, but in different incarnations that are correlated possibilities across time frames. Comprende?"

"I am trying, I am trying," said my darling wife, with a distinct frown of concentration.

"But remember, my skeptical darling, all past and future correlated incidents in experience are acausal coincidences. The meaning—remember? this is about the meaning of death—is in the mind of the experiencer, the particular individual consciousness that tunes in something from the nonlocal theme park, in that person's specific melodrama. And that person is free to disregard any nonlocal experience, to write it off as a hallucination—or to take it seriously as an opportunity for growth. Children, whose minds are relatively open, do; adults don't often. It doesn't mean any violation for the causal world, where relativity reigns."

"What a suave purveyor of answers you are!"

"No, love, I just have given up being afraid to ask a question, any question. Coming back to meaning. I hope you have begun to see a kind of tangled hierarchy between past, present, and future events. It's not a simple hierarchy where past effects present and present effects future; instead, each effects the other to form an interwoven network of events. Each nonlocal sharing perhaps reinforces the probability of further sharing, and so forth."

Putting her hand to her forehead, my wife suddenly went into a dramatic mock-swoon. "My limit is approaching. My head is spinning. . . ."

"See, ambiguity will do that to you," I persisted, laughingly catching her. "So instead of determinism, what we actually have is quite creative and full of novelty, an opportunity for new order to come from creative chaos. We have such freedom to choose the clothes we put on the invisible man! Glory hallelujah! As far as consciousness is concerned, the universe is constantly creative."

"Is creativity then the epitome of dying?"

"Yes. Within the wheel of karma, outer creativity, our arts and sciences, is the best thing. And when the creativity is inner-directed, inner creativity, we may even escape the wheel of karma. If we die consciously, at the moment of death we may be able to recognize the illusory nature of all experience; even the themes, creativity included, are illusions created by consciousness for play. That recognition is what people call liberation. There is no more identifying with the themes after that; there is no more rebirth."

"I agree with all that; it is your scientific theory that I have difficulty with. Does anybody else support this crazy theory?"

"Well, Seth has said similar things about our past, present, and future influencing one another."

"Who is Seth?"

"A disembodied being, supposedly from another plane, who spoke through the late medium and writer Jane Roberts."[11]

"A disembodied soul!" my sweetheart gasped. "Amit, if this gets out, your scientific colleagues will disembowel you. They'll crucify you for having too much fun!"

"Think nonlocally, woman. Well, you may be right about the reaction of my colleagues. Fortunately, my hard science colleagues don't read popular books, especially one on reincarnation."

"What I want to know is, is it your karma to write all this, or is it a creative choice? What is manifesting right now, nonlocal themes from the future or the past?"

"Why not both? Past, present, and future tangling, mixing, making up the quivering consciousness," I breathed in a suitably husky voice as I leaned toward her, "that wants to change the subject to amour."

"You've got to be kidding," my woman snorted. "I have a headache. That's your karmuppance."

---

[11]For a taste of the Roberts-Seth relationship, read Roberts 1975.

4.

THE NONLOCAL WINDOW: PUTTING THE TIBETAN BOOK OF THE DEAD IN MODERN TERMS

I hope that the last chapter has made you amply curious about quantum nonlocality as an explanatory vehicle for reincarnational data. In this chapter, I will be more formal to build such a vehicle.

The whole world is the various forms and identities of consciousness and their interactions. All phenomena, all things, all events express this play of consciousness. The most obvious plays are the modes of motion of matter and of the mind, our thoughts. If we observe carefully, we can see another movement in play: the modes of motion that underlie manifest life, what Easterners call prana, chi, or ki, what you sometimes feel in your body after a good massage or when you are under the spell of strong emotions, and which you may call vital energy. However, all this exists in consciousness and forms the physical, the mental, and the vital objects for consciousness to experience.

Clearly, there are qualitative differences between the experiences of physical, mental, and vital objects. This is because they arise from different contexts. Consciousness employs an intermediary, an interpretive field to manifest its physical vital idea forms, and mental meaning in its experiences. This field consists of contexts—the laws and principles that guide the movement of physical, vital, and mental objects.

An appreciation of the difference between context, meaning, and content is important here. Lexical meaning is the meaning(s) we assign to words by themselves. In contrast, the subjective meaning of a word changes with context. Take the two sentences "we all die" and "die before you die." The meaning of the first "die" in the second sentence has changed because the context is different.

Content is details, the actual story. The content of two stories can be different, but their meaning, their significance, may be the same. Romance novels are like that; two of them can have different characters, events, and settings, but the meanings they convey are always the same. This is because the context is fixed—looking at love as romance.

What are the contexts that consciousness uses for the operation of nonliving material objects? We already know most of them. They are force, energy, momentum, electrical charge, and so forth; these are contexts that are defined by the mathematical laws of physics (such as quantum mechanics and the law of gravity) and their derivatives. But the contexts for manifestations in life and mind are more subtle, more obscure, partly because research on them has been scanty. Still, these contexts undoubtedly exist.

Plato enumerated some of the contexts of mental manifestations—truth, beauty, love, justice. These can be considered themes of consciousness, an idea introduced in the previous chapter. The relevance of these contexts in the operation of the mind is not hard to see. Our mind evolves in stages of alternating creativity and homeostasis. As children, we have creative bursts as we discover new contexts for living; between bursts we explore the meanings of the various contexts learned. We can readily see, especially in the memories of our childhood, the play of contexts such as beauty and love in how our own creativity expresses itself, in how the exploration of truth and the pursuit of justice imbues our lives.

A common ancient way to depict the contexts of the movements of mind and of life, respectively, is to associate them with gods or goddesses and with devils, or demons or demonesses. All cultures have done this for millennia. There are pantheons of gods in the Egyptian culture, in the Indian, the Greek, Roman, Celtic, and Mayan. Some religions replace gods with the concept of angels, but they serve similar functions. Some cultures, like the Tibetan, depict demons as violent gods.

There are ways other than the Platonic archetypes or gods and demons to look at the contexts of mental processing. One is the Jungian archetypes, such as the hero, trickster, and so on (Jung 1971). The hero's journey begins with a questing in which the hero leaves home. Then the hero, through utmost creativity, finds the answer to his quest and returns to give to society the wisdom of the revelation. Buddha and Moses are prime examples of having lived the context of the hero, but many of us can recognize the same context expressed in substantial parts of our own lives.

The Monad or Sutratman

Each god or demon represents a specific context or theme of consciousness and expresses a specific aspect and attribute that has a correspondence with some movement or movements of mind or life. In contrast, sentient beings manifest many themes. Some idealists (for example, the Theosophists) imagine another type of contextual being called the monad that represents combinations and confluences of themes (Judge 1973).

In developing a scientific theory of reincarnation, my first thought was that the various reincarnations of each human individual are the immanent expressions of the various themes of a transcendent, universal human monad. We have more than one incarnation because there are many themes, and it is impossible to learn and live them fully in one life. Incarnations continue until each of us completes the manifestation of all the themes of the human monad. As Rabbi Simeon ben Yohai explains in *The Zohar*, "The souls [monads] must reenter the absolute substance whence they have emerged. But to accomplish this end they must develop all the perfections, the germ of which is placed in them; and if they have not fulfilled this condition within one life, they must commence another, a third, and so forth."

The monad is akin to the Hindu concept of *sutratman*. The Sanskrit word sutratman literally translates as "thread life," the golden thread of the transcendent contexts on which all the immanent incarnate bodies of each individual human are strung like pearls on a thread.

Interestingly, in Greek and Roman mythology as well, this idea of spinning thread occurs in connection with our life and death. There is a triad of old women spinning; these were the fates. Clotho is the custodian of birth who draws the thread of life from her distaff. Lachesis spins the thread and determines its length. And Atropos, the custodian of death, snips the thread.

Some people worry about the concept of the soul because they note that there are more people now than in earlier times; does this not conflict with some sort of conservation of souls, they ask? But if souls are simply contexts, not things, there isn't any need for such accounting.

Notice that the human individual defined in this fashion has both a finite beginning and a finite end. The finite beginning should not be surprising; we know life itself has a finite beginning. The finite end is also well-known in spiritual literature. It is called liberation.

I was happy with this picture as it first took shape in my mind—no dualistic souls, no accounting of souls. I became convinced that monads, thought of as a locus of human contexts, are the "souls" that reincarnate. Little did I know that this was only part of a much grander story.

Monads As "Souls" That Reincarnate

Many of us intuit that we are not only a body but also a soul. At the peak of our experiences of living, we all are able to feel this soul—for example, when we say "my soul is satisfied." In conventional soul-thinking, this soul is supposed to survive and escape the body when we die. Depending on the karmic situation, the soul then reincarnates in another body.

Now augment this soul-talk with the concept of the monad/sutratman as enunciated in the last section. Suppose that the purpose of your life is to live the contexts or the themes that the human monad represents (the themes are the same for all humans). So when something is soul-satisfying, you are living the context properly, you are fulfilling your destiny. If you are not successful in manifesting and living the themes of your monad fully in one life, you get another chance in another life.

To paraphrase the East Indian philosopher-sage Sri Aurobindo, the fundamental necessity of our embodied life is to seek infinite creativity on a finite basis. But the physical body, the basis, by the very nature of its organization, limits creativity. In order to continue our quest for creativity, the only option we have is to change the physical body as needed. This is the meaning of reincarnation.

Notice that it is not necessary to picture the monad as an entity (the soul) that leaves one dying body and enters another body being born. Instead, we can say that two lives are connected by reincarnation because they reflect a continuity of how the essence, the group of themes which is the monad, is played out. In a sense, it is the monad that lives us, that connects us in our various reincarnations, but the monad is not an entity, it is not a thing made of energy or even information, or any other mode of material being. It is the *context* around which the energy and information of a life are processed by consciousness. In the process of our living, content is generated, but always around these contexts.

There is, however, one problem. How do two different lives, one the reincarnation of the other, connect with each other? What exactly is the nature of the *sutra*, the thread of the sutratman that binds one incarnation of an individual to another? Mind you, one does not necessarily need an explanation here. This could be thought of as part of the movement of consciousness that manifests as synchronicity in creative experiences. But then we would be missing the creative process in death—death as a transformative experience.

Let's look at this from another angle. Most of us feel uncomfortable about reincarnation because we cannot believe in a continuity of our ego content. The ego content is so tied to our body-brain, to the particular incarnate experience, that it makes much more sense that the ego and the memories on which it operates are destroyed when the body dies. So we say that only the essence lives, the monad, after death. But then a paradox arises. Much of the data about reincarnation, much of the good data we have, are about people recalling their past lives, the ego content.

Face it. If only the monads, or the essential contexts, were the entire story of reincarnation, there would be no way we would know about reincarnation (except as an intuition). The truth is, we all live the same basic contexts—that's the wonder of being human—although the particular incarnate confluence of contexts differs from life to life and from individual to individual. The concept of monad makes sense, but in no way can I say that I recall the ego content of a past life from my monad; the monad as defined here cannot make records of incarnate lives because it is changeless.

It seems like a paradox. Listen to the philosopher Ken Wilber struggle with it:

> It is the soul [monad], not the mind, that transmigrates. Hence, the fact that reincarnation cannot be proven by appeal to memories of past lives is exactly what we should expect: Specific memories, ideas, knowledge, and so on belong to the mind and do not transmigrate. All of that is left behind, with the body, at death. Perhaps a few specific memories can sneak through every now and then, as in the cases recorded by Professor Ian Stevenson and others, but these would be the exception rather than the rule. What transmigrates is the soul, and the soul is not a set of memories, ideas, or beliefs (Wilber 1990).

Wilber's difficulty is clear. It is the soul [monad] that transmigrates—I agree with Wilber there. Yet Ian Stevenson's data is about the recall of past mental lives, contents. If we are philosophically astute, we must agree that Stevenson's data (see chapter 5) does not prove reincarnation. And yet it is good data; Stevenson has earned our respect. So Wilber equivocates by allowing that a few mental experiences can "sneak through" and transmigrate along with the monad every now and then. Sorry, Ken, that does not make sense. Actually, even the concept of transmigration of the monad does not seem necessary.

So let's take an intellectual risk and see if we can make sense of an Eastern model of reincarnation that admittedly looks dualistic in its original form (with use of pictures that can be interpreted as the transmigration of the soul), the model known as *Bardo Thödol* translated as the Tibetan Book of the Dead.

Putting the Tibetan Book of the Dead in Modern Terms

There were two ideas that first helped me reconcile the Tibetan Book of the Dead with my scientific skepticism. The first was the idea of the monad/sutratman—the transcendent locus of the contexts threading through our various incarnations. The second was quantum nonlocality. I assumed that the Tibetan description of the bardos—at least the way it was translated into English by Evans-Wentz (1960)—in death is misleading because it ascribed concepts of the material world to the soul world—the soul as a dualistic body very similar to the material body moving in spatial paths, taking physical time, and all that. Instead, we have to reframe the experiences of the bardos of death as nonlocal experiences in the nonordinary state of consciousness at the moment of death. (It is good to know that the Tibetan word bardo means "transition," not place.)

The moment of death offers us the opportunity for a creative experience of insight, but whether we have such an experience or what insight we may have depends on our preparedness. If we are ready, the insight would be that of the fourth bardo experience, an opening to the clear light, an insight that "my real identity is with the whole; I am that." With this insight, naturally, I become free, my karmic burden is burned away. And this moment can be eternal because it is outside of time.

If I am not ready for this creative recognition of liberation of the fourth bardo, then I still have the opportunity for insight. I may recognize my identity with the peaceful or the wrathful gods, an identity that frees me from any immediate reidentification with another physical incarnation. This insight may lead me to what is popularly called heaven, but it is not an eternal abode, by any means. I am not totally free yet.

Eventually, I may intuit my particular situation with respect to the human monad—the contexts that I have lived and those I was supposed to have lived—and synchronistically, partly in nonlocal time and partly in temporality, I may become aware of how this monad-identity is being reborn in a newly conceived fetus or even share awareness with it in the first few years of his or her life (of course, for the newborn, the correlated experience will remain in potentia for a while yet).

If I am dying in a special state of consciousness, having such an insight, then I am directly aware that the developing child is correlated with me (quantum mechanically) because consciousness is occasionally collapsing the same actuality in the child as in me (see figure 2.12). In that case, I am sharing the child's life, which is a glimpse of my future reincarnation. Likewise, the child may share the memories of my life (in potentia, to be actualized later) as and when they flash in my mind. And of course, in the vast majority of cases, we would expect the child to be so distracted with processes and patterns of the developing ego as to be largely inattentive to the processes that might reveal past life experiences. But even if the child doesn't pay particular attention to these glimpses of its past lives during its ego development, the experience will stay in memory and may be retrieved later (as in skillful past life regression sessions with a trained therapist).

So in the manifest domain where we live, the various reincarnations of a single life appear quite disconnected. But behind the scene, they are connected by the thread of quantum nonlocality and the themes of the sutratman in the domain of transcendent consciousness. Consciousness synchronistically collapses intentionally correlated possibilities into the actual events of individual incarnate lives. The correlation extends to the past as well as to the future; however, we have to remember that the correlated future exists only as possibilities, albeit definite. This is like Aspect's correlated photons. If one experimenter observes a photon, thus collapsing its state, the other correlated photon will immediately acquire this state, although it will stay in potentia, unexperienced until another observer measures it.

And it is not necessary to assume that this nonlocal window connecting ourselves to our various incarnations closes up at times other than birth and death. The nonlocal "window" is open all the time, except that when we identify with our ego, we don't look out it; we cannot. The moment of birth and the moment of death (potentially) are times when we are egoless (or as egoless as we are likely to be), so the opportunity is greatest then that we will perceive our nonlocal connection with our other incarnations. But the open window can be glimpsed in other moments of great intensity, too, such as in a trauma.

The philosopher Michael Grosso (1994) thinks similarly when he urges us to explore the next (after-death) world now. The nonlocal window is open if we are not closed to it by ego. The liberated ones among us do not identify with our egos; thus, it is said that one of the signs of liberation is spontaneously remembering past life experiences.

In the present picture, are life and death a continuous matrix? Yes and no. No, because the actual story lines are different. But yes, because the contexts are continuous, and all the incarnate lives of an individual are connected by nonlocally correlated experiences.

If it bothers you that this nonlocal transfer of information implies an immediate reincarnation, think again. The time frame of a nonlocal experience is very different from that of "real" physical time. You can see this to some extent even in dreams. In a dream, we sometimes cover enormous time territories, although in real time dreams pass pretty fast. See the film *Jacob's Ladder* for a good depiction of this.

So it is quite possible for a dying person to enjoy "years" in heaven (or demonland, which is not necessarily a fire-and-brimstone hell) before reincarnating. The Taoist master Chuang Tsu once dreamed that he was a butterfly. When awake, he wondered, "Was I dreaming of the butterfly, or was the butterfly dreaming of me?" Think about it. I am dying and having a ball as a "soul" roaming through heaven in my non-local dream. From the perspective of the soul, the soul in heaven is the real thing that incarnates as manifest humans between soul experiences.

However, the proof of the pudding is in the eating. If this is the meaning of the Tibetan bardo experience, what is the experimental consequence of such an idea? Simply this: In the formative years, a child who is the continuation of a previous incarnation may be able to recall memories of the past life when suitably stimulated. Tibetans make good use of this situation to find the reincarnates of their Rinpoches and lamas. In chapter 5, we will look at some evidence for this outside the Tibetan tradition—the data collected by Professor Stevenson and others. We will also look at the data of this whole business of survival after death and examine the data from the point of view of the new theory.

Unfortunately, a candid look at the data was humbling to me. Only part of the data fits this simple model, this attempt to eliminate dualistic soul-talk. Some important and well-investigated data stubbornly refuses to fit. A look at the literature told me that in proposing quantum nonlocality as the do-all for the survival and reincarnation question, I was siding with a class of theories called super-psi or super-ESP, according to which any and all evidence of survival of anything personal (such as an individual personal soul—the monad as proposed here is not really personal) can be explained away in terms of extrasensory perception. But several recent books have examined the data and their verdict is against any super-psi theory being the complete story. (See, for example, Becker 1993 and Gould 1983.)

In truth, the theory so far is not even a complete explanation of the Tibetan Book of the Dead. You may have noticed that I went directly from the explanation of the fourth bardo experience to that of the sixth bardo in the above scenario. According to the Tibetans, if I am not ready for total freedom yet, I may have the insight afforded by the fifth bardo: I may see the nirvanic path, achieving liberation in Sambhogakaya form. But what does that mean? Our simple model has no answer. In truth, our simple model cannot even answer the question, How does the monad keep track of what contexts have been learned and what is yet to be learned when it reincarnates?

It took many months, and several creative experiences, big bangs and little bangs, to develop the proper model for the soul, the quantum monad, which has sufficient explanatory power to fill in all the gaps. This will be the subject of chapters 6 and 7.

5.

IS THERE MORE TO THE STORY OF REINCARNATION THAN QUANTUM NONLOCALITY?

Several years ago, and this was before I started researching reincarnation, I was very intrigued when I read about a young man in Sri Lanka who as a child, although he was being brought up as a Christian, recited unusual Buddhist chants. When he was a little older, his parents took him to various Buddhist monasteries and he remembered living in one of them in his past life with his teacher. The child's parents recorded his childhood chants, and experts have said that his pronunciation of Pali (a derivative of Sanskrit used in early Buddhist texts) was quite different from contemporary pronunciation. Even though I did not at the time believe for a moment that we can develop a science of reincarnation, I also had no doubt about the authenticity of the story. It prompted me to read more reincarnation data.

Such stories as above are not that uncommon even in Western culture. Even more common are stories of near-death experiences (NDE). I personally know several people who had such experiences and were deeply affected by them. But many scientists remain deeply skeptical, entrenched in a Newtonian belief system. The physician Raymond Moody, the first researcher to write about NDE, tells a revealing anecdote that I will paraphrase. Once Moody was giving a talk on his work and somebody from the audience, a surgeon, stood up and chastised Moody. "You are citing so many of your revived heart patients having near-death experiences. I, too, have performed many such life-saving operations. No patients of mine have ever reported having any such experience." But then right from behind him, somebody else said, "We didn't tell you because you would not believe our experiences."

This reminds me of a story. A young boy drew a picture. When he showed it to adults, they praised him for drawing a fine picture of a hat. "But it's not a hat," said the young boy. "It's a dwarf elephant swallowed by a boa constrictor." But despite the young boy's protests, the adults could only see a man's top hat.

Recognize the scenario? It is from Antoine de Saint-Exupery's *The Little Prince*. Perhaps this story best represents the inability of many scientists to acknowledge that there is substance in the death, dying, and reincarnation research of the past several decades, enough substance to guide theoretical research. These scientists suffer from what is sometimes called the "I will see it when I believe it" syndrome. Perhaps this book will help establish a different belief system that will bestow credibility to reincarnation, NDE, and the data from other survival research even for skeptical scientists.

But to you, open-minded reader, the data are already sufficiently credible, so I am sure you won't mind if I use the evidence to guide my theoretical endeavor. There are three kinds of evidence (this list is not inclusive, however).

* Experiences in connection with the altered state of consciousness at death. Deathbed visions, near-death experiences, and life-review experiences fall into this category.

* Reincarnation data: evidence of past-life recall, details of which have been verified and have passed scientific scrutiny; past-life recalls under hypnotic regression, under drugs such as LSD, and under other techniques such as holotropic breathing developed by the psychiatrist Stan Grof; past-life readings

of others by people such as Edgar Cayce; people of unusual talent or psychopathology that cannot be explained as due to the conditioning experiences of this life alone.

* Data on discarnate entities: mediumship and channeling fall in this category, plus the data on angels, spirit-guides, automatic writing, etc.

The first kind of data is mostly explained as nonlocal experiences at death, more or less according to the model of the last chapter. The second kind of data fit that model to some extent, but not entirely. The third kind of data does not much fit that model. Prognosis: progress, but quantum nonlocality is not the whole story. Below I review some of the details of the data and the conclusions they lead to. Let me note, however, that my job is not to convince the reader about the authenticity of the data presented; the researchers whose data I discuss are credible scientists who have argued the validity of their cases as well as can be done. The skeptical reader should check the original references for their complete argument.

Deathbed Visions

Let's look at the full range of accumulated scientific data about experiences at death. Anecdotal data, of course, go back millennia, but collection of what today we may call scientific data goes back only to the nineteenth century, roughly coincident with the establishment of the British Society of Psychical Research.

One class of evidence relates to the threshold of death, the dying experience. Suppose a person you love is dying, but unfortunately, you are not with her. And yet, suddenly you see hallucinatory visions pertaining to this dying person. Experiences of such deathbed visions communicated psychically from dying people to relatives or friends are not that uncommon. In fact, this kind of data goes back to 1889, when Henry Sidgwick and his collaborators began a five-year compilation of a "Census of Hallucinations." Sidgwick discovered that a substantial number of reported hallucinations related to people who were dying (within a twelve-hour period) at a distance from the hallucinating subject.

More recent data is even more suggestive. In the study conducted by the psychologists Osis and Haraldsson (1977), the correlated well subject does not experience the hallucinations of a suffering, dying person; instead, the communications more closely represent ordinary ESP with another well person. But if a dying person can communicate the peace and harmony of a well person, must he not be experiencing a nonordinary state of consciousness? In such deathbed visions, the dying subject seems to transcend the dying situation which is, after all, painful and confusing (Nuland 1994). The dying subject seems to experience a joyful realm of consciousness different from the realm of ordinary experience. There is evidence that even Alzheimer's patients may recover lucidity when dying (Kenneth Ring, private communication with author).

Speaking of Alzheimer's patients, the physician-author Rachel Naomi-Remen (1996) tells the story of Tim, a cardiologist, whose father suffered from Alzheimer's when Tim was a teenager. During the last ten years of his life, Tim's father gradually became close to a vegetable state. However, one day, as Tim and his brother were sitting by him, he turned gray and slumped forward in his chair. Tim's brother instructed Tim to call 911. But before Tim could respond, the voice of his father that he had not heard for ten years interrupted, "Don't call 911, son. Tell your mother that I love her. Tell her that I am all right." And he died. Later, autopsy showed that the brain was quite destroyed by the disease. Shakes up our ordinary concepts of dying, doesn't it?

In my view, the deathbed visions corroborate the theoretical model of the last chapter just about perfectly. The joy or peace communicated telepathically in deathbed visions suggests that the death experience is an intense encounter by the dying with nonlocal consciousness and its various archetypes.

In the telepathic communication of a hallucinatory experience, clearly the identity with the painful, dying body is still strong. But subsequently, that identity is released; hence, the joy of quantum-self consciousness beyond the ego-identity is communicated unadulterated.

Near-Death and Life-Review Experiences

More well-known, of course, are near-death experiences in which the subject survives and recalls her own experience. In near-death experiences (NDEs), we find confirmation of some of the religious beliefs of many cultures; the experiencer describes going through a tunnel into another world, often led by a well-known spiritual figure of his tradition or by a dead relative (Moody 1976; Sabom 1982; Ring 1980). The NDE also gives direct support to the idea of the nonlocal window opening around the moment of death.

The psychologist Kenneth Ring (1980) has summarized the various, generally chronological aspects of the near-death experience. (See also Rinpoche 1993.)

1. Most NDEs begin with a feeling of an altered state of consciousness. A feeling of peace pervades the being, no bodily pain or sensations are felt, no fear.

2. Many NDEers find themselves out of their bodies looking over their own bodies which may be undergoing surgery. Some have the experience of passing through a wall. They feel light, and their awareness remains vivid.

3. Now they are at the threshold of another reality; they are aware of darkness. They go through a tunnel.

4. There is light, first at a distance, then it is upon them, a light of great nonglaring intensity, beauty, and love. Some see a being of light. Others see a spiritual figure like Christ. Others see relatives.

5. Many have life-review experiences—their whole lives flash before them as they judge their roles, good or bad.

6. Many people experience heavenly realms of great beauty and a oneness with all things and beings. A few experience hellish realms.

7. Now they are told to go back. Their Earthside experience is not yet completed.

The opening of the nonlocal window in the NDE is striking. NDEers (such as accident victims) see from above their bodies being operated on and often report extraordinary details (Sabom 1982). Clearly, there are no local signals to carry the information. So how else to explain this information transfer than quantum nonlocal viewing in conjunction with somebody else's (for example, the surgeon's) viewing (Goswami 1993). The most recent data is showing that even the blind can "see" in this way; they are not encumbered by the fact that their own vision is inoperative (Ring and Cooper 1995); they must be seeing telepathically (that is, nonlocally) in synchronicity with someone else's viewing.

There is no need to see a contradiction here just because the NDEers usually report seeing their bodies while hovering at the ceiling while the operating surgeon's (or of the assisting nurses') perspective, although one from above, is not exactly the same one. The explanation is similar to that of mental telepathy—while the surgeon looks at the operating table getting the actual information, consciousness collapses a similar actuality from quantum possibilities available in the correlated NDE subject's brain. Thus, minor differences, such as in the viewing perspective, can easily arise.

That near-death experiences are encounters with nonlocal consciousness and its archetypes is borne out by this direct data. A new dimension of NDE research is that when the survivors' later lives are studied, it is found that the NDE often has led to a profound transformation of the way these people live their lives. For example, many of them no longer suffer from the fear of death that looms in the psyche of most of humanity (Ring 1992). And, in general, survivors of NDE are able to live a life dedicated to love and selflessness, suggesting spiritual transformation manifesting from the insight gained in the near-death encounter with the quantum self.

What is the explanation of the specific imagery described by near-death subjects? Near-death patients have a lessening of the body identity—the ego is not busy monitoring the body. This state is much like a dream state, much like what Jungian psychologists call a "big" dream. So as in the big dream, in NDE also, one experiences archetypal images such as Buddha or Christ, but where do the images come from in big dreams or in the NDE? In agreement with neurophysiological models (Hobson 1990), I think that we construct the images out of the Rorschach of random electromagnetic noise always available in the brain. However, this noise is quantum in nature; it represents quantum possibilities and is not classical and deterministic as the neurophysiologists assume. Consciousness collapses suitable patterns into meaningful pictures as it recognizes them.

The key point in the NDE is the lessening, even release, of the ego-identity, which allows the subjects to remember archetypal images that they don't normally recall. The images visualized—spiritual figures, relatives such as parents or siblings—are clearly archetypal.

This way of looking at the near-death experience should also put to rest the debate about whether the experience of light reported in NDE is simply a physiological phenomenon or something deeper and significant. In my way of looking, it is both. What the materialists miss is that the near-death subjects work with what is physiologically available in their brain, but they make new meaning out of it, much as we do in a creative experience when we transform a mundane scene into a new insight. In other words, consciousness, and not the brain, orders the neurological events into a unique, spiritual experience.

Finally, many near-death subjects report life-review experiences during which their entire lives, or at least a significant portion of them, flash before their eyes. (For a review, see Greene and Krippner 1990.) This is crucial for our model to work. As the dying person has a life-review experience, the aborning child of the next incarnation shares the memory recall. And it becomes part of the childhood reincarnational memory of the next incarnation.

A disturbing discordance, however, exists with the super-ESP theory of the last chapter in the fact that the NDE subjects insist that they experience being "out" of their body; they experience being light and having no body feelings such as pain. Clearly their identity must shift away from their physical body during the NDE, but to what? Can it be to a discarnate soul as they seem to claim?

Reincarnational Data

The evidence for reincarnational memory is obtained mainly from children remembering their past lives in details that can be verified. University of Virginia psychiatrist Ian Stevenson has accumulated a database of some 2,000 such claimed-reincarnational memories which have many characteristics that have been verified.[12] In some cases, Stevenson actually accompanied the children to the villages of their remembered past lives. The children had never been to these villages; yet they seemed familiar with the scenery and were able to identify the houses in which they lived. Sometimes the children recognized members of their previous families. In one case, the child remembered where some money was hidden in his previous life, and the money was found in the remembered place.

Not only Stevenson has collected such data. Consider the case, studied by L. Hearn at the end of the nineteenth century, of the Japanese boy named Katsugoro who at age eight claimed to be Tozo, the son of a farmer in another village, in another

---

[12]Apparently, Stevenson is writing a several-volume book presenting this data. At this writing, the books are not out.

life a few years earlier. He also said that his father had died when he was five in his previous life and he himself had died a year later of small pox. He gave many details of his previous birth, for example, the description of his parents and of the house in which they lived. When Katsugoro was taken to the village of his previous life, he was able, unaided, to find the house in which he lived then. All together, sixteen items of his past-life recall checked out (Hearn 1897). (See also Stevenson 1961.)

Swarnalata Mishra, who was born in Shahpur, India, in 1948, is another remarkable case. Swarnalata began having past-life memory recall at age three when, on a trip to a nearby city, she suddenly asked the driver to go down "that road" which led to "my house." In the next several years, she related things and events of her past life as a girl named Biya Pathak, describing her house and family car (an unusual possession for an Indian family at the time). At one point, she met the wife of a professor whom she recognized as an acquaintance from that past life and remembered the wedding they had attended together. The professor's wife confirmed this and many other statements made by Swarnalata of her life as Biya. Swarnalata's case was investigated by a reputable Indian reincarnation researcher, Dr. Hemendranath Banerjee, and also later by Ian Stevenson, and many items from her huge paraphernalia of past-life recall checked out, especially the long list of acquaintances (Stevenson 1974).

Another remarkable corroborated reincarnation story, that of Nicola Wheater, comes from two researchers, Peter and Mary Harrison (1983). Nicola recalled her past life as a young boy named John Henry Benson of a nearby village in Yorkshire, England, during the last part of the nineteenth century (a hundred years before Nicola's time). When she was two, Nicola said things like, "Why am I a girl this time?" and "Why am I not a boy like I was before?" to her parents. Soon the little girl remembered many more things about her past life and expressed them so coherently and with such consistency that her mother felt compelled to take her to the village of her past life. Here Nicola guided her mother to the house where she had lived in the previous century. And to her great amazement, the mother found the local church registry showing the birth of a boy named John Henry Benson.

All of this data generally fits with the theoretical picture of the last chapter. You can find more details in the books and articles cited as well as in many recent books on the subject. Read, for example, Cranston and Williams 1984 and Viney 1993.

So far I have discussed cases in which only one life was recalled because these are the cases that could be corroborated to a large extent. There are, however, many cases of multiple-life recall, even as many as nine in the case of a South African girl.[13] Thus, the idea of a nonlocal window that connects past, present, and future incarnations of a monad and that opens during special moments such as the time of death seems to be vindicated.

If the current model is correct that reincarnational memory is formed at a very early age via nonlocal communication from the dying self of the previous life, there is one way to verify this. If adults can be induced to regress to childhood, they may be able to remember past-life experiences better. Indeed, Banerjee has a few cases in which he was able to obtain many more details from his reincarnation recallers under hypnosis.

The psychiatrist Stan Grof has elicited past-life recall in many subjects under LSD and with a new technique—holotropic breathing—all of which have given much good data about reincarnational-memory recall that basically confirms the model of the last chapter. This is what Grof says about his cases of reincarnational-memory recall:

---

[13]I read about this case in a book in the Bengali language, *Janmantarbad* (Theory of Reincarnation), on the research of H. Banerjee.

> They [the reincarnational memories] feel extremely real and authentic and often mediate access to accurate information about historical periods, cultures, and even historical events that the individual could not have acquired through the ordinary channels. In some instances, the accuracy of these memories can be objectively verified, sometimes in amazing detail. . . . The criteria for verification are the same as those for determining what happened last year: identify specific memories and secure independent evidence for at least some of them. . . . I have myself observed and published several remarkable cases, where most unusual aspects of such experiences could be verified by independent historical research (Grof 1992).

I leave it up to the reader to read specific cases that Grof found satisfactory.

If you grow up in India, it is not unusual to hear of a child who remembers his past-life experiences. Parents and siblings are quite sympathetic with that. The same is true in Tibet. "It is common for small children who are reincarnations to remember objects and people from their previous lives," says the current Dalai Lama. "Some can even recite scriptures, although they have not yet been taught them." In fact, Tibetans put this to good use in locating reincarnated lamas and rinpoches.

But it is relatively rare in Western culture. The English romantic poet Percy Bysshe Shelley believed in reincarnation. One day, while in a conversation with a friend, he came across a woman carrying a child. Immediately, he became interested. "Will your baby tell us anything about preexistence, madam?" he asked the mother. When the mother answered, "He cannot speak, sir," Shelley cried with an air of deep disappointment, "But surely the babe can speak if he will. . . . He may fancy perhaps that he cannot, but it is only a silly whim. He cannot have forgotten entirely the use of speech in so short a time."

But some babies, even in the West, do remember and do speak of preexistence as soon as they are physically able to speak. The following episode would have pleased Shelley. An autistic five-year-old was brought to Helen Wambach, a clinical psychologist. This child, Linda, was severely withdrawn and refused all contact with the therapist until through role-playing she was allowed to repeatedly force-feed her therapist from a baby bottle. Now Linda was able to reveal how much she hated the helplessness of infancy. Contact was now established and rapid progress followed, and soon Linda was like any other five-year-old.

Now what is also interesting in this case is that, as an autistic child, Linda possessed high math and reading skills, skills she lost when she became normal. Wambach says that Linda's autistic behavior was due to the child's holding on to the adult identity of a previous life. When she came to accept her new condition of a child with the help of her therapist, she gave up her adult identity and lost her adult skills (Wambach 1978).

But in Western culture, reincarnational-memory recall is still considered weird (although this is changing somewhat); so children who have it are not encouraged. Wambach reports another case in which a hyperactive child, Peter, was brought to her. After some reassurance, Peter began to confide to her about his former life as a policeman and how he resented not being allowed adult privileges like smoking. Of course, his parents had discouraged and forbidden him from talking about his previous life as a policeman (Wambach 1978).

Not all children who remember a past life become autistic, but repression of such memory is common in this culture. But such suppressed memory can be recalled under hypnosis. Although hypnotic regressions get a bad rap because too many subjects remember being such famous historical people as Cleopatra in their past lives (it is difficult to sort out fantasies from a genuine reincarnational-memory recall), there is good data of hypnotic past-life recall as well. (Read Wambach 1978, 1979; Netherton and Shiffrin 1978; Lucas 1993.)

But There's More: Not Only Memory Is Transmitted but Also Character

The phenomenon of reincarnational memory likely occurs through the open nonlocal window of the individual, but there are subtleties that do not fit. For example, take the above-cited case of Swarnalata. When Swarnalata met with the family of her previous incarnation as Biya, she was found to take on the appropriate character as well. She behaved like the child that she was in her usual surroundings of her current life, but when with the Pathak family, she became Biya in character; she behaved like the older sister to people who were many years her senior. Helen Wambach's subject, the autistic child Linda, retained math and reading skills from her past life. So what brings the conditioning of the past life into this life? The model we have at this point has no answer.

There are still other data that don't fit well either. Stevenson (1987) has correlated phenomena of special talents with reincarnational memory. But special talent is not the result of memories of content that the model of the last chapter can handle; instead, special talent refers to memories of a propensity or learned contexts of thinking. Xenoglossy, the phenomenon in which children (or even an adult occasionally) speak a language that they have not learned in this life, also falls in this category.

I have quoted the Dalai Lama above as saying, "Some [Tibetan children] can even recite scriptures, although they have not yet been taught them." But this ability of reciting scriptures cannot be explained as reincarnational-memory recall by itself. Furthermore, when Tibetans look for the reincarnates of their rinpoches and lamas, they depend more on such transmigrated qualities as the ability to read scriptures than reincarnational-memory recall.

Reincarnation researchers find that subjects of past-life recall often have character traits that cannot be explained from genetic or environmental conditioning. Says the psychologist Satwant Pasricha about her research data:

> The present study revealed certain physical and psychological characteristics in the subjects that were unusual for their families but that corresponded well with those of the identified previous personalities. Except in five

[out of sixty] cases, in which the subjects were biologically related to their claimed previous personalities, the hypothesis of genetic transmission cannot adequately explain such unusual behavior on the part of the subjects. Where the genetic theory has failed to explain the inheritance of physical and psychological traits, the hypothesis of reincarnation may offer an explanation for them (Pasricha 1990).

How is a Mozart able to play piano so well at the age of three or a Ramanujan able to become such an expert at summing infinite mathematical series without any exceptional mathematical training in his background? The usual answer, genetic or environmental conditioning, seems utterly inadequate in such cases. Genes are instructions to make proteins, nothing more. There are no special-talent genes that some people inherit. And the presence of environmental conditioning can be checked in each individual case of a child prodigy. Indeed, there are a substantial number of cases, such as Ramanujan, for whom appropriate environmental conditioning is conspicuously lacking to explain the special talent. These are the cases for talent due to past-life conditioning, no doubt, but our theory needs additional new ideas before it can explain such cases of predisposition from a past life.

Phobias and Regression Therapy

Stevenson has also correlated certain phobias with past lives. Phobias, in psychoanalytic theories, are avoidance conditioning connected with childhood traumatic experiences. But cases exist where no such childhood trauma occurred. In the same vein, there is neither any genetic nor environmental explanation of gender confusion, such as cross-dressing. So a logical explanation is that these are cases of conditioning flowing from a past life into this life (Stevenson 1974, 1987; Guirdham 1978), and never mind that this does not agree with the model of the last chapter. This is just another evidence that my simple model has to be extended.

The important thing to recognize is that if phobias are reminders of past-life traumatic conditioning, regression into a past life should have therapeutic advantage.

There is evidence that reincarnational-memory recall under hypnosis has been used quite successfully for therapeutic purposes. I will quote from the back cover of a bestseller:

> A blind woman cured when she confronts what she wished she had not seen a hundred years ago . . . An anorexic compensating for her prior life of insatiable greed . . . A coward who relives his own murder . . . (Goldberg 1982)

Such books relate how eliciting such reincarnational memory can be therapeutic. My first inclination, like so many hard scientists, was to dismiss this data as a mere therapeutic gimmick with little or no substance, but several things contributed to changing my mind. First and foremost, I myself underwent a past-life regression session back in the 1970s. Although I can see how difficult it is to distinguish between pure fantasy and what came up for me during the session, still two of the episodes remembered made a strong impression on me regarding my psychological tendencies. Second, I myself have discussed the subject with reputed past-life therapists such as Roger Woolger, and the methodology seems utterly credible to me. Third, over the years, I have listened to many past-life regression stories in connection with my travels and/or in connection with my teachings and several of them have stood out. I will give an example from a woman who took a course on "physics of the soul" from me. In her own words:

> My spiritual studies began . . . in what appeared to be an accidental way. I was a member of a traditional church, twenty years old, and recently married. I had no interest in learning about spirituality—feeling perfectly satisfied with life as I was living it. At that point my husband's air force career took us to a new location and I began a new teaching career. . . . Soon thereafter, things began to unravel for me.

The stresses of moving away from family and beginning a new career and a new marriage were compounded by my husband's job sending him away on a two-month training assignment. Something about this experience triggered an extreme reaction within me—one that I had never experienced before and had no way of dealing with. I became extremely anxious and afraid of the experience of being "left behind" by my husband going away on his assignment. I saw other air force wives in similar situations that were coping with this quite differently, so I knew my reaction was out of proportion to the experience. Up until that point in time, I had handled stress very well—working, going to school on a year-round schedule, and moving frequently as a child in a naval family. So when I began to experience severe anxiety which led to actual anxiety attacks, accompanied by depression, I was mystified. My state of mind had been so completely normal to that point in time that I did not even have words for the feelings I was having. . . .

This engaged all my coping mechanisms as I tried desperately to regain my mental and emotional balance. Having always had a spiritual connection through my religion, I turned to our minister for help. There was none available from that source. What I was experiencing was foreign to him. Something inside of me felt betrayed. I had dutifully followed all the church's rules in order to go to Heaven when I died—and yet I was living a veritable hell on Earth right then! I began to search for answers outside of my church, through reading everything that seemed to have answers for me.

During this time of searching, I came across the writing of Edgar Cayce, in which reincarnation was mentioned. This was my first exposure to the concept. It made sense to me, so I searched further. I found the writings of Ruth Montgomery, in particular, a book titled *Here and Hereafter*. That book was a godsend to me at the time. In the book, Ms. Montgomery explains the concept of reincarnation and gives examples of people who had found help and solace through discovering their past lives. And at the end of the book she explains how a person can go into a meditative state and actually begin to recall their own past lives. I began to practice this, and recall came to me quickly and easily. The puzzle began to be solved.

The first recall I had was a lifetime with my husband about one hundred years ago. In that lifetime I was living in Denver, Colorado, during the Gold Rush days. I was a saloon girl whose job was to entertain the men (certainly not a very respectable profession by my standards today!) However, at the time, and due to my circumstances, it was the only way I could support myself. Things were fine for me, until one day a stranger (my husband of today) came to town and into the saloon where I worked. There was an instant recognition between us. (As it turned out, we had spent many lifetimes together before that.)

I immediately felt the connection and wanted to go with him and leave behind my life in the saloon. However, he was a gold miner, living with all his belongings strapped to a single mule. He had no way to support a wife or family. So he left me there. What had been an acceptable life to me before that time now appeared sordid and undesirable. From that point on, in that lifetime, I sank into a state of despair and eventually was murdered in my bed.

The recognition of the similarities instantly clicked within me and I knew why I was feeling so anxious and afraid. While I wouldn't say the healing was instantaneous, it certainly opened up doors of understanding in my consciousness that led to my healing. [I might paraphrase: "Consciousness is the ground of all healing."] Something in me remembered that he had left me before, not actually of his own choosing then either. Something in me remembered that I became despondent. And something in me remembered that I wanted to die so badly that I actually attracted the circumstances for that to happen. I felt like it was happening all over again! Naturally, I was terrified of sleeping alone, for I knew what had happened before. The mystery began to clear up and my peace of mind returned.

At that point in time, I doubt that anything could have convinced me of the validity of reincarnation except a direct experience with it. Consequently, I am very understanding when others don't accept it. It is something that has to be experienced to be really believed. Otherwise it's just an interesting theory. For me, it is not a theory. It's a reality that quite literally saved my life or, at the very least, my sanity (Anonymous, private communication with author).

Surveys collected by serious researchers during regression sessions also support reincarnation. Consider for example the research of Helen Wambach. Wambach has researched 1,088 regression cases and has tabulated the distribution of the recalled past lives as a function of sex, race, and socioeconomic class, and has even correlated the data with the population-growth curve. She found that irrespective of the gender of the regressee, the past lives of her subjects were distributed quite evenly across sex: 50.6 percent male, 49.4 percent female, in almost exact correspondence with the gender distribution in the actual population. The same result was found for the distribution of race, even though Wambach's patients were mostly white. Similarly, the socioeconomic breakdown of the past lives followed historical trends. Among lives of older times that were recalled, only about 10 percent were upper class, the rest poor. But the percentages changed in more modern cases in agreement with the change of our socioeconomic spectrum.

And interestingly, the time distribution of the recalled lives was found to follow the empirical population growth curve. So here is another answer to the population paradox of soul-thinking. How can a fixed number of souls keep up with the population explosion? Wambach's answer: souls take birth at a greater and greater frequency as time progresses. (This research is reported in Viney 1993.)

Edgar Cayce and Looking through the Nonlocal Window

Legend has it that Buddha could see five hundred of not only his own but also others' past lives. This is not historically documented, but there are some historical cases of people, the best known recent example being Edgar Cayce, who are able to read other people's reincarnational past lives (Sugrue 1961). Cayce, under hypnotic sleep, gave about 2500 such past-life readings, sometimes more than once but never contradicting himself. Sometimes his readings involved period aspects of history that could later be checked. One time he read a person's past-life occupation to be a "stool-dipper," but he himself did not know what that entailed. Research showed that indeed such an occupation was part of early Americana; stool-dippers strapped supposed-to-be witches on stools and dipped them into cold water.

How could a person like Cayce look into the nonlocal window of another individual? Cayce's own answer was "Akashic memory," for which an acceptable translation is nonlocal memory, but I think a more tangible explanation exists in terms of the nonlocal window of our model. The point is that, in principle, consciousness is one; thus, any person's nonlocal window that connects all of her incarnations is open to everyone who knows how to look, but this is a very unusual capacity. In India, it is said that such capacity comes naturally with liberation. Clearly, Cayce had it.

We have been speaking of data regarding experiences that involve people in the manifest reality, but there is very controversial data of people—mediums, mostly—who claim to communicate directly with the dead person in the afterworld. Entire scenarios—all extremely dualist—of the afterworld have been built, based, perhaps, on this kind of evidence. I will discuss this evidence and how we may deal with it in more detail in the next couple of chapters, but here is a preview.

Data on Discarnate Entities

By far the most romantic, the most puzzling, the most controversial data regarding after-death survival are those in which a living person (usually a medium in a trance state) claims to speak for a person who has been dead for some time and inhabits a realm beyond time and space. Here seems to be evidence not only of the survival of consciousness after death but of the existence of a dualistic "soul" living without a physical body.

Naturally the evidence is controversial because there seems to be no way to ascertain whether the data is concocted by the medium, especially when cases of fraud are abundant. Even about data for which fraud is not an issue, the researcher Michael Grosso has this to say:

> After studying the best of the case material, however, one is driven to the conclusion that the great mediums were either (1) obtaining information from minds deceased and discarnate, or (2) creating compelling illusions of deceased people by obtaining all the relevant information by paranormal means, often from a variety of sources (minds of living people and written or photographic records) and then instantaneously synthesizing these scattered data and creating convincing personas of known deceased people (Grosso 1994).

But there is somewhat compelling evidence of survival, even in mediumship data, which is obtained via "cross correspondence," in which the deceased communicates an integrated message divided up into several pieces through several different mediums (Saltmarsh 1938). In this case, it is difficult to argue how a particular medium could get the information from a living person by telepathy. Against this data, one can still argue that maybe the mediums concerned were unconsciously creating the appearance of cross correspondence. Or perhaps they were synchronistically tapping into the nonlocal window of the deceased in just the right way; maybe the purity of the intention of the deceased along with that of the psychics was enough to create these synchronous events of intrigue. In any case, clearly, this kind of mediumship data need not be taken as evidence of what they are purported to be—communication with a conscious discarnate soul.

Anyway, this aspect of the mediumship data concerns content of the dead person's history and therefore, at best, proves the medium's ability to tune into the nonlocal window of the dead.

Of more significant importance is the data on channeling. Here again commercialism and fraud abound. Even so, there have been channels and channeled entities that are intriguing because the channelers seem to take on the character of the channeled entity, which is strikingly different from the channeler.

A spectacular example is provided by the case of "Lydia Johnson," a thirty-seven-year-old housewife, a case studied by Ian Stevenson and cited by Sylvia Cranston and Carey Williams (1984). Lydia initially was helping her husband with his experiments on hypnotism. But soon, with help from another hypnotist, she began to channel an entity named Jensen Jacoby, a name she pronounced as "Yensen Yahkobi," who lived in a tiny village of Sweden three centuries ago. As Jensen, Lydia spoke Swedish and recognized seventeenth-century Swedish objects; most tellingly, as Jensen she would forget how to use modern tools such as pliers. The case of the psychologist Jane Roberts and the channeled entity Seth is another outstanding example of the channeling of an entity very different in character from the channeler, and it showed. When channeling, Jane's character changed; she behaved like an intellectual male, for example (Roberts 1975).

I myself have witnessed a channeler in action, JZ Knight, who channels an entity named Ramtha, supposedly an enlightened being. In this case, also, there is a remarkable change in character when JZ channels Ramtha; literally, her behavior becomes that of a dominant male guru, quite different from her ordinary pattern of behavior. This change endures for hours at a time.

I will share with you one of my encounters with JZ while in the process of channeling Ramtha. I have checked with JZ herself and also with her associates and it seems that JZ is not much of a drinker. But on this occasion, JZ as Ramtha was giving a party when I found her guzzling wine, and yet she remained so unaffected that she shared, quite poetically, Ramtha's experiences of migrating from Atlantis to India when the Atlantis civilization was being destroyed. Never mind the content of what she said, but the change of her character was so remarkable that ever since I have never doubted the authenticity of the channeling phenomenon.

In another remarkable case of channeling in Brazil, the channeled being is a German surgeon, Dr. Fritz. Dr. Fritz has been channeled by a series of channelers, all of whom are ordinary people with no surgical skills. But while channeling Dr. Fritz, they successfully and rapidly perform complex surgery without anesthesia or proper hygiene.

Remarkable as these performances are, could such channelers be faking a change in character? The paranormal researchers Gilda Moura and Norman Don have done a study that substantially rules out fraud. Moura and Don wired up a channeler's brain to an EEG machine and found that his brain waves changed uncharacteristically from ordinary low frequency beta (around 30 Hz) to very high frequency beta (over 40 Hz) when he performed surgery. High frequency beta is characteristic of a great amount of concentration. Surgeons exhibit it in their work, but not ordinary people who are faking surgery (Moura and Don 1996).

A similar study has also been carried out on JZ Knight using eight simultaneous psychophysiological indicators. All of the indicators show significant changes between JZ's ordinary performance versus that when she is channeling. It would be impossible to fraudulently pass all eight indicators, conclude the scientists (Wickramsekera et al. 1997).

Angels

Another interesting class of data come from people purportedly communicating with angels and spirit guides. It seems that these entities lend character patterns to the subjects that make the subjects capable of fulfilling tasks that would normally be considered impossible for such subjects. For example, the Christian priest Padre Pio is supposed to have had the help of his guardian angel in translating Greek, a language unknown to the Padre (Parente 1984). (See also Grosso 1992.)

One of the most famous cases of angelic interference saving one's life happened to the best-known magician that ever lived, Harry Houdini. On December 27, 1906, Houdini was performing one of his best and riskiest tricks, jumping handcuffed in ice-covered water through a hole, escaping from the handcuffs, and coming out through the hole. On this particular time, though, something went wrong; when Houdini did not emerge after five minutes—the escapade usually took him no greater than three minutes—reporters declared him dead. Fortunately, Houdini did make it back after eight minutes. And he did not contract hypothermia.

What happened was that currents swept him away this time, disorienting him from using the usual air pockets trapped between the river and the ice sheets and preventing him from doing his trick. He was also contracting hypothermia fast and did not know where to swim and how to return. Suddenly he heard his mother's voice guiding him to swim in the direction the voice was coming from. He also felt sudden and inexplicable warmth. The combination enabled him to get out of the handcuffs and emerge through the hole.

Was his mother communicating to Houdini telepathically? But how would she know where to guide her son? Also that does not explain the inexplicable warmth. A better explanation is angelic lending of an extraordinary sense of direction (the mother's voice was an external projection), and of the unusual power of generating heat (Goldberg 1997).

To summarize, then, there seems to be enough data to warrant the hypothesis of discarnate beings, or souls. First, there are out-of-the-body experiences, in which the subjects claim to have shifted identity to a discarnate body, albeit temporarily. Second, there are unexplained propensities or tendencies; if they are reincarnational, how can propensies be transmitted without transmigration of some element of the ego-being? Third, mediums seem to be able to channel entities whose character they assume temporarily. Fourth, ordinary people often receive guidance from discarnate entities (spirit guides) because they, too, it seems, are able to take on character patterns very different from their ordinary being.

So we come to the quintessential question: Is there an individual soul? Do we have bodies other than the physical that bestows the monad/sutratman of the last chapter with individuality? Is there a discarnate body after death that transmigrates and brings to the next life the propensies acquired in this life? Is it possible that mediums communicate with discarnate bodies in transition? And are there permanent or semi-permanent discarnate bodies, angels and such?

6.

DO WE HAVE MORE THAN ONE BODY?

I assume that the summary of data in the last chapter has convinced you as strongly as it convinced me that there is more to survival and reincarnation data than quantum nonlocality can handle. We need more flesh on the backbone of the theory we have built, subtle though it may be.

Now if you consult the esoteric traditions about what this additional mechanism might be, the answer would be: this mechanism involves subtle bodies with individuality that we possess in addition to the physical body.[14] These individual subtle bodies—a vital body connected with our particular life processes; a mental body connected with our individualized ways of mentation; and a supramental intellect body that contains the learned themes of movement of the mind, the vital, and the physical body—like the physical body, are bodies made of substances, the esoteric traditions declare, but the substances are more subtle, more refined, less quantifiable, and harder to control. You cannot say this thought weighs five ounces but only that this is a "heavy" thought. You can say that this thought was brief but not that it measured one inch. You try to be quiet when you meditate, but uninvited thoughts invade your mind regardless.

---

[14]The Upanishads, the Zohar, and, more recently, the texts of the Theosophists all posit the existence of subtle bodies.

According to these traditions, when we die, we drop only the physical body; our subtle bodies survive. But what are these subtle bodies if not the products of the dualist notion of the individual soul? Are they not just another name for what we normally call the soul? And if we adopt the soul explanation of survival, however sophisticated its garb, aren't we going to fall into the difficulties of Cartesian dualism? That gives rise to troubling questions: What substance(s) mediates the interaction of these subtle bodies with the physical body? How is energy of the physical world conserved in the face of such interactions with these other bodies?

As I pondered the subtle bodies and the difficulties of interaction dualism, I explored the possibility of overcoming these difficulties with the new principles of our science within consciousness. It is not possible to postulate that the subtle bodies directly interact with the physical without digging a grave for the idea, agreed. On the other hand, if they don't interact with the physical, of what significance are they?

Well, there is another way of looking at the situation. Suppose that the subtle bodies neither interact with the physical nor with each other; suppose they run parallel, maintaining a correspondence with the physical. In other words, to every physical state, there is a corresponding supramental, mental, and vital state. Such a philosophy was formulated by the seventeenth-century physicist/philosopher Gottfried Leibniz to rescue mind-body dualism and is called psychophysical parallelism. The extension of the idea to include the supramental intellect and the vital body is straightforward; generalize the notion of the psyche, our internal world, to include the vital, the mental, and the intellect body. But psychophysical parallelism has never been popular because it is hard to see what maintains the correspondence, the smooth parallel movement of the disparate bodies. The question of interaction once again lurks behind the scene, doesn't it?

But wait, don't give up. The principles of our science within consciousness offer a solution. The problem of interaction is a tough one, no doubt, but suppose that the subtle substances of our subtle bodies are not Newtonian-determined "things," but are quantum in nature. In other words, suppose we assume that the states of the vital, mental, and supramental bodies are probabilistic like those of the physical body. Suppose these states are states of quantum possibility within consciousness, not actuality, and consciousness collapses these possibilities into actuality.

Although the vital, mental, and supramental intellect bodies do not directly interact with the physical, that is, they move parallel to it, suppose consciousness recognizes parallel simultaneous states of the physical and of the vital-mental-intellect trio of the subtle body for its experience. From Jacobo Grinberg-Zylberbaum's experiments (see chapter 2), we already know that consciousness can and does synchronistically collapse similar states for nonlocally separated brains that are suitably correlated. And the collapse of a unique state of experience is one of recognition and choice, not one of exchange of energy, so all the problems of dualistic interaction are avoided.

So our science within consciousness allows us to postulate that we have other bodies besides the physical without the pitfalls of dualism. We do not need these bodies to interact with each other or with the physical. Instead, we say that consciousness mediates their interaction and maintains their parallelism. The next question is: What is the rationale for postulating such subtle bodies besides finding an explanation of the survival and reincarnation data? You cannot make arbitrary postulates to explain data; that is not science. Are there other profound reasons to suspect that we have a vital, a mental, and a supramental intellect body in addition to the physical?

Law-Like and Program-Like Behavior

The causal laws of physics are deterministic laws. Given initial conditions on position and velocity and the causal agents (forces) acting on the system, the laws of motion determine the future of all nonliving systems.

For example, suppose we want to know the whereabouts of the planet Jupiter some time in the future. Determine the position and velocity of the planet now. These "initial conditions," plus the algorithms (logical step-by-step rules of instructions) generated by the knowledge of the nature of gravity and Newton's laws of motion, will enable any good computer to calculate the position of the planet for any future time. Even for quantum systems, statistical causal laws can predict the average behavior and evolution as long as we deal with a large enough number of objects or events (which is usually the case for submicroscopic systems). Nonliving systems are therefore cause-driven, and I call their behavior law-like.

But there is something peculiar about living systems. When we talk of the living, we not only deal with the movement of physical objects but also with feelings, feelings that need concepts such as survival, pleasure, pain, and so forth. These words are not in the vocabulary of the laws of physics; we never need such words to describe the nonliving. Molecules of the nonliving show no tendency to survive or to love. Nor do we need the concepts of pleasure and pain to describe molecular behavior. Instead, these concepts describe the contexts and meanings behind the contents or "feel" of living.

These "feels" are mapped or programmed in the physical body, and once programmed the physical body can carry out the function that the feeling is about. Thus, living organisms display "program-like" behavior giving away their secret—that they have another body that consists of the feels behind the programs that living organisms are capable of running (Goswami 1994). This is the vital body.

The biologist Rupert Sheldrake (1981) reaches the same conclusion by noting that the genes do not have the programs for morphogenesis or form-making. In Sheldrake's terminology, morphogenesis (development of the forms or organs that carry out biological functions) in living organisms is guided by nonlocal extra-physical morphogenetic fields. What is experienced as "feels" is operationally the morphogenetic fields; these are equivalent descriptions of the vital body.

Similarly, the biologist Roger Sperry, the philosopher John Searle, the mathematician Roger Penrose, and the artificial-intelligence researcher Ranan Banerji, all have pointed out that the brain which can be looked upon as a computer cannot process meaning that we so covet. Our lives center around meaning. Where does meaning come from? Computers process symbols, but the meaning of the symbols has to come from outside—the mind gives meaning to the symbols that the brain generates. You may ask why can't there be some other symbols for meaning, call them meaning symbols. But then we would need further symbols for the meaning of the meaning, ad infinitum (Sperry 1983; Searle 1992; Penrose 1989; Banerji 1994).

The feels behind the vital functions of a living organism come from the vital body of consciousness. Consciousness maps the vital functions in the form of the various functional organs in the physical body of the organism using its vital body.

Since only consciousness can inject meaning in the physical world, it makes sense to hypothesize that consciousness "writes" the meaningful mental programs in the brain. When we write software for our personal computer, we employ a mental idea of what we want to do in the programming. Similarly, consciousness must use the mental body to create the mental "software" (the representations of the meanings that mind processes) in the brain.

To summarize, the behavior of nonliving matter is law-like, but the behavior of living and thinking matter is program-like. Thus, logic dictates that we have both a vital and a mental body of consciousness. Consciousness uses the physical hardware to make software representations of the vital and the mental. What argument can we give for the essential existence of the supramental?

Why Supramental Intellect?—
The Nature of Creativity

What is creativity? Only a little thought is needed to see that creativity has to do with the discovery or invention of something new of value. But what is new?

The new in creativity refers to either new meaning or new contexts for studying new meaning (Goswami 1996, 1999). When we create new meaning using old, already-known contexts, we call it invention or, more formally, situational creativity. For example, from the known theory of electromagnetic waves, Marconi invented the radio. The radio gave new meaning to a particular portion of the electromagnetic spectrum, but the context for the invention was already present.

In contrast, the creativity of Clerk Maxwell, who discovered the theory of electromagnetic waves, is fundamental creativity, because it involves the discovery of a new context of subsequent thinking or inventions.

Thus, the fact that we have two kinds of creativity, situational and fundamental, invention and discovery, necessitates the hypothesis for a supramental intellect body which processes the context of mental meaning.

Actually, the definition of creativity, if you recall, speaks of something new of value. What gives value but our feelings of pleasure and pain? So the existence of the vital body is also implicit in the definition of creativity.

A little thought will show something else. The mental body not only gives meaning to the physical objects of our experience, we also use it to give meaning to the vital body feelings. So similarly, the supramental is used not only to give contexts of mental meaning but also to provide contexts for the movement of the vital as well as the physical. In other words, the supramental intellect is the very same as what I previously called the theme body—the body of archetypal themes that shapes the movement of the physical, the mental, and the vital.

Now, what of the quantum nature of these bodies that we postulate to avoid dualism? Let's tackle the mental body first.

In Search of the Quantum Mind

It has become customary in modern psychology to denigrate Decartes. But this great seventeenth-century philosopher/scientist noticed something undeniably profound about the differences between what we call the mind and what constitutes our physical body. He said that, while the objects of the physical world have extensions, localizations in space (they are *res extensa*), the objects of the mental world (*res cogitans*) do not have any extension; they cannot be localized in space. Thus, the idea that thoughts, mental objects, can be described in terms of objects that move in space, objects that have finite localizations, seemed unreasonable to Descartes. Hence, he proposed the mental world as an independent world (Descartes 1972).

It also follows from Descartes' argument that physical objects, having extension, are reducible to smaller components. The macro-physical is made of the micro, of atoms, which, in turn, are made of still smaller elementary particles. But mental objects, having no extension, cannot be reduced to micro subdivisions. The same idea is found in Indian philosophy where mind is referred to as *sukhsha*, which is usually translated as subtle but also implies indivisibility.[15]

But Descartes, profound as his ideas were, also made profound blunders. One blunder is interactionism, as we have noted many times. Another blunder is that he included consciousness as a property of the mental world. But now that we have corrected with our new science both his mistakes, can we seriously take what was profound in his thinking?

What is the difference between gross physical and subtle mental substances? One big difference is the grossness of the macroworld of our shared perception in the physical domain. We are postulating that both physical and mental substances are quantum substances. But the difference is that, in the physical world, micro-quantum objects form macro-objects. This is not so in the mental world.

Quantum objects obey the uncertainty principle—we cannot simultaneously measure both their position and velocity with utmost accuracy. Now in order to determine the trajectory of an object, we need to know not only where an object is now

---

[15]I am grateful to Swami Dayananda Saraswati for pointing this out to me.

but also where it will be a little later—in other words, both position and velocity, simultaneously. And this the uncertainty principle says we cannot know. So we can never determine accurate trajectories of quantum objects; they are subtle by nature.

But if you make large conglomerates of subtle quantum objects, they tend to take on the appearance of grossness. So, although the macrobodies of our environment are made of the micro-quantum objects that obey the uncertainty principle, they have grossness because the cloud of ignorance that the uncertainty principle imposes on their motion is very small, so small that it can be ignored in most situations. Thus, macrobodies can be closely attributed with both position and velocity and, therefore, trajectories. Thus, we can observe them at leisure, while others are observing them, and form a consensus about them.

Another way to see this is to recognize that the possibility waves of macromatter are so sluggish that between your observation and my observation, their spreading is imperceptibly small; so we both collapse the object virtually in the same place. In this way consensus is born and with it the idea of physical reality out there, in public, outside of us.

Incidentally, this idea that the behavior of macrobodies is given approximately by deterministic Newtonian physics is called the correspondence principle. It was discovered by the famous physicist Niels Bohr. The physical world is made in such a way that we need the intermediary of the macrobodies, macro "measurement" apparatuses, to amplify the micro-quantum objects before we can observe them. This is the price we pay—losing direct touch with the physical microworld—so that we have a shared reality of physical objects, so that everybody can simultaneously see the macrobodies.

So why are mental objects not accessible to our shared scrutiny? Mental substance is always subtle; it does not form gross conglomerates. In fact, as Descartes correctly intuited, mental substance is indivisible. For mental substance, then, there is no reduction to smaller and smaller bits; there is no micro out of which the macro is made.

So the mental world is a whole, or what physicists sometimes call an infinite medium. There can be waves in such an infinite medium, modes of movement that must be described as quantum possibility waves obeying a probability calculus.

You can verify directly that thoughts—mental objects—obey the uncertainty principle; you can never simultaneously keep track of both the content of a thought and where the thought is going, the direction of thought (Bohm 1951). We can directly observe thoughts without any intermediary, without any so-called macro measurement apparatus, but the price is that thoughts are private, internal; we cannot normally share them with others.

Profound ideas give us profound understanding. Thus, the idea that we have a mental body consisting of quantum possibility "objects" enables us to understand why our awareness of mental objects is internal as opposed to our awareness of the physical, which is external.

When we act in our conditioned modality, the ego, then our thoughts, indeed, thinking itself, seem algorithmic, continuous, and predictable, which gives them the appearance of objects of Newtonian vintage. But there is also creative thought, a discontinuous transition in thinking, a shift of meaning from conditioned to something new of value. When you recognize creative thought as the product of a quantum leap in thinking, any resistance to accepting the quantum nature of thought may decrease substantially.

Finally, although normally thoughts are private and we cannot share them with one another, there seems to be compelling evidence for mental telepathy in which thoughts are shared, suggesting quantum nonlocality of thought between minds that are suitably correlated (Becker 1993). The physicist Richard Feynman (1981) showed that classical Newtonian systems can never simulate nonlocality. So perhaps the nonlocality of thought, as in telepathy, is the best evidence of its quantum nature.

Mentation, at least, is a familiar beast, and you may have already intuited, even without my prodding, that the idea of a separate mental body is justified including its quantum nature. But is there any profound justification for the postulate of the quantum nature of the vital body?

The Vital Body

In our culture, thanks partly to Descartes, maligned as his teachings may have been by materialists before the current development of science within consciousness, and thanks partly to our familiarity with thoughts, we have always had friendship with ideas of mind-body dualism, the dual worlds of mind and physical matter. However, the same thing cannot be said of the idea of the vital body. To be sure, we sometimes are intrigued when somebody uses the words "vital energy" to describe his experiences. But we do not necessarily engage with notions of a separate vital world of vital substance; our experience of the vital energy is not confident enough.

To be sure also, biologists of the past sometimes have used the idea of a vital body and its vital force—a philosophy called vitalism—to explain the workings of a living cell. But with the advent and phenomenal success of molecular biology in explaining how the living cell works, all ideas of vitalism were banished from science. We have to look at the science of other cultures to access and examine ideas of the vital body, cultures such as the Indian, the Chinese, and the Japanese. In particular, how medicine is practiced in India and China is highly instructive as to the nature of the vital world and the vital body.

In India, yogic healing consists of a manifold approach to who we are. In the Upanishads, there is a description of five bodies of a human being (fig. 6.1). The grossest is physical, literally renewed constantly from food molecules and hence called *annamaya* (made of *anna*, food) in Sanskrit. The next subtler body is called *pranamaya* (made of vital energy, *prana*); this refers to the vital body of life associated with the movements of life expressed as reproduction, maintenance, etc. The next, even subtler body, *manomaya* (made of *mana*, mind substance) is the mental body of mind movement, thought, discussed above. The next body, called *vijnanamaya* (made of *vijnana*, discriminatory intelligence), is the supramental intellect or theme body, the repository of the contexts of all the three "lower" bodies. Finally, the *anandamaya* (made of nonsubstantial *ananda*, spiritual joy or bliss) body corresponds to Brahman—the ground of all being, consciousness in its suchness.

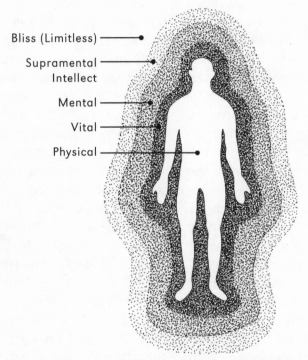

Bliss (Limitless)
Supramental Intellect
Mental
Vital
Physical

The five bodies of consciousness

Fig. 6.1. The five bodies of consciousness. The outermost is the unlimited bliss body; the next body is theme, or supramental intellect, that sets the contexts of movements of the mental, the vital, and the physical. Of these latter bodies, the mental gives meaning to vital and physical movements and the vital has the blueprints of biological forms of life manifested in the physical. Finally, the physical is the "hardware" in which representations ("software") are made of the vital body and the mind.

Accordingly, Indian medicine is divided into the study of five healing modalities: diet, herbs, and hatha yoga (*asanas* or postures) for the care and healing of the physical body; *pranayama*, the practice of which in the simplest form consists of following the inflow and outflow of breath, for the care and healing of the vital body; repetition of a mantra (incantation of usually a one-syllable word) for the care and healing of the mental body; meditation and creativity for the care and healing of the supramental body; and deep sleep and samadhi, or absorption into oneness, for the care and healing of the bliss body (Nagendra 1993; Frawley 1989).

Understand that pranayama is more than the following of breath. The Sanskrit word prana means breath, to be sure (it also means life itself), but in addition, it means modes of movement of the vital body, the body made of prana. The aim of pranayama is ultimately to access the movements of the vital body. These movements are felt as currents through channels called *nadis*. Two important nadis cross at the nostrils; hence, watching the breath as in alternate nostril breathing helps to veer us toward the awareness of the movement of prana.

When Western medicine came across such ideas as prana and nadi, attempts were made to understand them as some sort of physical entities. In particular, nadis were looked at as nerves, but to no avail; no correspondence was found.

The Chinese have developed the very sophisticated medicine of acupuncture, based on the idea of the flow of *chi* through channels called meridians. These channels have no correspondence to the physical nervous system, either. There is enough similarity of these meridians to the nadis of the Indian system (although the correspondence between the two, interestingly, is not unique) to suggest that chi is akin to prana, the modes of movement of the vital body.

The journalist Bill Moyers did a television series for Public Broadcasting Service that had a wonderful segment regarding Chinese medicine and the mystery of chi. In one segment, in answer to Moyers' question, "How does the doctor know he's hitting the right (acupuncture) point?" David Eisenberg, an American apprentice of Chinese medicine, said:

> It's an incredibly difficult thing to do. He asks her whether she feels the chi, and if she has a sensation, that's how he knows. He also has to feel it. My acupuncture teacher said it's like fishing. You must know the difference between a nibble and a bite (Moyers 1993).

But it takes years to learn to feel somebody else's chi. The feeling of chi is internal, normally not a part of our shared reality. How the acupuncturist shares in the chi experience of a patient is like mental telepathy.

To me, the most interesting segment of the Bill Moyers episode came when a *chi gong* master demonstrated his control of his chi field (and presumably of others) which others could not penetrate with all their physical might. They attacked this slight, elderly master, but were repelled by an invisible force without any physical contact whatsoever. Was the master repelling his attackers by controlling their chi fields? It sure seemed that way. Chi gong is a form of martial arts designed for learning the control of the flow of chi in the vital body. *Tai chi* is a dance form with the same objective.

The Japanese system of aikido is, likewise, designed to learn and access the movement of *ki*, the Japanese word for the modes of movement of the vital body.

I must tell you about my first direct experience of chi (or prana, or ki). This was in 1981; I was an invited guest speaker at a workshop given by John and Toni Lilly at Esalen Institute in Big Sur, California. The East Indian guru Bhagwan Shri Rajneesh was very popular then, and one morning I was participating in "dynamic" meditation to a Rajneesh music tape—a combination of first shaking your body vigorously, then doing a slow dance, followed by a sitting meditation. I got a good workout shaking my body; it was unusually invigorating. When the music changed to signify the beginning of the slow dance, we were instructed to dance closed-eye, and that was nice.

But I bumped into somebody and opened my eyes, and lo! a pair of bouncing breasts engaged my stare. I was a little uptight about nudity then (this was my very first trip to Esalen), so I closed my eyes immediately. Unfortunately, closing my mental body was a different matter. So the mental picture of the bouncing boobs and the ensuing embarrassment and, additionally, the fear of bumping into somebody else occupied me.

When the slow dancing ended, I was very relieved. I sat down to meditate, and concentration came easily. It was then that I felt a strong current rising along my spine from my lower back to about the throat area. It was extremely refreshing—utter bliss.

Later analysis suggested that this was indeed a flow of prana, sometimes called the rising of *kundalini shakti* (*kundalini* means coiled up, and *shakti* means energy; thus, kundalini shakti means coiled-up vital energy or prana), actually a partial rising. In later years, I have been to workshops (in particular, one given by the physician Richard Moss) where I experienced profound flows of prana throughout my body. More recently, I have been doing practices to stabilize my experience of prana.

My experience is not unique. Many people have experiences of the flow of prana or chi or rising kundalini, and it is now one of the anomalous phenomena under intense study by *avant-garde* medical researchers in this country and elsewhere. (Read, for example, Greenwell 1995 and Kason 1994.)

Let's come back to theory. Can the modes of movement of the vital body—prana, chi, or ki—be described as the quantum possibility waves of an underlying infinite medium of the vital world? Clearly, since both the Indian and Chinese systems talk about pathways or channels for the flow of vital energy, vital energy must be more localizable than its mental counterpart. However, notice that the Indian pathways of nadis do not exactly match the Chinese meridians. This can be understood if the localization is not laid in concrete; so there is scope for the validity of the uncertainty principle here. Additionally, in

Chinese medicine, chi is always thought in terms of complementary concepts such as yin and yang. So both uncertainty and complementarity prevail for vital energy movements suggesting their quantum nature.

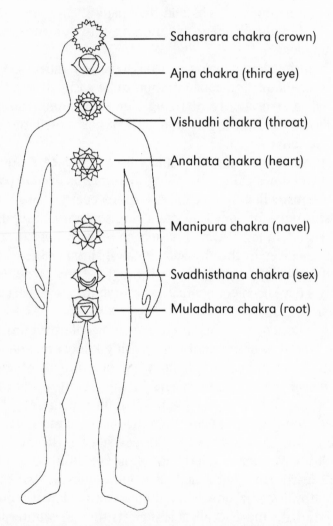

Fig. 6.2. The chakras. We feel emotions in conjunction with these points in the physical body. The chakras represent the places of the physical body where representations (the organs) are made of vital body blueprints for biological form-making, or morphogenesis.

I have already argued that vital energy is experienced internally, as is the mental, although these modes are less subtle (that is, more localizable) than the mental. This further confirms the play of the uncertainty principle for these modes. I will therefore assume that the modes of vital energy, like the mental, can be described as waves of quantum possibility in the ocean of uncertainty of the vital world.

Realizing that, like thought, the movement of prana also displays both conditioning and creativity further supports a quantum assumption. The truth is that there are conditioned aspects of pranic flow with which you are quite familiar. When you feel romantic, the feelings in the region of your heart are conditioned movements of prana. When you are tense and nervous, the knot you feel in your stomach or thereabouts is another example of this conditioned movement. Likewise, it is a conditioned movement of prana if you are singing before an audience for the first time and feel the sensation of choking in your throat area. These points where we feel the conditioned movements of prana are called chakra points in the literature, according to which there are seven major chakras (fig. 6.2) (Goswami 2000). On the other hand, the previously cited rising kundalini signifies the creative movement of prana; it breaks up the homeostasis of pranic conditioning and is the source of all the creative breakthroughs that kundalini rising often initiates.

I mentioned chi gong masters before. Scientific research in China indicates that these masters are able to effect biochemical reactions in cell cultures in vitro with their chi field. If they project a peaceful chi, it increases the growth and respiration of the cultured cells; the opposite happens with destroying chi—the biochemical reaction rate of cell cultures are reduced (Sancier 1991). This suggests that the movement of chi is nonlocal, and, therefore, quantum.

Thanks to the popularity of yoga, tai chi, and aikido in today's West, the vital body and its modes of movement are a little more familiar to the popular psyche. But don't think that the idea of the vital body is "Eastern" in any sense. In a famous poem, the English romantic poet William Blake wrote, "Energy is eternal delight." Blake was not writing about physical energy. He experienced vital energy; he knew chi.

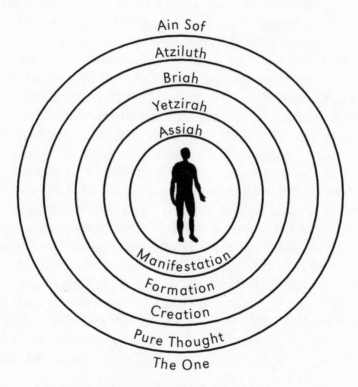

Fig. 6.3. The five worlds in the Kabbalah. *Ain Sof* is the ground of being. *Atziluth* represents the world of pure thought or archetypes of thought. *Briah* represents creation (of thought). *Yetzirah* represents (biological) form and *Assiah*, the manifestation of form.

Jesus said, "My Father's house has many mansions." He knew that we have more than the one physical body. According to the Kabbala, the divine manifestation of the one (Ain Sof, or bliss body) into many takes place via four worlds, all of which transcend the physical: *Atziluth*, the world of pure thought—

the archetypes, or themes; *Briah*, the world that gives creation its meaning; *Yetzirah*, the world of formation or morpho-genetic fields; and finally, *Assiah*, the world of manifestation (fig. 6.3) (Seymour 1990). It makes sense that we have not only a physical body but a body corresponding to each of these worlds.

Today's bias, thanks to our materialist pundits, is that mind is brain, although the two things are experienced quite differently. Similarly, when the question arises of whether life is entirely chemical, we expect materialist biochemists and molecular biologists to settle the issue. But actually, these issues are very far from being settled.

The mind-is-brain philosophy does not explain the simplest and most straightforward aspect of our experience, namely why the mind is experienced internally in a nonshare-able way while the brain can be experienced from the outside. With the help of such instrumentation as positron tomography, anybody can look at what's happening there (Posner and Raichle 1995). We model the conditioned aspects of the mind with our computers and think that the computer (brain) is all there is to mentation, avoiding the proper study of creativity, telepathy, and spirituality—the aspects of the quantum mind.

We depend on our creativity to write innovative programs to carry out our purpose with our computers. Is there evidence for such creativity of the programmer in the evolution of life? Repeated evidence. All big changes in complexity, such as the transition from reptiles to birds or from primates to humans, is not explained by a Darwinian gradual variation/selection mech-anism. Instead, they show the quantum leap of a creative con-sciousness choosing among many simultaneous potential variations (Goswami 1994, 1997, 2000). "Punctuation marks" in evolution, fossil evidence of periods of very rapid change, are evi-dence of such creative interventions (Eldredge and Gould 1972).

When we study the conditioned, programmed movements of life processes in a cell, chemistry works and we become complacent that all life is chemistry. But the philosophy that life is chemistry neither explains creativity in evolution nor how a one-celled embryo achieves a complex adult form whose integrity is a vital part of the definition of the organism (Sheldrake 1981).

The Five Bodies of Consciousness

Let us review the situation in regard to the question, Do we have more bodies than one—the physical? It has long been noted by philosophers that the contexts of movement in the physical domain—space, time, force, momentum, energy, and such—are quite different from, and utterly inadequate for capturing the essence of, some of the contexts important for life, such as survival, maintenance, and reproduction. A rock doesn't try to retain its pristine integrity of form when bombarded by mud that adheres to it. But throw some mud on your cat and see its reaction.

There are self-maintaining, inanimate systems with cyclical, chemical reactions that can go on and on, but there is no purposiveness in such self-maintenance. Living systems, particularly advanced ones, on the other hand, live their lives with a clear agenda. A brushfire may be said to reproduce when it spreads, but this kind of reproduction lacks the purposive evolution that is part of the agenda of the living.

And then we have physical-mental-vital contexts of movement that manifest as emotions such as desire. Can you imagine inanimate physical matter driven by desire?

Furthermore, we have mental contexts of the movement of thought, such as reflection and projection, and, finally, mental/supramental contexts such as love and beauty, that are very far removed from such physical contexts of movement as force and momentum. You may describe the eddies in a river or the play of colors on clouds during a sunset as beautiful, but the beauty is entirely in your mind.

Even greater is the difference in our experience of the physical and of the mental or vital. Physical bodies of our experience appear external to us; they are part of a shared material reality. This includes our own physical bodies which we and others can see, touch, feel. But not so with the mental.

We experience thoughts as internal and private; normally, nobody else can perceive them. Likewise, your feeling of "aliveness" after a physical workout and a shower, a feeling that Easterners would say is connected with the flow of prana in your vital body, is normally your private feeling. The exception occurs when quantum nonlocality connects two people as in telepathy.

The case of emotions is interesting because, in our experience of emotions, we can clearly see that all three "bodies"—physical, mental, and vital—are involved in the experience. Notice the difference in how our experience of emotion is expressed in the three bodies. The physical signs of emotion are for everybody to see or to measure with an instrument—your face is flushed, your blood pressure goes up. And there is associated mental chatter that nobody else can hear. There is also a vital flow of chi, which is quite distinct from the physical and mental aspects of emotion, that you may feel inside if you pay attention but that remains private and is much harder to control than the physical signs.

Materialists theorize that the aspects and attributes of life and mentation emerge from the movement of molecules at a certain level of complexity. But this idea of emergent life and mind remains utterly promissory. In contrast, the idea of a separate mental body makes sense even on a cursory look at our direct experience. The pictures on the TV set are nothing but the movement of electrons; however, they tell a story because we put meaning in those movements. How do we do that? We use mental pictures to dress up the physical movement of electrons that is taking place (Sperry 1983). To be sure, these mental states may be mapped into our brain now. But where did they come from originally?

Similarly, the states of the vital body manifest the contexts of the movement of life—for example, in the structure of the morphogenetic fields for the development of adult form from the embryo. When consciousness collapses the parallel physical (cellular) state of the physical body, it precipitates a physical memory (a representation) of the state of the vital body. Isn't

113

that how you use your computer? You start with an idea in your mind and make a representation of your mental idea in the physical body of the computer. Now the computer can be said to have made a symbolic representation of your mental state.

Somebody else could carry out a conversation with the computer maps of your mentation and may find it quite mental, quite satisfactory. It would be like conversing with Data of *Star Trek: The Next Generation*, all of whose data-rich responses come from his built-in programs that map the mentation of his creator. But there is no need to assume that Data has mental states or the experience or understanding of what he is talking about.[16] To have mental states, Data would need access to a mental body, and for experience and understanding, he would need conscious awareness, he would have to be a self-referential quantum-measurement device.[17]

The *Star Trek: The Next Generation* shows have a running plotline of Data trying to get a chip that would give him emotion. (He even got it in one episode.) An emotion chip may be able to capture the mental component of emotion, but this is not how nature programs the vital body into the physical. Vital functions are programmed as a conglomerate of living cells that actually carry out the vital function it represents, and emotions are felt (at the previously mentioned chakra points) in connection with these organs (Goswami 2000). Also, the experience of emotion would require additional vital and mental bodies and, most importantly, consciousness to mediate and coordinate the movement of all three bodies and to experience it.

So it makes sense to theorize that there are separate and distinct vital and mental bodies that manifest the vital and mental contexts of living and mentation into content and that consciousness uses these states to map physical body and brain

---

[16]This point is especially emphasized by the philosopher John Searle 1992. See also Varela et al. 1991.

[17]This point is also made by the computer scientist Subhash Kak, private communication with author. See also Kak 1995.

states that correspond to them, just as we can build computer software to map mental functions (the programs that artificial-intelligence researchers write) into computer hardware.

This brings us to the question of the quantum nature of the supramental intellect or theme body, the body of contexts—the contexts of all the other three bodies, the physical, vital, and mental. The supramental body is the most subtle of the subtle bodies, so subtle that we are not at the point of evolution yet when it can directly be mapped onto the physical. But we do have evidence for the discontinuous collapse of the supramental in fundamental creativity and evidence for its nonlocality as well.

In chapter 4, I introduced the concept of monad as the body of contexts in which we live, which would make it equivalent to the supramental intellect body in the present parlance. To fully deal with the issue of survival and reincarnation, we now must generalize the concept of monad to include the vital and mental bodies as well. And to circumvent dualism, we must recognize the quantum nature of the monad.

Both the physical body and the quantum monad (now looked upon as the conglomerate of the supramental intellect, mental, and vital bodies) are embedded in the bliss body of a transcendent consciousness as possibilities. The manifestation of possibility into actuality is only an appearance (see chapter 7). Ultimately, there is only consciousness, and there is no dualism.

The perceptive reader will notice that in this chapter we have used the ideas of the subtle worlds (vital, mental, intellect) and subtle bodies interchangeably; we have not quite succeeded in showing how we acquire individual subtle bodies without dualism. This will also be done in chapter 7.

Behold! We Are Extending the Arena of Science

When I speak to nonscientists about subtle bodies, they often think of the question, Why can't there be subtler and subtler substances, ad infinitum? When the physical body evolves to an adequate complexity, states that correspond to the life functions and mental functions of the vital and mental worlds can be mapped into it—this is how life and mind evolve in the physical world. Can the future evolution of more complex biological beings enable it to map worlds that are even subtler than the mental? Of course, we cannot really know the answer to that question, but I mention it here only to point out that nonscientists are quite willing to ponder subtle bodies and their ramifications. (I believe that at least one more evolution of the human being is compulsory: the evolution of the capacity for mapping the supramental intellect onto the physical.)

It is also my experience that at about midnight, especially under an open sky and with a little spirit (of the alcoholic nature) in their bellies, even hard scientists become a bit spiritual. At those moments, the idea of the spirit and its five bodies would make sense to them. Even Freud is supposed to have admitted this to a friend: "I have always lived only in the basement of the building. You claim that with a change of viewpoint one is able to see an upper story which houses such distinguished guests as religion, art, etc. . . . If I had another lifetime of work before me, I have no doubt that I could find room for these noble guests in my little subterranean house."

But the problem is with daylight. Buoyed by the solid illusion of the daytime material reality around them, these hard-scientific types profess total disbelief in anything but matter and behave as if the existence of substances other than the physical bothers their scientific sensibility to no end. Can the concept of the subtle body compete with the persuasiveness of the solid, material reality?

The first point for you to recognize here is that words such as "substance" or "bodies" have a very different meaning in quantum mechanics than in familiar, Newtonian-classical mechanics. This is true even for physical quantum objects. "Atoms are not things," said Werner Heisenberg, the codiscoverer of quantum mechanics. The "thingness" of our familiar macroworld arises because large, massive, macro objects camouflage their quantum no-thingness; their possibility waves spread, but very sluggishly. But in truth, as the physicist Casey

Blood has emphasized, even the macroworld of our observation is the direct result of the interaction of consciousness with mathematical wave functions of potentia (Blood 1993).

It will also help to give up the Cartesian subjective connotation for the mental (and the vital) body and recognize that in the Eastern tradition, as clarified above, these bodies are defined objectively (only their experience is subjective). In consonance with that tradition, I postulate that the vital, mental, and supramental substances also obey a quantum probability dynamics describable by objective mathematics. The physicist Henry Stapp agrees partway with me. "There is no intrinsic reason why sensible qualities and the directly knowable 'ideas of objects' cannot be represented in precise mathematical form," he wrote once (Stapp 1996). Is there any mathematics that describes mental movements of meaning and vital movements of feeling? Spiritual traditions talk about sacred geometries of meaning, so perhaps we should pay more attention to such things. In truth, scientific work in this direction has already begun.[18]

When we hear or think of other worlds or bodies, we visualize structures like Chinese boxes-within-boxes. The Upanishadic bodies are sometimes referred to as *koshas*—sheaths—evoking a similar picture.[19] We have to eradicate such habits of conception. The four quantum worlds remain in potentia until manifested (as appearance) in a quantum measurement. There is no substantiality in any of these bodies in the sense of classical physics; consciousness gives them substance via manifestation. In other words, the experience of the solidity of a solid table is not an intrinsic quantity of matter,

---

[18]For example, physicist Saul-Paul Sirag is developing a model of the mind based on group theory, a branch of mathematics. See Mishlove 1993.

[19]A reference to *Taittiriya Upanishad* (Nikhilananda 1964), where the idea of the five bodies of consciousness first appeared, will show that it is not necessary to interpret the bodies as sheaths. I am grateful to Swami Dayananda Saraswati for a discussion on this point.

but is the result of the interaction of the appropriate material mathematics with consciousness. Likewise, the experience of mental meaning is not inherent in mental objects but results from their interaction with consciousness.

Furthermore, a quantum measurement always requires the physical body (see chapter 7). Thus, the subtle worlds never manifest in experience without an incarnate physical body, and they manifest as bodies that usually are experienced privately.

In this way, we have physical, vital, mental, and supramental worlds of existence in potentia, and the manifestation of physical, vital, mental, and supramental bodies occurs only with quantum collapse. Consciousness is responsible for recognizing and choosing manifest actuality from all the possibilities, physical, vital, mental, and supramental, that it has available, and for experiencing that actuality moment to moment. Only this experience is subjective and beyond any scientific treatment.

In spite of the rise of a monism based on the primacy of matter, the idea that we need explicit mental substance with mental states in order to have a mind has been emphasized by many great modern thinkers, among them the philosopher Karl Popper and the neurophysiologist John Eccles (1976). But their work has been ignored because of the use of dualism in their model. With science within consciousness, with the idea of consciousness simultaneously collapsing the parallel states of our four parallel bodies, we retain these dualists' valid point and still avoid the difficulties of dualism. And importantly, by positing that the subtle bodies are objective, we open the door for science into what, in Western tradition, has been called "the mind of God."

To those who raise the objection of Occam's razor, the parsimony of assumptions, against the proliferation of "substance" bodies in which reality manifests, I quote Einstein. "Everything should be made as simple as possible," he said, "but not simpler." We must also recognize that internal consistency, objective experiments, and our subjective experiences are the final arbiter of what metaphysics believe: a material monism or a monism based on the primacy of consciousness that allows five different levels—physical, vital, mental, supramental, and bliss—of our experience.

A science based on the supremacy of matter gets bogged down in stubborn paradoxes—among them, the quantum measurement paradox—that expose the lack of internal consistency of this metaphysic. A science within the metaphysics of the primacy of consciousness resolves these paradoxes, including the quantum-measurement paradox. The present theory is the first to indicate why we experience the physical as external/shareable and the subtle as internal/private without us getting bogged down in dualism. The theory also explains the stubborn nonlocality of some of our supramental, mental, and vital experiences. This is genuine scientific progress.

By postulating, in accordance with esoteric traditions, that we have not one but five bodies that define our existence, we are enlarging the scope of our science.[20] Let's now return to our main subject: how does the existence of these additional bodies, the enlarged definition of the monad, help with the fundamental question of reincarnation? Namely, *what is it* that transmigrates from one incarnate body to another so that these bodies can be said to form a continuity, and how does this happen?

---

[20]For a taste of the scope of this extended science, see Goswami (in press).

7.

THE QUANTUM MONAD

The German philosopher Arthur Schopenhauer believed in reincarnation. He clearly saw that the existence of a new-born has its origin in the worn-out and perished existence of another being in another time. But he also saw this as a riddle. Said he, "To show a bridge between the two (existences) would certainly be the solution of a great riddle." In this chapter, we will construct this bridge based on the concept of a new kind of memory.

I have spoken of macrobodies of our physical world having grossness because their possibility waves are sluggish. The macrobodies have a property that adds to their grossness. Because of their complexity, once they are "excited" by some interaction, they take a long time to return to their normal "ground" state; in other words, they have a long regeneration time. This allows macrobodies to make memories or records that are practically permanent, that seem irreversible; a tape, audio or video, are examples. I call this classical memory since all you need to understand it is classical physics. An important difference between physical and subtle substances is that the subtle substances do not form classical memory, which requires the grossness of the macrobody.

Do any of our bodies other than the physical form memory of any kind? This is a most important question, because this is the quintessential test of whether they can carry some kind of an identity of lived experience from one incarnation to another. Brahman, the bliss body, comprises all creatures, great and small; manifestations happen within it but do not affect it. But how about the intellect, mental, and vital components of the subtle body?

To their credit, both the Buddhists and the Hindus have always postulated that reincarnation carries learned habits and tendencies from one life to another. Buddhists call these *sanskaras* and Hindus call them *karma*. But even these ancient traditions fall short of suggesting a mechanism for transferring the tendencies. This is where our science within consciousness is elucidating.

In the event of every quantum measurement involving us as observer, consciousness not only collapses the possibility wave of the external object of our observation, but also the quantum possibility wave in the brain that gives us self-reference. The collapse in the brain also involves classical memory making. This is clearly content memory, much like an audio or video tape, even though it could be holographic as suggested by the neurophysiologist Karl Pribram,[21] and contributes to the personal history with which we identify. For example, I am Amit Goswami, born in Faridpur, India, raised in Calcutta; I moved to United States in my youth, etc.

But another kind of memory associated with quantum measurements in the brain is more subtle. The classical memory made of each measured event is played back whenever a similar stimulus is presented. Because of such repeated measurements of a confined quantum system (that is, not only the stimulus but also the memory playback is measured), the mathematical equation of the system acquires a so-called nonlinearity. This other kind of memory has to do with this nonlinearity due to memory feedback.

Don't get bogged down by mathematical terms such as nonlinearity and what that means; leave it to the mathematician. I am just preparing the context so that you may

---

[21]However, the known laws of physics do not allow such memory to be completely irreversible.

appreciate the discovery story below. Ordinary quantum mathematics, unencumbered by nonlinearity, gives us waves of possibility and freedom to choose from possibilities. In 1992, a sudden flash of insight convinced me that the nonlinearity of the quantum mathematics for the brain with memory feedback is responsible for a loss of freedom of choice, in other words, what psychologists call conditioning. But how to prove it? The solution of nonlinear equations is notoriously difficult even for mathematicians.

One afternoon I was pondering the problem while devouring a large glass of diet Pepsi at the "fish bowl" (so named because it is surrounded by glass walls) in the University of Oregon student union building when a physics graduate student, Mark Mitchell, joined me, saying, "Why do you look so distraught?" To this I said, "How can one be happy when one has a nonlinear equation to solve?" We got to talking and I continued complaining to Mark about the difficulty of solving nonlinear equations. Mark took one look at my equation and said, "I know how to find a solution. I will bring it to you tomorrow."

When Mark did not show up the next day, I was not surprised. One learns to accept the limitations of youthful enthusiasm in my profession. So I was doubly surprised when Mark did bring a solution the following day. There were still some glitches, but nothing that could not be worked out (here my greater experience paid off), and the solution was genuine. What we found is this. The more our burden of memory and its playback is, the more compromised our freedom to choose becomes. For any previously encountered stimulus, the probability increases that we will respond to it the same way that we responded to it previously (Mitchell and Goswami 1992). This, of course, is a well-known property of memory; recall enhances the probability of further recall. But the tendency for conditioned behavior lies not in the memory itself, which is physical. The tendency comes from the biasing of the probabilities of those quantum possibilities that we have actualized and lived in the past. The conditioning is contained in the modified quantum mathematics; this I call quantum memory.[22]

Reader, behold! Objects obey quantum laws—they spread in possibility following the equation discovered by Erwin Schrödinger—but the equation is not codified in the objects. Likewise, appropriate nonlinear equations govern the dynamical response of bodies that have gone through the conditioning of quantum memory, although this memory is not recorded in them. Whereas classical memory is recorded in objects like a tape, quantum memory is truly the analog of what the ancients called *akashic* memory, memory written in *akasha*, emptiness—nowhere.

Let's now remember that our experiences of the world as observers not only involves the brain but also the supramental, the mental, and the vital body. In the beginning of the chapter, I noted that subtle bodies cannot make classical memory like a tape recording. This is one of the reasons these bodies are called subtle. The important question now is, Can they make quantum memory?

We have already noted that the physical is needed for the mapping and manifestation of the vital and mental functions that involve movement in space and time. This mapping includes classical memory. Subsequently, if the physical body is excited in this memory state due to some stimulus, consciousness recognizes and chooses to collapse and experience the corresponding correlated states of the vital and the mental body. This repetition is how the mental and vital bodies acquire quantum memory.

Thus, the memory of the vital and mental bodies is entirely quantum memory that occurs through conditioning

---

[22]Physicist Howard Carmichael (private communication with author) has shown by statistical "Monte Carlo" calculations that the solution of nonlinear Schrödinger equations for a photon in a resonant cavity also acquires conditioning, thus providing an independent verification of the idea of quantum memory.

of the possibility structure due to repeated experiences, and it results from the same basic dynamics as the quantum memory of the physical body. With many repeated experiences, the quantum memory tends to prevail for any response to any stimulus; this is when our vital and mental bodies can be said to have acquired individual character (fig. 7.1).

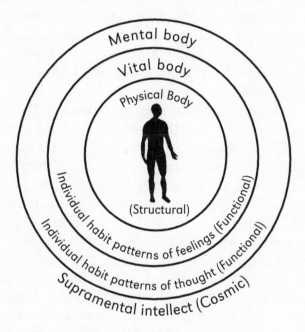

Bliss body (Ground of being)

Fig. 7.1. The individualization of the vital and the mental bodies.

The identification with this mental and vital character and the classical memory (history) recorded in the brain gives us the ego. Note that since the supramental cannot be mapped in the physical, it cannot be conditioned either. In other words, there is no supramental component to the ego. Interestingly, the Theosophists intuited this distinction between the supramental (which they call "higher mental") and mental-vital parts (which they call "lower mental") of the subtle body.

Let's study the message of figure 7.1 carefully. The core of our individual fixity is the physical body; it has a concrete structure. Next comes the vital and the mental bodies: here there is no individual structure, but their fixity comes from our identification with conditioned pattern of habits that we acquire for vital and mental responses. We habitually invoke certain vital energies (feelings) more than others when we respond to emotional situations. We think in character (as a mathematician, as an artist, as a businessman, etc.) when we solve a problem. Thus, our vital and mental bodies are entirely functional. Finally, our supramental intellect and bliss bodies remain unconditioned and universally shared.

Neurophysiologists tell us that there is a full half a second time lag between the time a stimulus arrives and the time of our verbal response (Libet et al. 1979). What happens during this half a second? When a stimulus first arrives, we have many possible quantum responses to it, and we are free to choose among them. The corresponding event of collapse (let's call this the primary collapse event) gives rise to our subject-object split awareness: subject looking at an object. But this subject has freedom of choice, it is not compromised by memory replay, it has no individual habit pattern to respond from. I call the experience of this subject a quantum self experience. It is characterized by creative spontaneity. Now begins memory playback and the conditioning that brings.

The figure 7.2 shows this by the compromise of choice between past (physical, mental, and vital) images and new modes of perception, meaning and feeling included: the probability of choice is greater (indicated by the longer arrow) for the past image than for a new mode. In the secondary collapse event that follows, it is more likely that the past image will collapse than a new perception. As the stimulus percolates down through repeated reflection in the mirror of past memory, the secondary collapse events display more and more tendencies for collapsing a past image rather than a new mode of perception.

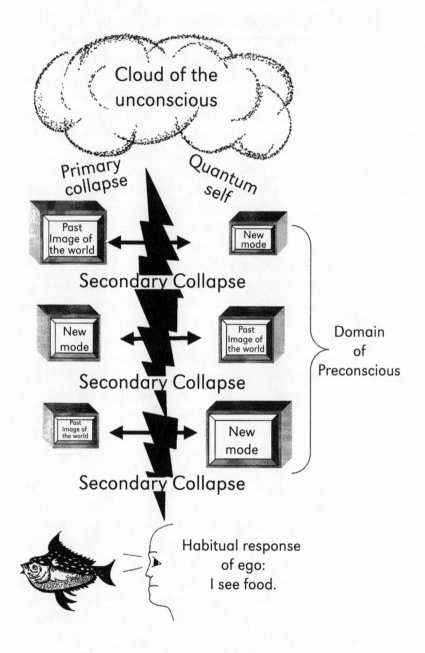

Fig. 7.2. The domains of the ego, the preconscious, and the quantum self experiences.

However, in these preconscious stages, there is still some freedom of response. If we exercise this freedom, we experience our quantum self. But by the time the half a second is over and we make our usual verbal response, it is almost a hundred percent conditioned response. If I am looking at a fish (the stimulus), my conditioned mind says "food" if I am a fish eater. I am responding from my ego, strictly according to conditioned patterns of thinking and feeling.

Of course, this is familiar territory for you. You get a new hairdo and dress up nicely in preparation for dinner with your significant other. Your loved one comes home, looks at you but doesn't "see," and says, "What's for dinner?" You also must have noticed the difference when the response is from the preconscious quantum self: it is spontaneous and joyful, worth dressing up for.

With the ego-response firmly established, there is also a continuity in response. Virtually gone is the discontinuity of the creative response available only in the quantum self.

Let me emphasize once again that it is through this quantum memory processing that we acquire an individual mind and vital body (what we call individual intellect is really part of the individual mind, because the real intellect is supramental and cannot be mapped directly in the brain). Potentially, we all have access to the same mental and vital worlds that are structurally indivisible, but we acquire different propensities and habit patterns that manifest the mental and vital functions in individual ways. Thus, our individual mental (which includes the intellect as intuited and elaborated in the mental) and vital bodies are functional bodies, not structural ones as with the physical body.

Now you can see what happens when we die. The physical body dies with all its classical memories. But the subtle body, the monad, has no structure; there is nothing there to die. The monad with its quantum memory, with its conditioned vital and mental components, remains available as a conglomerate of conditioned vital and mental possibilities. This monad with quantum memory, let's call it a quantum monad, is a viable model of what the Tibetan Book of the Dead and other spiritual traditions identify as the surviving soul.

If somebody else in some future time and place uses a conditioned quantum monad from the past, then, even without the classical memory or prior conditioning in the current life, the vital and mental patterns with which he or she will respond will be a learned pattern, the learned pattern of the quantum monad. In principle, the use of such quantum monads is available to all of us. It seems, however, that certain incarnate individuals are correlated via quantum nonlocality; they have privileged access to the events of each others' lives via nonlocal information transfer (see chapters 4 and 5). It seems that it is these individuals who share the same quantum monad in an ongoing fashion; it is they who can be called the reincarnations of one another. The past life mental and vital propensities that one inherits in this way is called *karma* in the Hindu tradition.

Thus, the monad, the survivor of the death of the material body, forms a continuum with the physical incarnations because it carries, via its subtle vital and mental bodies, part of the individual identity (fig. 7.3); not the melodrama, not the ego-content, but the character, the tendencies of mental thinking and vital feeling, the (mentally) learned repertoire of contexts, also phobias, avoidances of certain contexts—in other words, both good and bad habit patterns that we call karma. It should now be clear that the propounders of life and death as a continuum are right, and therefore, the Tibetan Book of the Dead is correct—we have proven the validity of its essential point!

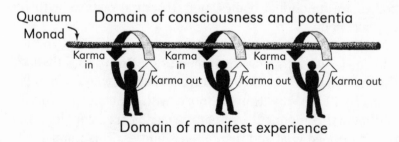

Fig. 7.3. The quantum monad and the wheel of karma.

The monad is not only a theme collective that is common to all humanity, as I suggested in chapter 4. It is individualized, possessing vital and mental memory of which contexts have been learned in a particular reincarnational history, a learning that takes place through the modification of the vital body's and the mind's quantum dynamics. At birth, the monad brings karma to the present incarnation. At death, the monad continues, with additional karma accumulated in this life.

Renee falls in love with Sam and learns about romantic love—love expressed as romance. The content—the particular story with Sam—is stored in her brain and is not a part of the quantum monad. But the learning about romantic love is, and it is this mental learning that goes forth from one incarnation to another. The totality of all such learnings forms the quantum memory of the quantum monad.

What entails learning of a context? Quantum leaping to the supramental intellect in a creative insight, we have a momentary mental map of the new context discovered in the insight for which the brain makes a memory. But this does not alter the existing propensities of the mind substantially. That happens when we repeatedly live the insight. The repeated feedback of the brain content memory into the dynamics of experience produces quantum memory in the brain as well as in the mind. Then only can we say that the context has become a learned context of the quantum monad. The same can be said of the vital component of the quantum monad.

For the after-death journey, the idea of the surviving quantum monad complements the nonlocal consciousness of the at-death experience elucidated previously (see chapter 4). Lived content is transferred between incarnations via the nonlocal window; learned contexts and habit patterns are transferred via the vital and mental components of the quantum monad. As discussed in chapter 5, currently there are plenty of objective data that stand witness to the validity of these ideas (also, see below).

Tangled Hierarchy: Why New Experience Is Impossible without a Physical Body

When we are alive, we have a public domain of experience—the physical body; but we also have a private domain—the subtle body of the quantum monad. When we die, the public domain disappears, but why should the private disappear since the quantum monad survives?

Many people imagine, in fact, that conscious awareness in the subtle body is lighter, livelier, and presents far greater opportunity for being creative than while living in conjunction with a gross body. Some Hindus think that it is possible to work off karma, even strive toward liberation, while in the subtle body, even without a physical body. And it's not only the Hindus. In a Gallup survey, it was found that fully one third of all adult Americans believe that they will grow spiritually in Heaven (Gallup 1982).

Souls, looked upon in the way developed here as discarnate quantum monads, cannot have subject-object awareness, cannot grow spiritually in any tangible sense, and cannot be liberated by doing spiritual work in the heavens. They carry the conditioning and the learning of previous incarnations, but they cannot add to or subtract from the conditioning by further creative endeavors, which can be done only in conjunction with earthly form. The reason is subtle.

The truth is, collapse of the possibility wave requires a particular self-referential dynamics called tangled hierarchy (a circularity of hierarchies as explained below) which only a material brain (or a living cell and its conglomerates) provides.

I have already mentioned that there is a circularity, a breakdown of logic, when we consider the role of the brain in relation to quantum measurement and the collapse of the quantum possibility. Undeniably, collapse creates the brain in the sense that it is our observation that collapses quantum possibilities of the brain to actuality. On the other hand, how can we deny that there is no collapse without the presence of a sentient observer's brain? This tangled hierarchy characterizes the quantum measurement in the brain.

It will help to understand the difference between a simple and a tangled hierarchy. Consider the reductionist picture of the material world. Elementary particles make atoms, atoms make molecules, molecules make living cells, cells make brains, brains make observer/subjects, us. At each stage, cause flows from the lower level of the hierarchy to the higher level. That is, the interaction of atoms is believed to be the cause of the behavior of molecules, interaction between cells (neurons) causes the behavior of the brain, and so forth. Ultimately, the interactions of the lowest level, the elementary particles, are believed to cause everything else. This is a simple hierarchy of upward causation.

But when we say that quantum measurements take place as a result of our observations, we are violating the rules of a simple hierarchy. We are acknowledging that the elementary particles, the atoms, all the way up to the brain, are waves of possibility, not actuality. And we, the observers, are required to choose (collapse) actuality from possibility. We are here because of the brain, no doubt, but without us the state of the brain would remain in possibility. This is suggestive of a fundamental tangled hierarchy involved in the quantum measurement in the brain.

To see this, consider the liar's paradox, the sentence, "I am a liar." Notice that as the predicate of the sentence defines the subject, the subject of the sentence redefines the predicate; if I am a liar, then I am telling the truth, but then I am lying, and so on ad infinitum. This is a tangled hierarchy because the causal efficacy does not lie entirely with either the subject or the predicate but instead fluctuates unendingly between them. But the real tangle of causal efficacy in the liar's paradox is not in the sentence "I am a liar"; it is in our consciousness, in our knowledge of the metalanguage rules of English (Hofstadter 1979).

Try the paradox with a foreigner; he will ask, "Why are you a liar?" failing to appreciate the tangle because the rules of metalanguage are obscure to him. But once we know and abide by these metalanguage rules, looking at the sentence from "inside," we cannot escape the tangle. When we identify with the sentence, we get caught: the sentence is self-referential, talking about itself. It has managed to separate itself from the rest of the world of discourse.

Thus, realizing that the quantum measurement in an observer's brain is a tangled-hierarchical process helps us to understand our self-reference—our capacity to look at the (collapsed) object of our observation separate from us, the subjects. Note also that this subject-object split is only an appearance. After all, the self-referential separation in the liar's paradox of the sentence from the rest of the world of discourse is only an appearance. The same thing happens for the quantum measurement in the brain. The subject—that collapses, that chooses, that observes (or measures), that experiences—dependently co-arises with awareness of the object(s) that are observed and experienced; they dependently co-arise (as appearance) from one undivided, transcendent consciousness and its possibilities.

A tangled hierarchy in the brain's mechanism for quantum measurement is responsible for the self-reference, the appearance of the subject-object split in consciousness. Since we identify with the self (which I call the quantum self) of this self-reference, the appearance takes on the aura of reality. This identification is also the source of the apparent subject-object duality. However, ultimately, we, who are the causal force behind the tangle of the self-referential sentence, transcend the sentence and can jump out of the sentence. Can we similarly jump out of our self-referential separateness from reality? We can. This is what is referred to by such exalted concepts as moksha and nirvana.

Ordinary quantum amplification by a measurement apparatus, such as in our observation of an electron using a Geiger counter, is simple-hierarchical. The micro quantum system that we are measuring (electron) and the macro measurement apparatus (Geiger counter) we are using for amplification to facilitate our seeing is distinct; what is quantum system and what is measurement apparatus is clear. But in a self-referential system, be it a brain or a single living cell, this distinction is blurred since the supposed quantum processor of the stimulus and the supposed amplifying apparatuses are of the same size.[23] There is feedback, and in effect, the quantum processor and the amplifying apparatuses "measure" one another, creating an infinite loop because no number of such "measurements" can by themselves ever collapse actuality from possibility, as only consciousness can from a transcendent level. This is a tangled hierarchy.

It's like the Escher picture of drawing hands (fig. 7.4) in which the left hand draws the right and the right hand draws the left. But in truth, neither can ever quite do the drawing; their drawing each other is only appearance. It takes Escher from outside the system to draw them both.

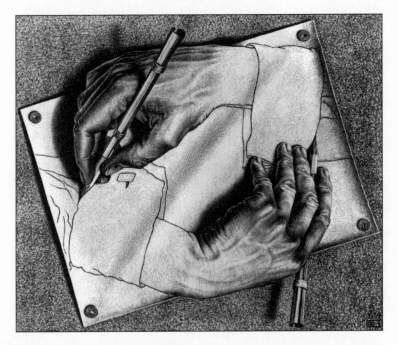

Fig. 7.4. "Drawing Hands" by M. C. Escher. From the "immanent" reality of the paper, the left and the right hands draw each other, but from the transcendent inviolate level, Escher draws them both.

---

[23]This point is particularly emphasized by Stapp 1993.

The subtle supramental, mental, and vital bodies do not differentiate between micro and macro; in effect, this makes it impossible to precipitate a tangled-hierarchical quantum measurement of the vital, the mental, or the supramental body by itself. Therefore, no tangled hierarchy, then no collapse of the quantum possibilities.[24]

Of course, the possibility waves of the vital, mental, and the supramental bodies collapse when they are correlated with the possibility waves of the physical body (even the correlation with a single cell is sufficient for collapse, although the mapping of the mind is only indirect in living organisms until the brain develops, and the direct mapping of the supramental is waiting further evolution) in one fell swoop of self-referential quantum measurement of the latter. But there is no collapse of the quantum possibility waves of a discarnate quantum monad without the aid of a correlated physical body/brain. Consequently, a discarnate quantum monad is devoid of any subject-object experience. We cannot be overoptimistic about the possibility of working off karma while in after-death sojourns. We may have to settle for a less melodramatic existence.

(Are you disappointed that there is no melodrama after death? I sympathize. When I was a teenager, I read a most wonderful novel by a Bengali writer, Bibhuti Banerji, about a spiritual love story in Heaven. I even fantasized translating the book into English, so enamored was I with its message. I guess truth is sometimes more disappointing than fiction!)

If, in the nonlocal consciousness of the state of death, the dying person recognizes the dim light of pure consciousness of the fifth bardo, the person has a choice. He can choose to reincarnate or to assume the Sambhogakaya form of the quantum monad and be free from human reincarnations. For such a

---

[24]The question can be raised: Can a physical body alone, if it has a tangled-hierarchical dynamics built into it, precipitate self-referential collapse without teaming up with a mental or a vital body? We may have to build a quantum computer to find the answer!

person, the only karma left is one of joyful service to all those who need it. (How does such a person render service? See below.)

In the Mahayana Buddhist tradition, it is a high ideal to not take personal salvation but to remain in service, helping all people to arrive in nirvana. In death, this consists of deliberately not seeing the clear light of the fourth bardo and choosing to recognize the dim light of the fifth bardo instead. What is the hurry?

Comparison with Data

As mentioned in chapter 5, some of the reincarnation data consists of reincarnational-memory recall of content, for which the opening into the nonlocal window of the individual is enough. But there are also data of transmigration of special propensities or phobias that now can find explanation in terms of their actual transmigration via the quantum monad from one incarnation to the next.

What gives rise to the propensities? The quantum memory of the inherited quantum monad makes sure that contexts learned in the previous incarnations are recalled with greater probability. How do phobias arise? They are due to the avoidance of certain responses, the avoidance of collapsing certain quantum possibilities into actuality because of past-life trauma. Why does hypnotic regression therapy work? The recall of a past-life trauma amounts to reenacting the scene, thus giving the subject another opportunity to creatively collapse the suppressed response.

With the quantum memory from a past life helping us, it is now easy to understand the phenomenon of genius. An Einstein is not built via childhood learning in one life; many previous lives contributed to his abilities. The inventor Thomas Edison intuited the situation correctly when he said, "Genius is experience. Some seem to think that it is a gift or talent, but it is the fruit of long experience in many lives. Some are older souls than others, and so they know more."

Even the conditioning of the vital body can be transmitted. Consider the following case, investigated by Ian

Stevenson. The subject, an East Indian man, clearly remembered that in his previous life he was a British officer who had served in World War I and was killed in battle by a bullet hitting his throat. The man was able to give Stevenson many details of the Scottish town of his previous incarnation, details quite inaccessible to him in the present life. These details were later verified by Stevenson.

So far it is all a case of reincarnational-memory recall via the nonlocal window. What is spectacular in this man's case were twin birthmarks on both sides of the throat, which Stevenson thought were consistent with bullet marks. It seems that the past-life trauma, recorded as a propensity of the vital body, had followed this man to this life and given him an unforgettable memory, carried in his body through the scars. Read Stevenson's vast work for this and many other cases of transmigration of the vital body's conditioning (Stevenson 1974, 1977, 1987).

"I find myself thinking increasingly of some intermediate 'nonphysical body' which acts as the carrier of these attributes from one life to another," says Stevenson. I agree: the subtle body of the quantum monad is the carrier of the attributes from one life to another.

By fleshing out the notion of survival and by identifying what survives from one incarnation to another, this extended model enables us to understand aspects of mediumistic communication that go beyond communication through the nonlocal window. How does a medium communicate with a discarnate quantum monad in "Heaven"?

Consciousness cannot collapse possibility waves in a quantum monad in the absence of a physical body, but if the discarnate quantum monad is correlated with a medium, collapse can happen. Clearly, channelers are those people who have a particular talent and the openness to act in that correlated capacity; by the purity of their intention, they can establish nonlocal correlation with a discarnate quantum monad. It is well-known that while a channeler channels, his or her habit patterns—manner of speaking, even thinking—undergo amazing changes. This is because, while the medium is in communication with the discarnate monad, the subtle body of the medium is temporarily replaced by the subtle body of the discarnate quantum monad whose habit patterns the medium displays. Note that historical information—for example, in xenoglossy, speaking an unknown foreign language—still has to come in through quantum nonlocal channels, but the information would be very difficult to process without help from the propensities that the deceased had that remain latent in the discarnate quantum monad.

The philosopher Robert Almeder (1992) has discussed the case of the medium Mrs. Willett, making the same point that I am making. Mrs. Willett displayed philosophical savvy demonstrating that she was in touch with propensities she did not have—the know-how of philosophical argumentation. These propensities could likely have come from discarnate quantum monads that learned and retained the propensities.

In the case of the channeler JZ Knight, whom I have seen in action when she channels the entity called Ramtha, there are records of her channeling extending over two decades. As Ramtha, JZ becomes a spiritual teacher of considerable originality. The records suggest that the content of Ramtha's spiritual teaching has changed over the years following the changes in the models of new-age spirituality. It makes sense to say that JZ supplies the content while Ramtha provides the contextual ability to shape the content.

There are cases of automatic writing that deserve similar explanation. The prophet Muhammad wrote the Koran, but he was practically illiterate. Creative ideas, spiritual truths, are available to everyone, but creativity requires a prepared mind, which Muhammad did not have. The problem is solved for Muhammad because the Archangel Gabriel—a Sambhogakaya quantum monad—lends Muhammad a prepared mind, so to speak. The experience also transformed Muhammad. A spectacular recent case of automatic writing is *A Course in Miracles*—a book that gives a modern interpretation of many Biblical teachings—which was channeled through the work of a couple of psychologists, one of whom was not particularly sympathetic to what she was channeling.

On the negative side, possession is a similar phenomenon as channeling, except that the discarnate quantum monad that becomes correlated with the possessed is not one of angelic character.

Angels and Bodhisattvas

Previously, I introduced the idea that angels belong to the transcendent realm of archetypes. These are the formless angels.

People who take rebirth in Sambhogakaya form, which is another metaphor for saying that these people no longer identify with any incarnate bodies, have no further need for quantum monads to transmigrate propensities and unfinished tasks from one life to another; they have fulfilled their contextual obligations. Thus, their discarnate quantum monads become available to all of us, to lend their mind and vital bodies to us, if we are receptive to their service. They become a different kind of angel, an angel in the form of a fulfilled quantum monad (the Sambhogakaya form). (For recent perspectives on angels, read Parisen 1990.)

In Hinduism, there is the concept of *arupadevas* and *rupadevas*. Arupadevas—devas without form—are purely archetypal contexts, part of the theme collective. But rupadevas, I believe, represent different entities; they have individual vital and mental (that includes the mental maps of the intellect) bodies. They are the discarnate quantum monads of liberated people.

Similarly, in Buddhism, there are archetypal, formless bodhisattvas, for example, *Avalokitesvara*, the archetype of compassion. In contrast, liberated Buddhists, when they die, become bodhisattvas in the discarnate form of the fulfilled quantum monad; they choose to go out of the death-rebirth cycle and be born in the Sambhogakaya realm. This rebirth as the discarnate quantum monad beyond the birth-death cycle is part of what Tibetans call the fifth bardo experience.

Buddhists, in general, are asked to become bodhisattvas— to stay at the doorway of merging into the whole but not to merge until the whole humanity becomes free of samsara. Hence, the famous Quan Yin vow: "Never shall I seek nor receive private individual salvation; never shall I enter the final peace alone; but forever and everywhere, shall I live and strive for the redemption of every creature throughout the world." A similar prayer is found in the *Bhagavata Purana* of the Hindus: "I desire not the supreme state . . . nor the release from rebirth; may I assume the sorrow of all creatures who suffer and enter into them so that they may be made free from grief."

Think of it in another way. Ellen Wheeler Wilcox wrote about the idea of meeting God face to face, or of seeing the clear light in her poem, "Conversation":

God and I in space alone . . .
and nobody else in view . . .
"And where are all the people,
Oh Lord" I said,
    "the earth below
    and the sky overhead
and the dead that I once knew?"
"That was a dream," God smiled
and said: "The dream that seemed to
be true; there were no people
living or dead; there was no earth,
    and no sky overhead,
there was only myself in you."
"Why do I feel no fear?" I asked,
"meeting you here in this way?
For I have sinned, I know full well
and is there heaven and is there hell,
and is this Judgment Day?"
"Nay, those were but dreams"
    the Great God said, "dreams that have ceased to
    be.
There are no such things as fear and sin;
there is no you . . . you never have been.
There is nothing at all but me."

Yes, that is the reality of the clear light; in the clear light nothing ever happens, and that must include seeing the clear light itself. For the creation to continue, the appearance of separation must continue. And since consciousness continues its illusory play, why not continue to play in it? First play in the physical body, and then without it. But play you do, because play is joy!

So the Vaishnavites in India postulate that the individual monad (called *jiva* in Sanskrit) always retains its identity. It makes sense. If the play is eternal, so is the (apparent) separation of the jiva from the whole.

The service or joyful play of angels, rupadevas, and bodhisattvas comes not only in spectacular automatic writing that gives us the Koran or *A Course in Miracles* but also as inspirations and guidance in our most difficult moments. Bodhisattvas and angels are available to all of us. Their intention to serve is omnipresent. When our intention matches theirs, we become correlated; then they act through us and serve through us.

When the East Indian sage Ramana Maharshi was dying, his disciples kept asking him not to go. To this finally Ramana said, "Where would I go?" Indeed, a discarnate quantum monad such as Ramana's would live forever in the Sambhogakaya realm, guiding whoever wanted his guidance.

Can We Be or See Quantum Monads?

Is it possible to "be in" the quantum monad while living, while in our incarnate bodies? In out-of-the-body and near-death experiences, people have autoscopic vision (vision of themselves) from a vantage point of hovering over their own body that can be explained as nonlocal seeing (see chapter 5). In these experiences, however, there is more than nonlocal viewing. People who have these experiences report that they were out of the body, that their identity shifted from the usual physical-body centered identity. To what?

I think the identity shifts to one centered in the subtle body conglomerate of the quantum monad. A woman, for example, was out of her body while she was being operated upon. She later reported that in that state she was totally unconcerned about the outcome of the surgery, about her physical well-being, which was "absurd" since she had small children. But the absurdity gives way to making sense when we realize that in these experiences people do not identify with their present situations, their body and brain and the accompanied history; instead, they identify with their quantum monad, which has no history, only character.

There is some controversial data that people and animals (for example, dogs) see something (a "ghost?") at the very places where subjects later report having been during their OBE (Becker 1993). Do we "see through" a quantum monad while the quantum monad (and its parallel physical body) is nonlocally "seeing through" us? Such a reciprocity between correlated entities would certainly make sense. When we see an apparition, perhaps we project what we see inside to the outside where we perceive the event to be taking place.

I think that spiritual visions also have a similar origin. Many people have experiences of seeing Jesus, the Virgin Mary, or Buddha, or their deceased spiritual guru. At the Hollywood Vedanta Society, where I occasionally give workshops, people sometimes have visions of Swami Vivekananda, the founder of the society. These visions could be the result of inner experiences projected outside.

Let me briefly mention one of the latest, extremely controversial, data regarding communication with discarnate quantum monads. In this data, discarnate quantum monads are supposedly communicating with specific groups of experimenters through machines—tape recorders, radios, TV, even computers (Meek 1987). This is referred to as the electronic voice phenomenon (EVP). If substantiated, this will eliminate the question of fraud in survival data. Of course, then a very difficult question arises: how does the discarnate quantum monad without the help of a physical body and physical interaction (which is forbidden) affect a material machine?

I think the discarnate quantum monad, first of all, becomes correlated with a medium, so that its possibility waves can collapse along with those of the medium. The rest is perhaps psychokinesis with amplification. Similar psychokinetic powers are witnessed in the poltergeist phenomenon. Perhaps discarnate quantum monads add greater psychokinetic power to a medium via some mechanism of amplification that we have yet to understand. Clearly, the idea of the quantum monad gives us a new way to think about a great deal of unexplained data. We will learn more as we continue with the adventure in the new science.

In the *Republic*, Plato tells a story in which the idea is conveyed that we choose our incarnations, "Your destiny shall not be allotted to you, but you shall choose it for yourselves." To what extent is this true? Let's find out in the next chapter.

Physics of the Soul and the Meaning of Life

In the preface of the book, I promised that the basic questions of reincarnation will be addressed and answered in this book with the adequate development of a physics of the soul. Let's summarize and see to what extent the promise has been kept.

Recognize once again that if you think of the soul without the backing of the right physics, you fall prey to dualism, and questions like, How does the nonmaterial soul and the material body interact without a mediator? haunt you. The dualism problem is solved in quantum physics by realizing that both the nonmaterial soul and the material body are mere possibilities within consciousness and consciousness mediates their interaction and maintains their parallel functioning.

Classical Newtonian determinism-oriented physicists say things like, The more we study the universe, the more we find it meaningless. Our soul sets the contexts in which meaning enters our lives. This contextualizing aspect of the soul is the supramental intellect or the theme body. Meaning is processed by the mind and expresses itself through a body whose plan is unfolded via the making of the representations of the morphogenetic fields of our vital body. Quantum physics, by making the concept of the nonmaterial soul a viable scientific concept, also revives meaning as a scientific pursuit of our lives.

But I call the soul a quantum monad, an individualized unit. How does the soul become individualized? The answer is: through the individualization of the mind and the vital body. This many-splendored individualization takes place through what I call quantum memory.

What is quantum memory? Memory that you are familiar with takes place because of the modification of the structure of something physical. Large macrobodies take a long time to regenerate from any such modifications of structure; hence, the modifications are retained as memory, and I appropriately call them classical memory. A magnetic tape recording is a good example. In contrast, quantum memory takes place via the modification of probabilities of accessing the various quantum possibilities that we collapse as actualities in our experience.

Every quantum possibility, be it of the brain, the mind, or the vital body, comes with an associated probability determined by quantum dynamics. The first time you actualize a possibility in response to a stimulus, your chance of actualizing it depends on the probability given by the appropriate quantum dynamics. Suppose for a particular possibility, the probability is 25 percent. Your consciousness has the freedom to choose this particular possibility into actuality anytime with the caveat that for a large number of such collapse events the probability constraint must be fulfilled, that is, for a large number of collapse events involving this possibility, this possibility may become actuality only one fourth of the time. But with subsequent experience of the same stimulus, the probabilities are modified; they are biased more toward recapitulating the past responses; this is conditioning. So now with conditioning, the probability of the aforementioned possibility to be actualized may be biased toward near 100 percent, in which case the response is no longer free at all. It is now a habit, a memory—quantum memory.

The complete model of reincarnation, the one that agrees with all the reincarnational data, can now be stated: Our various incarnations in many different places and times are correlated beings, correlated by our intentions; information can transfer between these incarnations by virtue of the quantum nonlocal correlation. Behind the discreteness of the physical body and lived history of these incarnations, there exists a continuum, a continuum of the unfolding of meaning. Formally, the continuum is represented by the quantum monad, a conglomerate of unchanging themes and changeable and evolving vital and mental propensities, or karmas.

8.

THE COMPLETE STORY OF THE TIBETAN BOOK OF THE DEAD

It took me a couple of years to intuit, comprehend, and manifest the ideas put forward in the preceding pages. In the beginning months of 1996, I was well into writing the first draft of this book when I noticed that something was still bothering me. You know the phrase "when the shoe fits." Well, in the case of this work, the shoe fit, but there seemed to be some irritating sand still in the shoe.

Gradually, I began to recognize what the thorny issues were. I intuited the idea of the nonlocal window through which sometimes reincarnational-content memories break through before I intuited the quantum monad. Being lazy, I was assuming that the two ideas just complement one another—one for content memory, one for the reincarnational propagation of context memory—and there was no need to further integrate them. I was wrong.

The pointers were there, but I was refusing to see them. In chapter 4, I proposed that all the Tibetan Book of the Dead after-death bardos were nonlocal visions of the dying person at death. But now, with the idea of the quantum monad, it is possible to define individual existence after death—we exist as discarnate quantum monads. Shouldn't the after-death bardos logically pertain to the quantum monad then? So the logic is inescapable: the nonlocal window opens before death, in the third bardo of transition from life to death.

Another hint came from the near-death experiences that supported my scenario—nonlocal experiences, archetypal visions, panoramic life-review experiences, and all that. But there are also differences between those and the after-death bardos: NDErs seldom report hell realms or wrathful Gods. They also do not usually report establishing rapport and communication with their future incarnations. And also, the undeniable fact is that the near-death experiences are just that—they are experiences of events before actual death.

As a scientist, I have a habit that is both good and bad. During the time I am working on an original idea, I don't like reading too many of other people's ideas. This saves me from becoming prematurely prejudiced or influenced. The bad side is that I miss the opportunity of seeing further "by standing on the shoulders of giants," so to speak.

It turned out that the famous Evans-Wentz translation of the Tibetan Book of the Dead that I took as my source omitted the pre-death stages which are part and parcel of the death scenario that originated with the famous Padmasambhaba, the founder of Tibetan Buddhism. As I was reading Ken Wilber's article in the wonderful compilation *What Survives?* the final pieces of the story came together (Wilber 1990). This final synthesis is the main subject of this chapter which we will delve into after an in-depth discussion on the subject of death and dying.

One final, face-saving comment: The near-death experiences have such commonalities with the description of the after-death bardos that even a sage as wise as Sogyal Rinpoche was tempted to associate the two (read his book, the *Tibetan Book of Living and Dying*). Sogyal, however, asked his master Dilgo Khyentse Rinpoche, who asserted that NDE is "a phenomenon that belongs to the natural bardo of this life."

Death As the Withdrawal of Consciousness

In my childhood in India, it was a common occurrence to see people carrying dead bodies to the burning *ghat* while chanting various names of God. The first time I saw such a thing, I asked my mother curiously, "What are they carrying?"

She explained, "It's a dead body."

"What is dead?" I asked, my curiosity increased even more.

"Death is a passing away to the next world; we all die," my mother explained.

The answer mystified me. "What passes away, Mother?" I asked.

"The soul, of course, the real you," my mother replied. Then she left on some errand, leaving me even more mystified.

In today's American culture, if a child, upon seeing a corpse at a funeral home, asks the same question of a scientifically-minded mother, a likely answer might be, "Death is an irreversible cessation of life processes."

"What are life processes?" the child may ask.

The mother will say, "Metabolism, breathing, thinking."

"How do we know that life has ceased irreversibly?"

Ordinary mothers may be a little puzzled at this point, but a sophisticated mother is ready, "You see, there is brain-dead, heart-dead, and cell-dead. A person is brain-dead when the brain has irreversibly ceased to function. A machine called the electroencephalogram records brain waves as a wavy line on a TV monitor. When the monitor shows a flat line, it indicates brain death. You understand?"

Today's child is no less sophisticated than his mother. He has seen many a scene on TV with brain waves going flat on the monitor. "So what is heart-dead, Mom?"

"Heart-dead is when the pulse stops. But today we can keep a person alive with an artificial heart that will indefinitely pump blood in the body to keep it alive. So heart-dead is no longer enough as a signature of death."

The child is pleased with his mother's savvy. He has learned about artificial hearts, too. "So what is cell-dead?"

"Cell-dead is when all the organs of the body start decomposing because the individual cells are not functioning properly. You see, there may be genes that regulate the life processes at the cellular level. When these genes stop acting, there is no more metabolism, and the organs will decompose and die."

Well, this is a very knowledgeable mother, as you can see, and the child is equally sophisticated, thanks to television's preoccupation with hospital scenes and medical concepts. But now the child asks, "What happens to me, Mom, when I die?"

Now the modern mother has to leave for an errand. She doesn't know what "me" is; her materialist models fail there, she is honest enough to know that. But she is hesitant to give a spiritual answer. Actually, many modern mothers at this stage may change over to a spiritual worldview, and say, "You go to Heaven." In an episode of the TV show *Picket Fences*, a mother—a medical doctor at that—did exactly that.

In past times, determining whether a body was dead employed only crude methods, and there have been cases when a person was buried or burned alive. Today, we use sophisticated methods, and we have all these definitions of bodily death (mostly developed to avoid legal hassles), and still determining when death has occurred remains tricky.

There is the case of a patient who was found to be brain-dead but was kept "organ-alive" with various machines hooked up to the body as needed because the doctor had an intuition about the patient. After several weeks, the flat EEG stirred and began to show slow brain activities. Soon the patient recovered and lived a normal life in good physical and mental condition. So, should we depend on a doctor's intuition when deciding death? Doctors are trained to make judgments based on the readings of instruments, not on intuition!

What to do with dying patients haunts the medical profession as medical costs skyrocket because of the cost of prolonging the last three weeks or so of life in dying patients in hospitals. No, today's medical practitioners have their hands full with practical and legal questions; they don't engage much with questions like, "Who am I? What happens to me when I die?" But perhaps the two types of question are not entirely unrelated. When we find the answer to the latter, a better answer to the former also emerges.

In idealist science, life is the arena in which consciousness self-referentially collapses the possibility waves of the living, in the process identifying with the living being. This identification begins with a single cell. In a complex, multicellular being with a brain, such as a human, self-referential quantum measurements take place not only at the level of the living cell but also at the conglomerate level of the brain. Now consciousness identifies with the brain and this supersedes the cellular identity. I suspect that not only the brain, but also other cellular conglomerates of the human body, such as the immune system, the gastrointestinal system, and the circulatory system, may be centers of such quantum measurement and conscious identification. It is well known that the immune system distinguishes the body from intruders of the body, thus maintaining the kind of body self-integrity that characterizes self-referential systems.

Thus, consciousness identifies with a complex organism at several levels. First, it identifies with the cellular level of operation, a cellular self-identity. Then there may be identification with organs such as the immune, the gastrointestinal, and the circulatory systems. Of course, the most important identification for humans is the identification with the brain which supersedes all other identifications.

So what is death? Death is the withdrawal of these identifications. With science within consciousness, we can say that the withdrawal of identification coincides with consciousness ceasing to collapse the quantum possibilities arising in the various components of the complex organism. This is a gradual process; consciousness withdraws first from the brain, then from the organs (although this ordering is sometimes reversed), and finally from the individual cells. For all practical purposes, a person is dead when consciousness ceases to identify with its brain.

Have we solved the inherent materialist problem of defining death? Materialist medical models give us the signs of death, stoppages of certain functions, as the sufficient conditions of death but cannot tell us the necessary condition as to which functional stoppage exactly means the stoppage of life. Religious models tell us exactly this necessary condition—the soul's leaving the body—but get hung up in dualism. Our present way of looking at death brings the two pictures, medical and religious, together. What leaves the body upon death? The conscious identification with the physical body or any part thereof. Exactly what necessary function has irreversibly stopped? The elaboration of macroscopic possibility waves in the brain (and in other relevant cellular conglomerates and eventually in every cell) for consciousness to collapse.

Notice that although the philosophical problem is solved, we still cannot say from external signs when there is finality in the withdrawal of conscious identification with the brain (or any other part of the body). The brain can go on in the unconscious (evolving in possibility) even if consciousness is not collapsing any of the brain's possibility waves and there is no conscious awareness; such a situation occurs with comatose patients when the body is kept "alive" by modern technology. There is unconscious processing in comatose patients, as is evident later when they wake up and sometimes remember conversations around them while they were in coma. In this way, it is good to speak nurturingly to comatose patients. Although there is no subject-object listening, there is processing of the possibilities that arise in response to such talk to the patient. These possibilities will remain uncollapsed. When and if she wakes and a particular pathway of possibilities is chosen, she will remember bits of the one-way conversation that were part of the collapsed (chosen) pathway.

In comatose patients, it is possible, unless the brain apparatuses have been damaged, that consciousness will choose at some future point to begin collapsing the wave functions again. So it becomes crucial to decide if the brain apparatuses have been irreversibly damaged in such a manner as to make tangled-hierarchical quantum measurement impossible, so no collapse of the wave function will occur and awareness will never again manifest. That is the time to declare the patient brain-dead.

The physician will have the responsibility to decide the question of irreversible damage, and that decision will always involve some ambiguity. Decisions about dying patients in the idealist scenario must leave room for physician's intuition, as in the current materialist scenario. The difference, however, is that this is to be expected in a science within consciousness, which incorporates and values subjective intuition.

The Stages of Dying

Dying, then, is a withdrawal of consciousness, of conscious identifications. But there is even more subtlety in this withdrawal than recognized above when we realize that besides the physical, we also have vital, mental, theme, and bliss bodies. In the Tibetan outlook, this withdrawal is imagined in graphic ways based on the idea that we are made of four elements:

> As death approaches the earth element, the feeling of the solidity and the hardness of the body begins to melt. . . . As the earth element continues to dissolve into the water element there is a feeling of flowingness, a liquidity, as the solidity that has always intensified the identification with the body begins to melt, a feeling of fluidity. As the water element begins to dissolve into the fire element, the feeling of fluidity becomes more like a warm mist. . . . As the fire element dissolves into the air element . . . a feeling of lightness, as of heat rising, becomes predominant. . . . As the air element dissolves into consciousness itself there is a feeling of edgelessness (Levine 1982).

Today, we can get lost in all that earth, water, fire, and air talk, but there is unmistakable wisdom here. We have to see the metaphorical nature of the "elements."

Earth is the grossest of all the elements—it corresponds to the gross physical body. Thus, the process of death begins with the dissolution of much of our identification with the gross physical body. The next elements—water and fire—refer to the vital and mental components of the quantum monad. After consciousness ceases to identify with the gross physical body, it identifies with these components of the subtle body, although it continues to collapse correlated possibility waves of both so that experiences may continue. But these are experiences of lightness, of being out-of-the-body, just as the NDErs report.

The next element is air—hardly substantial. It stands for the theme or supramental intellect body, the abode of the archetypes. When we identify with it, we have access to archetypes from which we can construct visions. The last identification is the identification with consciousness in its original, unlimited, edgeless bliss—the *Brahman* or *shunyata*.

Note that the dissolution process in death is an ascent of consciousness to complete freedom, and the death-time bardos are complementary to it—the descent of consciousness to bondage once more.

Clearly, near-death experiencers are catapulted by the jarring life-threatening incident that triggers their experiences into a shift of the center of their identity to the vital and mental components of the quantum monad. From this new center, they are able to make occasional forays to the theme body identity—hence their archetypal visions; they can even dimly see the light of consciousness itself. But as Sogyal Rinpoche's guru pointed out, they are not having a true dissolution experience leading to death. Theirs is a practice round. It is a genuine samadhi, the experience of a state of consciousness beyond ego, to be sure, but it is not a true experience of the bardo at the moment of death; it is not deep enough.

Hence arise the differences with the experiences of the nonlocal window that I intuit opens both in NDE and at the bardo at the moment of death, the third bardo. NDErs have experiences of the heavenly realms but seldom of hell realms. NDErs have life-review experiences but seldom any vision of future lives. All because they don't go deep enough. Often they have the experience of being told to come back. Who is telling them? Ultimately, they themselves.

An aside: What happens if one goes deep enough? For example, deep enough to see the clear light. In progressive states of samadhi, arrived at in the waking state itself via meditation and some grace, one goes through the same kind of ascent and descent, as in the bardos. Samadhi, in which the subject-object split is maintained, and thus some residual identity with the physical body, *savikalpa samadhi*, is the more common samadhi experience. But there is also mention in the literature of the rare variety, *nirvikalpa samadhi*, in which there is no division of subject and object and one's identity completely merges with the bliss body, albeit temporarily. In India, there is a strong belief that no one can survive such a complete shift of identity to the bliss body—to the clear light—for more than twenty-one days.[25]

Coming back to the NDE, I am convinced that in a genuine death experience, these shortcomings of the rehearsal are overcome, the nonlocal window is more fully open, and a true communication and mutual influencing between incarnations takes place more commonly.

Good. But now how do we explain the after-death bardos? The opening of the nonlocal window in the bardo at the moment of death explains Stevenson's and other past-life recall data; the shift of the center of the identity from the gross to subtle to bliss bodies all fit the Tibetan description of the bardo at the moment of death. But after death there is no physical body, there is only the now discarnate quantum monad. Gone with the physical body is the possibility of subject-object split experience. In truth, there is only unconscious processing, as in deep sleep. How, then, are the death-time bardos to be explained?

There is fortunately a way out of this dilemma. To see it, let's ask how the great Tibetan sages intuit the death-time bardos while still alive. Another hint comes when we realize that there is data, under hypnosis or under holotropic breathing, of subjects remembering experiences of death-time bardos, such

---

[25]I have read that the sage Ramakrishna himself made such a statement.

as choosing their parents, that fit the Tibetan description. For example, one of the subjects of the researcher Helen Wambach says, "I was so surprised to find that I wasn't really in the fetus much at all. The strangest part of the experience to me was the feeling that somehow I was helping to create the fetus" (Wambach 1979). This statement is suggestive of nonlocality as well as of the karmic shaping of the fetus during the period of unconscious processing that connects the fetus to his discarnate quantum monad.

So we can put together these hints and suggest the following. In the quantum monad, there is no subject-object experience, but there is unconscious processing of the quantum possibilities of the subtle bodies. This creates various possible paths. At birth, when a physical body is available, one of these pathways manifests, and then the events of the entire pathway happen retroactively. They are not perceived as conscious events but their memory is available. They can be remembered as such if the memory can be triggered, for example, by hypnosis.

Helen Wambach's study of hypnotic regression to the birth experience, involving 750 subjects chosen carefully to represent a cross section of the American public (thus including many Christians and even practicing Catholics), revealed that fully 81 percent thought they had chosen to be born. And 100 percent revealed that they had very little identity with the fetus until the fetus was about six months old; they felt going "in" and "out" (Wambach 1979). This kind of data sounds dualistic at first. But look at them from the vantage point of the theory presented here. Don't they make sense? Yes, there is choice between alternative pathways in the birth experience. At conception, the identity with the physical body is still rather weak, thus the tendency to be out of the body. The identity still resides to a large extent in the quantum monad.

The Tibetan Book of the Dead in Modern Idealist Form: Revised Version

So finally we are ready to reinterpret parts of the Tibetan Book of the Dead in a language that suits our modern mind and that reflects our quantum understanding of its message. But let's do it playfully, staying close to the format used in the original.

Noble-born, listen carefully. It seems from all the outward signs that you are about to enter the bardo of the moment of death. This is a once-in-a-lifetime opportunity for spiritual work and liberation. So remain aware, although it will be difficult because consciousness is beginning to show signs of imminent withdrawal from your physical body.

Be alert. As you enter the bardo at the moment of death, the world may look very different. In all likelihood, you never had an out-of-the-body experience; well, this is the time to have one. You never thought you could fly, did you? Well you can. You are light and probably lighthearted also.

Oh, noble-born. Listen carefully. If you are out of your body, this is quite normal. It just means that you are now identifying more with your quantum monad—your vital and mental facilities—that from behind the scenes helped you put form to your experiences while alive.

You are having nonlocal experiences. You can see your own body lying on the bed. Do not worry. Death is a rite of passage, a great samadhi. Be calm and restful and aware. The greatest experiences are yet to come.

Oh, noble-born. If you have missed the out-of-the-body experience, let it go. Concentrate on your visions. Are you going through a tunnel? Well, you see what you create. That's how you have always envisioned it, isn't it? The tunnel to the other side. But you are not on the other side yet. You are still capable of guiding your experiences, as in a lucid dream.

Your primary identity being with the quantum monad, you now have great powers to construct visions, to give form to the theme world that guides your mental and vital bodies. Can you see the light from afar? That's the light of consciousness, the one and only, beckoning you. These visions are a prelude. Pay careful attention to them. Much karma can be destroyed by paying attention now.

Are you seeing a being of light? Jesus, Buddha? Good. They should help. You may have to review your life now. Let it come. If the review includes your past lives, that's even better; let them in.

Be aware, be aware, my friend. Are you getting a glimpse of your future incarnation? The nonlocal window you are seeing through is open to all your incarnations—past and future. You are creating experiences of synchronicity for your future, just as you are reaping the benefit of past synchronicities you created the last time. You have been on this journey for a long time, O noble-born.

If you missed reviewing your life and sharing it with your next life, it's okay. You are relaxed about your life, you are not judgmental about it. You don't have to judge yourself before you let yourself enter the next realm, although if you saw clearly into your past and future incarnations that would be a good sign. But no matter.

Pay attention. Whatever you are seeing now, you are constructing it from the archetypes of your own theme body. Be brave. Don't get stuck with the usual images that kept you busy during life. See your emotions naked, even though it means encountering violent gods and angels. It's a passing show of your own creation. Don't be distraught because it feels like hell.

If you suppress your emotions now, they will get you on the other side when you will be unconscious. Why not be brave now and be done with it? You have been hiding from your emotions long enough.

Remember, Hell or Heaven all depends on your emotional mind-set. Remember that Taoist story? One goes to Hell and finds that it is a big banquet, nothing like the fire-and-brimstone depiction in some traditions. People are sitting in big round tables with heaps and heaps of every kind of delicious food imaginable. There is only one problem! The forks, spoons, and knives are all the same size as the tables; and people are struggling in vain to feed themselves with those big cutlery. When one enters Heaven, one finds the same banquet with one difference: people sitting on opposite sides of the banquet table feed one another.

Well, if you missed the violent gods, that's okay. Prepare to meet the good gods of the peaceful realm. You have always wanted to go to Heaven. Well, here is Heaven now. Are you aware? Feel that love from your favorite goddess of compassion. See a world where justice is manifest. Your vision of a benevolent and just God is manifest in the reality you are in now. But listen, kid, if you have come this far, why not hold out for more?

Sure, you can identify with this realm and become an angel yourself or a bodhisattva, if you prefer, after you die. But ahead is the clear light of all that is: consciousness in its suchness. Your identity is now virtually withdrawn from your physical and subtle body, even your theme body. You are hanging on to life by the tiniest of threads. If you are still aware, let go of all identities. This is the final peace, this is the final light. This is nirvana. This is moksha. This is eternal Heaven. *Om*, peace! peace! peace!

Now you are dead. You are on the other side, O noble-born. You are unconscious, capable of processing only in possibility. The words we speak to your ears can no longer reach you via the regular local channels. But glory to quantum nonlocality!

If you did not miss the clear light, you are now one with God, and my salutations to you. *Namaste*. If you missed it, let's go through the possibilities that await you. It may be useful later.

In truth, if you identified with the peaceful heavenly realm coming into death, it is very likely that you have transcended the death-rebirth cycle. You chose the path toward Heaven, but in your compassion, in order to help other beings, you did not choose your own salvation. You will forever remain radiant in your quantum monad, till the end of time, if you intend, or, should I say, if it is God's will. You know what I am saying— your intention is God's intention.

If you missed the heavenly realm coming into death but did recognize and identify with your emotional-hell realm, you are still free from further births. You are still an angel-helper. You will help us to cleanse our shadows. My salutations to you.

If you missed both the hell and heavenly realms while entering death, the possibilities above are not relevant to you, my friend, O noble-born. You are going to be reborn, you are in the bardo of becoming in death, the sixth, *sidpa*, bardo. There are possibilities before you that you are processing, unconscious though you are. When you are reborn, you will have chosen one of these possible paths.

If you did not identify with either the hell or the heavenly, archetypal, theme realms going in, but enjoyed a glimpse regardless, your sojourn in possibility is going to embrace those realms. You are in no hurry to be reborn. When you are reborn on Earth, you will welcome it as another opportunity to serve life, serve consciousness. I am not worried about you, my friend.

If you were aware going into death doing a life review, if you correlated and communicated with the child that you will be in the next go-round, the possibility path for you, you have chosen already. In your wisdom, you know what you need, the kind of life that will give you the best opportunity to work out your karma and to fulfill your monadic responsibilities.

If you are so aware, later on in your next life you may be able to remember what you did in the sidpa bardo, since what is now possibility, will, by then, become actuality. Maybe you witnessed your parents, as you were conceived. You were not identified with your fetus yet; you were out of the body and watching telepathically through your parents' eyes, so to speak, and maybe you felt the stirrings of desire. It is that desire that determined your sex at birth—the appropriate sperm will get the ovum, that's secondary. If your desire was directed to your mother, you were born as a boy; if, on the other hand, your father was your desire object, you ended up as a girl.

If you acquired good propensities this life, I hope you will choose parents and family that will further your propensities next time around. If you did not have a good life this time, if you never found your purpose of life, I hope you will find it next time. Be good, be true to yourself, fulfill your individual journey; then help others if you can. *Om*, peace, peace, peace.

9.

FROM THE EGO TO THE EVOLVING QUANTUM MONAD: DEVELOPING A NEW CONTEXT FOR LIVING

It should be clear from the last three chapters that quantum physics enables us to develop a satisfactory model of survival after death and reincarnation, a model that also agrees with the wisdom of the traditions as laid out in books such as the Tibetan Book of the Dead. So who are we? At the most obvious level, of course, we identify with our ego. But our creativity, our love experiences, times when we make deep moral decisions, give us a glimpse of who we may be at a deeper level—the quantum self.

At some point of our development we also begin to suspect that we will never fully realize our creative potential, or our potential to be perfectly happy, or develop our ability to love another unconditionally, as long as we identify with the ego. At this point, we begin the spiritual journey toward shifting our identity toward the quantum self. However, the reincarnational schema adds some new perspectives and insights about how we should go about the spiritual journey. This is the subject of this chapter.

Notice also that in a way, the model of the soul, quantum monad, developed in earlier chapters is still incomplete; there is still one piece of datum that needs to be explained. In chapter 7, I spoke of accumulation of karma; with each incarnation, the karma keeps accumulating. So in this model, one would continue forever on the wheel of karma burdened with more and more karma as reincarnations keep on happening. Also in chapter 7, I spoke of angels and spirit guides; but how does the soul arrive in these exalted states? How does it get out of the karmic wheel and achieve liberation? In this and the following chapter, we will consider the evolution of the soul beyond the wheel of karma.

Pay attention. In some real sense, we are now talking about the intellectual fruit of the reincarnational model and how it aids our experiential journey of spiritual development. Part of the chapter is a review of fairly traditional stuff; the quantum model just lays a satisfactory foundation of what the traditions have to say. But laced through the traditional stuff, do notice the quantum enrichment with ideas such as quantum leap of creativity and tangled hierarchy of relationship and incorporate them in your own journey.

The Atman Project

We usually think of ourselves in terms of an ego with a personality. We believe that our ego, from which our actions seem to flow continuously as a river flows from a glacier, chooses our actions. And the entire world becomes the playground of this ego and its "free will."

The ego becomes the organizer and interpreter of all of our experiences. Our experiences of other people, thus organized, become secondary—epiphenomena of our ego. So long as it is my family, my friends, others are tolerated, even loved. But the other who is outside my ego boundary loses validity and can even be destroyed, put to death.

At the top of the ego's agenda is self-protection, which the philosopher Ken Wilber calls the "atman project." Every moment, says Wilber, we stand at the crossroads of two polarities—life and death, eros and thanatos. Eros drives us toward life and toward ego-immortality, we become movers and shakers, we build empires. Thanatos, the archetype of death, drives us toward the cosmic unity that entails the sacrifice of the ego.

But the ego is clever; it perverts the drive toward the cosmic unity of death into a false one of even more separation. The ego-death wish becomes a sacrificial ritual, wishing the death of others, or even carrying it through literally (Wilber 1980).

Eros and thanatos. When they express themselves in our lives in a balanced way, life is a beautiful dance on the razor's edge. Since death is permitted every moment, creativity is possible—in fact, imperative. The poet Rabindranath Tagore wrote:

> *On the day when death will knock at thy door*
> *What will thou offer him?*
> *I will set before my guest the full vessel of my life,*
> *I will never let him go with empty hands.*

In contrast, when thanatos is perverted to the ego's service, we develop a deep fear of death, and creativity dries up. Such a life is without a rudder, lost in space seeking an immortality in a body that by its very nature is mortal.

Recent death research by Elisabeth Kübler-Ross and others with terminally ill patients confirms these egoic tendencies (Imara 1975). Such patients seem to go through the following clear stages:

1. Denial: In the shock of discovery, the patient denies that death is imminent. "This can't be happening to me. Not to me. Me with a malignant tumor? Me with only a few months to live? Nonsense."[26] This denial leads to noncommunication about the fear of death. The patient feels lonely and isolated, riddled with internal conflict and guilt. The meaninglessness of existence hits especially hard.

There is a story in the Indian epic *Mahabharata*. Once Prince Yudhisthira, his brothers, and their one common wife

---

[26]These comments were written by the author Thomas Bell, quoted in Imara 1975.

161

were traveling through a forest looking for water. There seemed to be a lake in the distance to which Yudhisthira sent first his wife and then each of his four brothers in succession to bring water, but to no avail; none returned. Finally, the prince himself went and found the lake to be guarded by a superhuman being who refused to give him water unless he answered some riddles. The first riddle was, What is the strangest thing in the world? To this, Yudhisthira replied, "Millions of people die every day; and yet, even knowing this, people do not believe that they will ever die." This, indeed, was the correct answer. Truly, denial is not restricted to terminal patients. Most of humanity suffers from denial of death.

2. Anger: Eventually the denial gives way to expression, emotions, especially anger—Why me? Why not the bad guys? "Okay, so I am dying, but why does it have to be so painful? I don't want your sympathy."

3. Bargaining: This is the "I will be good if I can live" phase. Miserly people promise to become givers. People who feel guilty about their overzealous sexuality offer to become celibate—that sort of thing. But hardly anyone really means it and keeps the bargain. Bargaining is always conditional, not motivational. The ego will sacrifice only if it gets something it wants or covets in return.

4. Depression: When bargaining fails, reality starts to sink in—yes, I am going to die, I will be no more. There is now a deep intuition of our powerlessness before death. It is the equivalent of what in spiritual practice is called "the dark night of the soul." There is surrender, there is much unconscious processing, and there is an intuition of the unreality of the ego.

5. Acceptance: The depression stage ends with an open mind from which a creative quantum leap can take place beyond the bondage of ego-limits that refuse the cosmic possibilities of death. When the leap occurs, a certain inner peace

comes. People at this stage live more in the moment and often are creative.

Two things need to be mentioned. First, the stages are not as chronological as a list implies. People fluctuate a lot. Acceptance becomes true acceptance after many such fluctuations (Levine 1982). This fluctuation is also common in creative acts.

Second, not everyone goes through all five stages. People who do are more communicative with their significant other to talk about their situation. These people also do not become defensive; they share their experience with their peers and talk about things that are happening to them rather than about inconsequential matters. Finally, these people accept life as both good and bad; they do not polarize (Imara 1975). In short, they are already aware that there is life beyond ego and, therefore, they fear death less.

The fact is, when we look for this ego/hero of our actions in our psyche, we don't find it. In truth, the ego is, first of all, mere content, a confluence of personal his (or her) stories. And, of course, ego also invents and plays various personas to match our various story lines. (The concept of persona originated from the Greek idea of wearing a mask in theatrical performances). Ego and personas are fictitious and, naturally, impermanent. If we knew them to be impermanent from the beginning, we would never feel the need to deny death.

Rethinking Ourselves

Actually, a more sophisticated way to think of ourselves, causally speaking, is as a character—a group of tendencies or dispositions. Most of our actions arise from these habit patterns in our minds. It is this character that behaviorism recognizes as the result of our psychosocial conditioning, hence the behavioral creed: there is no freedom of action at the individual level.

Is the behaviorist correct that we have no free will at the egoic level of identity? Partially, yes, because experiments in which your brain is connected to an EEG machine reveal that in such demonstrations as raising your hand of your own free will, somebody looking at the machine will be able to foretell that you are going to "free willingly" raise your hand. What kind of free will is that which can be predicted? But ultimately, no, because the neurophysiologist Benjamin Libet (1985) has shown that even after you start your predictable action of raising your arm, you can stop yourself. This gives powerful credence to the popular injunction to "just say no."

Our character has more to it than psychosocial conditioning. Some of our habits result from creatively learning contexts of action; they cannot be taught, only exemplified and facilitated. A ready example is mathematics. Teaching mathematics is such a challenge because it sometimes requires a creative participation from the learner; some of it requires discoveries of new contexts. Other examples are love and justice.

In the course of our development, we creatively discover the contexts that shape our character. The French psychologist Jean Piaget (1977) has described this process as a series of what he calls "equilibrations"—reaching homeostasis. The child uses simple and reciprocal equilibrations to maintain a homeostasis, and hierarchical equilibration to change to a new level of assimilation, a new homeostasis. Give an infant a finger and it will start sucking—this is a child who has accomplished a process of simple equilibration. Simple equilibration consists of developing a one-to-one fit between object and action, for example, finger and sucking. Reciprocal equilibration consists of equilibrating two simply equilibrated schemes and objects into one whole. For example, a baby that has learned to grasp an object and to suck her fingers will put the two skills together to bring a pacifier to her mouth. The third type of equilibration, hierarchical equilibration, is a process in which equilibrated systems and schemes are integrated contexually. Hierarchical equilibration requires creativity—creative learning.

As a child, when I first memorized numbers and learned to count up to a hundred, I did it because my mother drilled me.

She fixed the context, and I did rote learning—memorization; the numbers themselves had no significance for me. Next she told me to consider sets of two—two fingers, two pots—or sets of three—three books, three marbles. Then one day, all of a sudden, the difference between two and three (and all other numbers) became clear as daylight to me, because I had learned to view the numbers within a new context, the concept of the set (although I would not be able to express it this way then). And although the people in my environment facilitated my "getting" it, in the ultimate reckoning it was I who discovered the meaning. This is an example of hierarchical equilibration.

Our new science supports Piaget's ideas. We are capable of two different modalities. In the quantum (atman) modality, in the tangled-hierarchical creative mode, we discover new contexts. In the simple-hierarchical ego mode, we explore the breadth of application of the new discovered contexts to further elaborate our character.

A reincarnational framework for looking at ourselves adds further body to our character. Our character is defined not only by our tendencies, habits, and discovered contexts acquired in this life but also by the habits and discovered contexts of previous lives. As the Buddha said, "You are everything that you ever thought," including your past lives. But this calls for a reexamination of the structure of our self.

At one level, we identify with our ego, our story lines. At a deeper level, we realize that we depend on a deeper self, the quantum self, to discover the context of our story lines. Our quantum self gives the context for the content that weaves the ego. An offshoot of this process is the character, the disposition we arrive at, the bundle of our learned repertoire. And we do identify with it.

Without a reincarnational framework, it is easy to mistake the character wholly as a part of the current ego-identification, as most authors have done, including this one (Goswami 1993). In a reincarnational framework, this changes, because the character continues but the specific story lines (the ego content) of a particular life do not survive that life. But the disposition that acted as the context for those stories does survive. It is this identity, the quantum monad, that survives from one incarnation to another and defines a level of individuality that is intermediate between the ego and the quantum self.

If we are to make sense of our lives, our failures and successes, the mere analysis of this life will not do. The novelist Norman Mailer wrote in his biography of Marilyn Monroe:

> If we are to understand Monroe, . . . why not assume that [she] may have been born with a desperate imperative formed out of all those previous debts and failures of her whole family of souls. . . . To explain her at all, let us hold that karmic notion as one more idea to support in our mind while trying to follow the involuted pathways of her life (Mailer 1973, 22–23).

This appeal applies to all of us.

In the East Indian tradition, to avoid confusion, the atman—the quantum self, in our terminology—is called *paramatman*, or the great atman. In contrast, the intermediate level of individuality is called *jivatman*, or *jiva* for short. In other words, jiva is the Sanskrit name for the quantum monad (see figure 7.3).

Karma

The contexts that we discover and develop in one life stay with us in subsequent lives and make them richer. This is good karma. But it is not a case of being rewarded for doing something good; it is more one of the contexts learned in a past life serving as innate wisdom to carve out our destiny better in this life. An Einstein may be predisposed to a life as a genius in physics because of wisdom acquired in past lives.

You have to remember also that the learned repertoire is not all that the character in one life contributes to your individual quantum monad. As part of your character, you also build up defenses and barriers against creativity, against love, against the transcendence of the ego-identity, in general. This is what Ken Wilber (1980) has called the atman project of the ego—it is the project to keep atman, the quantum self, away.

This negative conditioning, these ego-defenses achieved by avoidance of the creative contexts, also becomes part of the habit pattern, the disposition that the subtle body carries through its quantum memory. You may acquire a phobia in this life from the negative conditioning of a past life. This is bad karma.

Other individuals may become involved with you for more than one life through karmic correlation. It may be that a particular individual (or individuals) becomes involved with you in your quest for the discovery of, say, the nature of love. This invariably involves the conscious manifestation and integration of what Jung called the archetypal female (anima) in men and the archetypal male (animus) in women; but integrating the anima or animus in our living is a tough job, often requiring more than one lifetime. The realization of anima or animus also most commonly requires a partner of the opposite sex. Thus, you may become involved in a relationship roller-coaster ride with another individual quantum monad as you try to integrate love in your character in the dance of manifestation of the theme of anima or animus. If you are one of a pair of individuals that are so entangled for several lifetimes, you may perceive one another as soul mates.

On the negative side, you may pick up an adversary in this life in what Jung called your hero's journey. Since adversaries help to energize the hero in his or her quest, they are really helpers in disguise. And over several lifetimes, the roles of the hero and the adversary may alternate. This gives rise to the notion that if you do harm to somebody in this life, that person may exact revenge in the next. I doubt that it is as melodramatic as that. And yet, it is certainly true that if we act unethically and hurt somebody, we have not understood love or trust, important archetypal themes. You can be certain that if this remains the case when you die, you will return again with the opportunity to realize these great themes in your life. And it may well be that the individual quantum monad, the jiva, you wronged in the previous life will be entangled with you in this life's attempt. In the least, the quantum memory of wrongdoing will haunt you:

> *Or ever the kindly years were gone*
> *With the old world to the grave,*
> *I was a king in Babylon*
> *And you were a Christian Slave.*
> *I saw, I took, I cast you by,*
> *I bent and broke your pride. . . .*
> *And a myriad suns have set and shone*
> *Since then upon the grave*
> *Decreed by the king of Babylon*
> *to her that had been his Slave.*
> *The pride I trampled is now my scathe,*
> *For it tramples me again.*
> *The old resentments last like death,*
> *For you love, yet you refrain.*
> *I break my heart on your hard unfaith,*
> *And I break my heart in vain.*[27]

With bad karma haunting you, you cannot count on what the English poet John Masefield romanticized:

> *With sturdier limbs and brighter brains*
> *The old soul takes the road again*
>
> (Quoted in Cranston and Williams 1994, 378).

Thus, the wise burns up his bad karma and the avoidance propensities through appropriate penance. Recently, the idea of closure has gained importance in relationships that end. This is good, but the connoisseur of reincarnation must achieve closure also with broken relationships of past lives.

---

[27]These beautiful lines by the poet William Henley are quoted in Cranston and Williams 1994, 343.

There is the idea of shadow cleansing in Jungian psychology. But, as emphasized by Jungian psychologist/past-life regression therapist Roger Woolger (1988), you have to go through past-life regression therapy to really clean up the shadow repressions that haunt you.

Why good things happen to bad people or bad things happen to good people are all mostly questions of past karma. We get befuddled by our present situation because we are looking at too small a slice of our entire individual drama that the totality of our lives carves out.

Clearly, from this perspective reincarnation is progressive, or at worst it involves the maintenance of the status quo; but it does not backtrack, it is not regressive. The ancient Chinese need not have worried—the contexts of living as a human embrace an arena vastly greater than that of a cockroach; it does not make sense that a human being would be reborn as a cockroach to pay off karmic debt.

What about stories in Hindu mythology that say otherwise? For example, there is the story of a sage who at the time of death saw a deer and had a momentary desire to be a deer. Instantly, he was reborn as a deer. Such stories can easily be reinterpreted as the rebirth with the quality of the deer that so enchanted the dying sage.

On the other hand, you can also see that the karmic law is ruthless. If you don't discover and learn to live a context in this life, karma will keep you in the death-rebirth cycle indefinitely until you learn.

It's like the character in Bill Murray's film *Groundhog Day*. Every morning he wakes in his hotel in a small town in Pennsylvania only to find that he has to live over the same day when people gather to find out whether the groundhog will be able to see his shadow to predict the duration of the winter. At first, the character in the film is bored and despairs, but it does not take him long to catch on. He learns to watch himself; he discovers relationships; he starts to help people; he becomes creative; and eventually he discovers love and moves on to the next day.

The karmic repetition is similar, but perhaps with a little twist. Maybe if you don't learn as a rich person, you can try as a poor person in the next life. But on and on you go until you learn, until you're ready, until you get bored and begin to inquire into the meaning of life and the nature of the self, until you understand the meaning of relationship and the beauty in helping others. And oh, yes, there is a judgment day, but there is no God judging you. The judge is *you*, and only if you are there, conscious as you enter the bardo of the moment of death. A character Woody Allen played in a movie said, "I'm not afraid of dying. I just don't want to be there when it happens." It is this escapist tendency that perpetuates the karmic wheel.

We create karma as we learn our assigned lessons, the contexts of our theme body. With experience, we get better at learning. If we learn creatively with closure, we "burn" karma, those propensities that are no longer needed. The truth also is, we have the ability to be creative without creating new karma. Unfortunately, in spite of this ability, we have other drives that get us into karmic involvement. Let's try to understand these drives for which the East Indian word is *guna*, which means quality.

The Gunas

East Indian philosopher-sages believe that people can be classified according to which of the three gunas—*sattwa*, *rajas*, and *tamas*—are dominant in their psyches. Sattwa means illumination; it is the quality that illuminates, such as the ability to love, or creativity. Rajas is the quality of activeness; and tamas is the quality of laziness, becoming mired in conditioning.

In my earlier work, I recognized the gunas as what we now call—following behaviorism, Freud, and Jung—psychological drives (Goswami 1993). Thus, tamas is the unconscious drive due to psychosocial conditioning that includes repression; rajas is the libido of genetic origin; and sattwa is the drive of creativity, a drive from our collective unconscious.

Although this classification is valid, it does not explain why people seem to be dominated by this or that quality.

People born of similar genetic heritage end up displaying different degrees of rajas. People growing up under more or less the same psychosocial conditioning display different degrees of tamas. The same can be said of sattwa; why some people seem to be born with sattwa as the dominant drive is a mystery—until we consider a reincarnational framework, that is.

Let's now recognize that the East Indian philosopher-sages, when they were talking about the gunas, were implicitly assuming a reincarnational framework. The gunas not only are the result of the conditioning of this life but they also carry the cumulative tendencies of past lives. People who are heavily tamasic not only underwent heavy childhood conditioning in that respect in this life but also had the same predicament in earlier lifetimes. This gives a different view to the issues of welfare or homelessness, doesn't it? Money alone will not help people who have spent several lives in tamasic soddenness; they must be educated to recognize their patterns of many lives so that they can change this life toward greater activeness or even creativity. (This is not to deny social contributions to the creation and maintenance of these problems and their solutions.)

However, people can get stuck in rajas, too, also perpetuating the karmic cycle. Activeness often leads us to exploit the less fortunate. This fuels the karmic roller coaster between people for many lives. And activeness becomes a barrier to creativity because it is fickle, because it favors fads. Thus, too much rajas keeps us from fulfilling our creative purpose.

Even sattwa, creativity, the basis for fulfilling our destiny of living our themes fully, can get us stuck in karma. In creative activity, if we are not careful, we may be incurring horrendous karmic debt. The scientists in wartime Los Alamos were highly creative, but the product of their creativity, the atomic bomb, has been a karmic nightmare for the entire human species.

From Ego-Persona to the Quantum Monad

In the closing lines of Eugene O'Neill's play *The Great God Brown*, there are a couple of evocative lines, "So long ago! And yet I am the same Margaret. It's only our lives that grow old. We are where centuries only count as seconds, and after a thousand lives our eyes begin to open." If our eyes are open now, how do we look at spiritual work? If our eyes are not open, what can we do to open them?

Spiritual work is usually looked upon as part of a journey beyond ego. I call this journey inner creativity because consciousness moves inward to discover that the ego has no self nature apart from Being, a deep unity. A branch of psychology, transpersonal psychology, is involved with this spiritual dimension of ourselves and how to facilitate it. Here we talk about self-realization, the realization that we are actually the universal quantum self, the atman, that we have the real freedom of the Holy Spirit to which we occasionally surrender our limited free will.

But in the absence of a reincarnational framework, transpersonal psychology has often left out death, dying, and after-death states from its equations. So the question we ask now is: in view of the intermediate level of our existence, which I call the quantum monad and which is called jiva in India, intermediate between the atman and the ego, what should our strategy be for our spiritual path? In other words, how do we live like a jiva and not like an ego? Can we? Is it strategically preferable to live as a quantum monad that transcends the ego?

I have read about a practice that Swami Sivananda, a great sage of India who lived in the twentieth century, prescribed to a supplicant to revive his reincarnational memory. The practice is to remember. At the end of every day, you write down all that you remember of the events of the day. At the end of the week, in addition to writing down the day's remembered events, you also write down all you remember about the entire week. At the end of every month, you do the same for the entire month. And at the end of the year, you do it for the entire year. Sivananda said that if one carries out this arduous practice for two years, one will remember past lives and propensities.

As the ideas expressed in this book took shape, I thought about doing Sivananda's practice, but where is the time in this busy American life? Finally, it occurred to me to do a shorter experiment. For two weeks, I meditated with the sole purpose of recalling my childhood to retrieve any sign I could of innate reincarnational propensities—propensities that could not be explained from either genetic or environmental conditioning. At first, the going was slow. But gradually, I began to realize that there was a special reincarnational gift to me—the ability to synthesize, to integrate diverse systems of knowledge.

I remembered that at age eight, I was already pondering world history from not only the British and Indian point of view, which is not unusual for an Indian child, but also from the perspective of Russia, China, Africa, and so forth. None of my family members had ever gone into science, and yet, at age fourteen, I abandoned history, my favorite subject, and plunged into science. Was the unconscious destiny of unifying science and spirituality driving me then? I am convinced that it was.

I am also convinced that if you seriously ponder your childhood or delve into childhood memory with the help of meditation or hypnosis, you will gain much in getting a perspective of the individual jiva that you are. It will not help you to remember specific events of your past lives, but it will tell you about the bigger you that you are.

Now here is something interesting. The East Indians divide karma into three categories. The first is called *sanchita* (accumulated) karma—all the karma accumulated through all the past lives of an individual quantum monad. The second is called *prarabdha* karma—the karma brought to bear in the current life. The third is called *agami* (future) karma—karma you accumulate in this life.

Psychologist David Cliness has developed a therapeutic method for investigating past-life tendencies, propensities, and unresolved contexts that affect the pains and sufferings of this life. From his data, Cliness concludes that the contexts that we center on in our present life are a composite of the unresolved contexts of not one but many previous lives. We also take on the abilities learned in more than one of our past lives to deal with the contexts we undertake in this life. Cliness compares the situation to playing a game of poker. The deck has fifty-two cards, but we get only five in any particular deal. The total number of cards metaphorically represents the propensities we learned in all the previous incarnations we have had. The five that we are dealt now represent those propensities of those few incarnations which are now coming to focus.[28] Notice how similar this is to the previously mentioned notion of prarabdha, of karma that we bring to bear in this particular life which is only a small fraction of all the accumulated karma.

Unconsciously, you are already following a destiny, the right path for you to creatively and ethically resolve the issues dealt to you by your quantum monad, a destiny that East Indians call *dharma*. (This is dharma with a small "d"; Dharma with a capital "D" stands for consciousness, the one and only, and also sometimes the god of justice.) When this destiny becomes conscious, however, leaving the ego behind in the journey of creativity becomes a lot easier. Furthermore, dharma includes ethics in action. So if you are clear about your dharma and pursue it with pure intention, you can do no wrong, you can easily avoid creating new karma.

According to Hinduism, there are four goals of human life: dharma (usually translated as right action or ethical duties); *artha* (money or security); *kama* (desire); and *moksha* (liberation). People often wonder—what is dharma doing there first, even before one has pursued security and desire? The reason is dharma is not just ethical duties but a creative destiny I have chosen even before I was born. Thus, our pursuit of security and desire must be guided by dharma. And moksha, liberation, is, of course, the ultimate goal of human life, according to Hinduism.

There was a rich, capable, and right-minded king who lived in ancient India. Lots of people lived in his palace, doing this or that, and they all respected the king very much. One day, a pretty woman asked his refuge and, as was his usual tendency, the king granted it. But this event began to have an unexpected effect on

---

[28]Cliness's as yet unpublished work is described in Bache 1991.

the king's household, because the woman was evil and continued to practice her evil ways even under the king's shelter.

First, the head security man complained. "O noble king," he said, "this woman you have granted shelter is evil incarnate, Alakshmi. I've been watching her for days. I do not wish to serve her. Please throw her out, or I will have to leave." The king was sad because he knew that the man was telling the truth. Yet he declined the offer and let the security man go.

This became a trend. One by one the king's servants, relatives, and even the queen left in tears. The palace became forlorn, a place of gloom. Finally, the king saw a grand old man with a golden aura leaving the palace one night.

"Who are you, and why are you leaving?" the king inquired.

"I am Dharma," came the reply. "I am leaving you because I do not like the proximity of evil, Alakshmi." Dharma is the great god of justice and goodness.

"But O Dharma, you are leaving unjustifiably," exclaimed the king. "Behold! Undeniably the woman to whom I have given shelter is Alakshmi. And yet, how could I refuse her? It is my dharma to protect any person who wants my protection. I am the king presiding over both good subjects and bad. I cannot discriminate and still remain within my dharma."

The god of justice saw his mistake and silently returned to the palace. With the god returned, gradually, all the others came back. Finally, Alakshmi came to the king and said, "Since you chose Dharma over me, I have to go." Now the king gladly let her go.

There are stories like this in every culture. A good example are the heroics of the knights of King Arthur's round table. These knights lived for their dharma; they honored their character; they did their duties.

Living As an Evolving Quantum Monad

So the first thing about living as an individual quantum monad is to discover your dharma, your destiny, your bliss, and follow it! The mythologist Joseph Campbell used to say "follow your bliss," but, of course, in order to follow your bliss you have to know what brings you bliss. As an individual quantum monad, or jiva, your character is more important to you than your particular melodrama, your story line. You learn to honor your character, your duties. This will often mean sacrificing your egoic demands for selfish melodrama. So be it. You do it because it does give you bliss, because it does satisfy your soul.

But suppose you intuitively discover your dharma and find a mismatch between the dharma you brought with you and the life you live. Some shamanic traditions have a remedy for this—soul retrieval. The idea is that part of the soul is lost and has to be brought back. The translation is: since your present life is not matching your intended dharma, adjust your dharma to match your life. It may be simpler than to change your life at a late date toward your intended dharma.

As a person of destiny, you also know your ultimate duty— to serve the creative purposiveness of the universe as long as you are tied to the wheel of samsara. So knowing, creativity is your steadfast goal.

Creativity is the discovery of a new context or seeing new meaning in an old context or a combination of old contexts and inventing something new to display that meaning. There are two kinds of creativity. In outer creativity, you delve into finding contexts and meanings in the outer arena of our living—the arts, music, the sciences. But in these actions, your adult character remains static. So you are serving the purposiveness of the universe in the way you came prepared this time around, but you are not developing your character further. You are not thinking of your next life. Because you are unconscious to a large extent about your patterns, you are also prone to create unnecessary (bad) karma along your trail.

Outer creativity is designed to generate more information on which civilization thrives. The goal of inner creativity is transformation on which the quantum monad is centered. In inner creativity, you work to develop your character further. You work to enlarge the arena of your duties. Both these tasks involve enlarging the contexts that you live now. These tasks also involve discovering the contexts of inner transformation—knowing firsthand that you are bigger than your ego. In inner creativity, you also meditate to obtain a greater awareness of your karmic patterns. Knowing these patterns helps you to free yourself by burning karma and to avoid creating new karmic involvements.

The new science I've been discussing in this book suggests five paths for the journey of self-discovery that are essential for a shift of your identity with ego. Not surprisingly, these paths were discovered long ago through empirical means; they are well-known in the great esoteric traditions. I will use the Hindu parallels because they are the most familiar to me.

One path is to take the question, How do I go beyond ego? as a burning question and investigate the question via the creative process. Recall that the creative process consists of four stages—preparation, incubation, insight, and manifestation. For preparation, you read the available literature and practice meditation (preferably, with a teacher). Incubation is unconscious processing, during which you let the ambiguities of life build a plethora of uncollapsed superpositions of possibilities in your mind. Insight happens suddenly when you quantum leap from your mind into your supramental intellect and bring back a new theme for awakened living.

Then manifestation is the process of gradual awakening to a new, more fluid self-identification beyond ego, an identification that I call the awakening of *buddhi,* which is best translated as supramental intelligence (Goswami 1993). With the awakening of buddhi, sooner or later you are going to become aware that as you live your life, a greater identity, the jiva, an evolving confluence of learned dispositions, is living you. So in this method, which is sometimes called the path of wisdom (*jnana* yoga, in Sanskrit), you use your mind to quantum leap from the mind, to transcend the ego.

There is a second strategy called *raja* (king) yoga in which one focuses on the creative discovery of the nature of awareness (of mental processes) itself to go beyond. Raja yoga is based on the famous first-century sage Patanjali's *Yoga Sutra*. Patanjali gave detailed instructions for achieving samadhi—quantum self experience, and no book on raja yoga has yet surpassed the quality of his comprehensive treatment.

Central to the method is the trio: concentration, meditation, and samadhi. You can look upon concentration as the preparation stage of creativity. But the object of your concentration is an object in your awareness, not an object of knowledge. For example, meditation on a mantra falls in this category. What Patanjali calls meditation is more subtle. Partly it is meditating on the witness consciousness, becoming the indifferent watcher of your thoughts (similar to relaxed incubation stage of the creative process).

A crucial step, however, is the encounter of the ego and the quantum self which happens only when you enter the preconscious, only when there is an (almost) effortless flow between your awareness of the subject and that of objects. From this state, quantum leaping is possible because the probabilities of the possibilities you choose from are no longer close to hundred-percent prejudiced in favor of the past response. When you leap to a new response, you have identified with the quantum self, which is samadhi.

The path of devotion or love (*bhakti* yoga, in Sanskrit) is quite different than the above two. In this one your creative burning question is, How do I love? But this is not an intellectual question, so reading or meditation is of limited help. Instead, you begin by undermining the ego's simple hierarchy structures in favor of the tangled hierarchy of the being that lies beyond ego. If you take notice, in our ego, our love for others is very self-centered; we love other people and things for what they can do for us or because implicitly we regard them as extensions of us. We maintain ourselves as the head honcho of our simple-hierarchical relationships with the rest of our limited worlds. When we undermine this structure by such practices as loving our neighbors as ourselves, or loving our enemies, or seeing God in everyone, a sudden quantum leap takes place in which we directly discover the "otherness" of others. We see that other beings are individual jivas, as we are, with the same kind of creative aspirations, pursuing their dharma and playing out their karma. We even glimpse that we all, ourselves and others, are rooted in the same self, the universal self.

The fourth method is called karma yoga in the literature. Karma yoga is sometimes translated as the path of ritual action, but that is an incomplete definition. Karma yoga is another way to undermine the ego's simple hierarchy in favor of the tangled-hierarchical self beyond ego. In the tangled hierarchy, there is no doer, there is only doing; the emphasis is always on the verb. So in this practice we give up doership. Things happen—I am simply the causal connection, usually according to my character patterns and karmic necessities but occasionally with freedom and creativity.

The fifth method, tantra yoga, centers around creativity of the vital-physical body. Ordinarily, you are totally identified with your mind as mapped into your physical brain. In this method, you engage in yoga practices (*hatha* yoga) and breathing techniques (pranayama), meditating on the flow of prana. You do movements to activate and feel your chi, as in tai chi. You energize your ki with the practice of aikido (martial arts); you activate your vital energy through sports and dancing. Prana, chi, ki, or vital energy are, of course, the same thing—the quantum modes of movement of the vital body. Now ordinarily, we experience only the conditioned movements or modes of the vital body tainted by the mind-brain. A sudden insight takes place when you directly experience a new mode of prana, chi, or ki, without the interpretive intermediary of the mind-brain.

You are now experiencing the opening of what are called in esoteric traditions the *chakra* points and which are now being rediscovered by many scientists of the vital-physical body in both East and West. (See, for example, Motoyama 1981; Joy 1978.) I think that these chakra points are ancient names of those regions of our body where quantum collapse of the physical takes place with correlated collapse in the vital body. In other words, these are the places for mapmaking of the vital body onto the physical (Goswami 2000).

The opening of the chakras is important because the experience opens the door for you to gain access to your vital-physical body identity so that you can control the movement of vital energy (in other words, your feelings or mood swings). You

can even create new maps or representations of your vital morphogenetic fields in your physical body as necessary for healing.
Sometimes, all the chakras may open at once and integration of
all the vital-physical identities at the various chakras takes
place. In esoteric traditions, this is called the rising of the kundalini shakti, latent prana, from the root chakra to the crown,
the highest chakra. The myth is that this pranic energy lies
latent at the base of the spine, which is the lowest chakra point.

Rising of the kundalini signifies renewed direct access to
the vital body and its energies and the creative potential for
making new representations of the vital onto the physical.
Most importantly, as the kundalini experience is integrated
into your life, your identity with the brain-based ego begins to
shift irreversibly.

All the methods support one another. You can have a great
and wonderful jnana insight about the nature of your self, but
when you try to manifest it in your life, you have to do it in the
context of your relationships. That needs yoga of sensitivity
and love—bhakti yoga. Similarly, bhakti without jnana is too
mushy. Furthermore, without gaining some understanding
and control of our vital-physical bodies, which the practice of
tantra yoga gives us, how can we truly manifest "otherness" in
relation to the opposite sex? And as I see it, all the other yogas
support karma yoga, whose goal is appropriate action.

The truth is, all these yogas continue to be useful even after
the identity has shifted beyond ego, even after the awakening of
buddhi. Jnana yoga never ends until we arrive at that jnana
which is the source of all jnanas. The yoga of love never ends
until the whole world has become our family, which happens
only when we have surrendered our will to the will of that One.
Kundalini yoga does not end until the body, mind, and spirit are
integrated. Karma yoga does not end until we are steadfast in
appropriate action. We will discuss this further in chapter 10.

Once your identity is firmly established within the fluidity
of the buddhi level of being, you will find that following your
destiny and maintaining your dharma have become easy and
straightforward. Now you can be creative in the outer arena

without creating new karma. You now can serve the purposiveness of the universe through outer creativity from your more inclusive level of being. You can examine your life for missing themes and concentrate on discovering them. This involves working with archetypes, much emphasized by Carl Jung—archetypes such as the hero, the anima, the trickster, and so forth (Jung 1971). Now you are consciously working toward identifying with your individual quantum monad, your jiva—a process that ends in individuation, fulfillment of your monadic contextual responsibilities, a term that Jung coined. When this identity is arrived at, all your karma is "burned." *You* did not need it anymore.

Somebody once said, "It's not hard to die, it's just hard to stay dead." Most likely, after you die, sooner or later you will reincarnate. Do you want some choice in the matter, or do you want to be thrown around by unconscious forces of chance and necessity? If you want choice, you will do well to heed to what the great Indian Sufi poet Kabir wrote:

If you don't break your ropes while you're alive
do you think
ghosts will do it after?

The idea that the soul will join the ecstatic
just because the body is rotten—
that is all fantasy.

What is found now is found then.
If you find nothing now,
you will simply end up with an apartment
in the city of death.

If you make love with the divine now, in the next
life
you will have the face of satisfied desire
                                        (Bly 1977, 24–25).

181

10.

DEATH YOGA: CREATIVE DYING

One of the great paradoxes of death is the issue of the fear of death. Generally speaking, people believe that death is a hard thing, a bad thing. They fear death, hence the tendency to deny its inevitability.

It is interesting that primitive people are not particularly afraid of death but are afraid of the dead. They are more sensitive to the dead and seem to be affected by them. And the more they are affected by them, the more they are fearful of them. It took the discovery that the dead can affect us only if the living cooperate (by being afraid, by being sensitive) to change our fear of the dead. Disbelief became the protection against any harm by the dead.

And then a new fear gripped us—the fear of death itself. Or rather, the loss of fear of the dead revealed our fear of death itself. We intuited in the early days of civilization that the after-death state is a journey of the soul into dark Hades, and we became afraid. As a Greek poet wrote, "Death is too terrible. Frightening are the depths of Hades." This fear continues today. "Now I am about to take my last voyage, a great leap into the dark," wrote the author Thomas Hobbes, echoing this fear.

The development of materialist science should have eliminated our fear of Hades. If we are simply matter, only atoms (or genes) that do survive death, then why fear Hades? But what science has tried to accomplish philosophically has not changed people's (scientists included) personal fear of death.

The point is that the fear of death is irrational in materialist science. The fear of the irrational has become irrational fear.

Why is death feared as a bad thing? How can we consider something bad before we have experienced it? From where does the idea of badness of our personal death arise? Materialist/behaviorist models of ourselves cannot answer such questions very well.

And yet a different perspective of death also exists. The psychologist Carl Jung put it well when he wrote, "Death is the hardest thing from the outside and as long as we are outside of it. But once inside you taste of such completeness and peace and fulfillment that you don't want to return." Jung's statement was prompted by a near-death experience he had when he suffered a heart attack in 1944.

Many people in our culture have benefited from near-death experiences. Such people often experience being out of the body and often have spiritual experiences. As a result of such experiences, freed from the dominant body identity, they shed their fear of death. This is a good thing to remember: death may be very different from inside than it appears from outside.

Admittedly, and especially when we look at death from a materialist worldview, from the outside, death looks terminal for our life, mind, and consciousness. But from the inside Jung felt (as do subjects of near-death experiences in general) that death is a freeing of consciousness from the shackles of the body. It is impossible to make sense of such a statement in a materialist model of the world.

You may argue, correctly I believe, How can near-deathers be "inside" death when they don't really die? But this raises the still more intriguing question: Is it possible to understand death without dying, without even the near-death experience, in such a way that the fear of death disappears?

Jung's statement implies that consciousness survives death. And it does not necessarily take a near-death experience to reach that conclusion. Many people living normal lives intuit that their consciousness is not limited to their body and that, even when their bodies die, consciousness will survive in some way. It is this kind of direct intuition that rids people of the fear of death.

The point is that only truth can set us free from fear. If materialism were truth, all true believers of materialism, including most scientists, would be free from their fear of death. But they are not. On the other hand, people who deeply realize that consciousness extends beyond the material world, beyond their ego, are more or less free of the fear of death. As Dorothy Parker said, "Death, where is thy sting-a-ling-a-ling?"

It is known that in cultures where reincarnation is accepted the fear of death abates considerably. The person can relax, because in some way or other she will not die but will come back. We are not afraid to lose consciousness in sleep! As you can see, reincarnation is another way of achieving a sort of immortality, not in the same body but through the continuity of some "essence of life." The poet Walt Whitman, a connoisseur of reincarnation, expressed the same sentiment:

> *I know I am deathless,*
> *I know this orbit of mine cannot be swept by a*
> *   carpenter's compass. . . .*
> *And whether I come to my own today or in ten*
> *   thousand or ten million years,*
> *I can cheerfully take it now, or with equal*
> *   cheerfulness I can wait . . .*
> *I laugh at what you call dissolution,*
> *And I know the amplitude of time. . . .*
> *To be in any form, what is that?*
> *(Round and round we go, all of us, and ever come*
> *   back thither) . . .*
> *Believing I shall come back again upon the earth*
> *   after five thousand years. . . .*
>
> (Whitman; quoted in
> Cranston and Williams 1994, 319)

To some of us, "I will come back" is certainly reassuring, but how much more reassuring it would be if we knew *how* we'd come back. Can we gain some control over what happens at death? This question gives rise to the idea of dying consciously, dying creatively.

Creative Dying

When I think of creative dying, I sometimes think of Franklin Merrell-Wolff. I met this wonderful spiritual philosopher and teacher when he was 97 years old. During the next year, his last, I spent about twelve weeks in his presence, including a one-month period which I consider the happiest time of my life. I still refer to it as Shangri-la.

During my time with him, I noticed that one of Dr. Wolff's preoccupations was, not surprisingly, death. He wanted to die consciously, he repeatedly said to me. But most times, we would just sit quietly. I felt, for the first time, *being* in Dr. Wolff's presence.

I think he wanted to die in this state of pure being. Did he succeed? I was not there when he died; actually, nobody was with him. He died from pneumonia at around midnight after he was left alone, apparently sleeping, for a few moments. When Andrea, his nurse-companion and student, returned, Dr. Wolff was dead. The reports I got from all those who attended Dr. Wolff during his two-week illness was that he maintained his sense of humor, his kindness, and being, if you will, until the very end.

How can one die consciously? Is it important to die consciously? Death is this wonderful opportunity to be liberated or, at least, to communicate via our nonlocal window with our entire string of reincarnations; thus, the importance of conscious dying cannot be overstated. The first question—How can one die consciously?—is the much more difficult one to answer, although there is a whole yoga called death yoga, which can teach us that.

The essence of reality, when you comprehend it with a science within consciousness, is that there is no death, there is only the creative play of consciousness. And ultimately, the play is only appearance. The Hindu philosopher-sage Shankara is emphatic: "There is neither birth nor death, neither bound nor aspiring soul, neither liberated soul, nor seeker after liberation—this is the ultimate and absolute truth." So creative dying, death yoga, liberation itself, has this one goal: to comprehend this true nature of reality that is consciousness.

We are afraid of death because we don't realize the truth that we are one with the whole, and we suffer as a result. In the last chapter, I spoke of the various stages patients go through when they discover their imminent mortality—denial, anger, bargaining, and all that. You have been there, too, if not in this life (yet), many times in your past incarnations. You have denied that your ego will die, you have been angry about its inevitability, you have tried to bargain with God, thinking that God is separate from you. Where has that got you? As long as you are convinced of the reality of your ego, the suffering recurs.

Sure, when you are young and healthy, you can philosophize. Life and death, joy and suffering, sickness and health—these are the polarities of the human condition. Perhaps the best strategy is to accept these polarities. Meditate "this too shall pass" when suffering hits. When death knocks on your door, you can remind yourself that you will be born again in another life, so there is no big deal about dying in this one. The problem with this kind of thinking is that a true acceptance of this philosophy does not come easy. In fact, it requires liberation or a state of being that is pretty close to it.

Twenty-five hundred years ago, a prince in India who was kept isolated from all suffering for his first twenty-nine years, went on an unsanctioned tour of his city and discovered that there is sickness, that people get old and die. This prince Gautama, who later became Buddha, the enlightened one, realized that life is recurrence of suffering. He discovered the virtue of nonattached living, meditating on "this too shall pass" not only when suffering but also when pleasured in order to move toward nirvana, the extinction of desires—liberation.

A true acceptance of the polarities of our being can lead to desirelessness—a falling away of desires, an abatement of preferences; many sages throughout history have stood witness to that. But look at some people striving for liberation in the spiritual path, embracing pain (if only the pain of boredom), and you wonder, "Aren't these people just trading off?" They may remind you of a story. Two old friends are talking. One of them complains of gout. The other one gloats, "I never suffer from gout. A long time ago, I taught myself to take a cold shower early every day. That's a sure prevention of gout, you know." The other friend scoffs, "Yes, but you've got cold shower, instead."

You want to be free (of suffering), but you don't want to take cold showers for it. The good news is that there is an avenue to liberation even for you, a way to escape the birth-death cycle. Welcome to death yoga, learning how to die consciously, with creativity, and so be liberated. Any creative experience is a momentary encounter with the quantum self, but in a creative experience—outer or inner—while you are living fully, you have to return from the encounter back to ordinary reality where your ego-identity usually takes hold once again. But in a creative encounter with God at death, there is no coming back. Such an experience can truly liberate you.

And if, perchance, you are not convinced that this philosophy of liberation is for you because "life is fun in spite of death, pleasure is fun in spite of the pain that follows," you need to expand your concept of liberation. You have intuited a philosophy deeper even than liberation philosophy. Liberation philosophy is based on "life is suffering," and it suits some people just fine. After all, all this is *maya*, an illusory play of consciousness. But wait! The illusory play has a purpose—to comprehend creatively all that is possible, all that is potential in consciousness. And creative comprehension is ananda—spiritual joy. So in this philosophy, the play is the thing, and life is joy. In this philosophy, what is the role of liberation? It is to achieve true freedom of choice and to live creatively all the time.

For "life is suffering" seekers, liberation is freedom from the birth-death cycle, and death leads to a merging into the unity of reality forever. For "life is joy" seekers, liberation is having the choice, to be born or not to be born is a question they would like to keep forever open, forever having the option to partake of all that life offers, including its polarities, but to partake of it creatively.

So you can look at the ultimate aim of death yoga either as a way to opt out of the birth-death cycle or a way to achieve ultimate freedom—freedom to choose if and when to take birth again. At the least, death yoga can enable you to stay conscious in parts of the dying process, crucial in order to have a real choice in your next incarnation.

Why Is Death Such an Opportunity for Creativity?

Try to meditate in the midst of a marketplace. It is quite a challenge to concentrate on your breath or a mantra when there are so many distractions. Sounds and sights, smells and tastes abound. People buying and selling have a frenetic energy; that too sends your efforts awry. Isn't it easier to meditate in a quiet corner without distractions?

Similarly, life is full of distractions. In a sense, it is also a marketplace of buying and selling, exchange of possessions and relationships. Comparatively speaking, death is a quiet corner where things and possessions, people and relationships, leave you alone.

Creativity is an encounter of the ego and the quantum self (May 1975; Goswami 1996). At death, as we have seen, consciousness begins to withdraw from the physical body. While it continues to collapse correlated possibility waves so that experience goes on, the center of identity shifts first to the vital-mental body, then past that to the realm of archetypes (the theme body). When the identity shifts in this way, the ego becomes more fluid, as in a dream; it has a minimum of the fixity that we experience during our ordinary waking hours, a fixity that is the utmost obstruction against the creative encounter.

A good analogy is the flow experience that you have when you forget yourself in the dance of creation with the quantum self. Flow is when the dance dances you, the music plays you, the pen writes on the paper as if it is just happening and you are not doing it. We sometimes naturally fall into this state in our pursuits, but we can also practice to maximize the chance of falling into them. Practicing to be in the creative state of flow as we die is a purpose of death yoga.

In the Upanishads, it is said that people at death go to *Chandraloka*—the realm of the moon (obviously a station between Heaven, the transcendent, and Earth, the ordinary immanent realm). Here they are asked, "Who are you?" Those who cannot answer are destined for reincarnation as determined by their karmic bondage. But those who answer "I am you" are allowed to proceed on their great journey (Abhedananda 1944). But notice how paradoxical the phrase "I am you" is. I am separate because I can see "I am," and yet I also see my identity with you. This is the nature of the encounter between the ego and the quantum self.

Creative acts require four stages: preparation, incubation (unconscious processing), encounter and insight, and manifestation. Creativity in death is no exception. In the following pages, let's look into the details of these stages. One good thing about death is that you don't have to go through hoops to achieve it. It costs you nothing and has the potential to give you everything. What a treat!

Preparation for Death

When should you begin preparing for death? There is really no reason why you should not start right now. Some people regard their whole life as a preparation for death (somewhat like people who eat their whole dinner in preparation for the dessert), and they are not wrong to think and act in this way (death is their "dessert"). But if you have lived "normally," then when to prepare for death has special significance. It is the beginning of your particular practice of death yoga.

You must begin such preparation when you know you have a terminal disease—that's easy. But when there is no such clear indication, what then?

When you are old, if you watch for them, some preliminary symptoms of the eventual withdrawal of consciousness from life become clear to you. The physical body may get weak.

You may experience periods of dry mouth and difficulty in breathing. You may also have difficulty in recognizing people. These withdrawal symptoms may also appear as a general reduction in the need to conceptualize, a tendency toward less aggressiveness in doing or accomplishment, and a lessening of desire for things. These symptoms are further accompanied by a natural tendency to fall into nondoing, a disinterest in the contents of the mind that is close to emptiness. Why these tendencies? There is a gradual decoupling of the correlated actions of the mental and physical, or of the physical, mental, and vital. When this becomes fairly frequent, it is time to prepare in earnest.

Of what does preparation consist? Although documented best with terminally ill patients, the truth is that most of us go through the stages of denial, anger, bargaining, and depression when we are confronted with death, even vaguely (as and when we are old and not so healthy and begin to notice the preliminary withdrawal symptoms above). The first essential step of preparation is to go through these stages, ending in acceptance. Acceptance is the opening of the mind toward the creative possibilities of death. The psychologist Carl Rogers gave high value to an open mind for creativity.

In a Zen story, a professor goes to see a Zen master to learn about Zen. While the Zen master prepares tea, the professor begins to give the Zen master an earful of what he knows about Zen. When the tea is ready, the Zen master starts pouring the tea into the professor's cup. But he goes on pouring, even after the cup is full, until the professor cries out, "The cup is overflowing." The Zen master calmly says, "So is your mind with ideas about Zen. How can I teach you when your mind is so full?"

And yet preparation also entails reading the literature of death, dying, and reincarnation. You are going to discover what happens after death. The literature tells you about other people's intuitions—it provides you with useful hints. But you must remember the lesson of the story above. You must be careful not to make what you read part of your belief system.

Alternative Preparation
and Unconscious Processing

What we normally call dying of old age is actually death from some illness or other. As the physician/author Sherwin Nuland says, death is painful and grubby. Preparation means that you strive to make your death a creative experience, a death with dignity. It is also a letting go.

The truth is, you are already that which you seek—the immortal one and original consciousness. What you are looking for is the one that is looking. But in the process of looking, there is separateness and pain. This separateness dissolves when you don't strive. That's when unconscious processing occurs.

Remember the double-slit experiment? Electrons go through both slits of a two-slitted screen to make a multifringe pattern on the fluorescent plate behind the screen (see chapter 2 and figure 2.1). But this quantum wonder happens only if the electrons are not looked at so they pass through both slits; if you look, there are only two fringes (fig. 10.1) because your looking collapses each electron at only one of the two slits through which it now travels. This is the thing. Striving is always looking. Process, don't look. Unconscious processing lets us accumulate and proliferate ambiguity through the quantum dynamics of the brain-mind/vital-physical bodies.

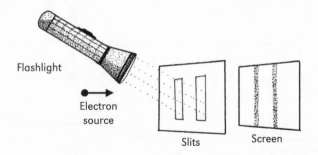

Flashlight

Electron
source

Slits

Screen

Fig. 10.1. In an arrangement where a flashlight is aimed at the slits so we can see which slit an electron passes through, the interference pattern disappears and electrons behave like classical, tiny baseballs.

So when pain comes, you may respond to it with both doing and nondoing. Doing means something active, for example, doing some of the practices described below. Nondoing means just that, just letting go—not resisting and not identifying with the pain. The first requires will, the second surrender. This interplay of both may lead to the preconscious encounter, the encounter between your ego and the quantum self, between who you think you are and God.

The filmmaker Mel Brooks said, "If you're alive, you got to flap your arms and legs, you got to jump around a lot, you got to make a lot of noise, because life is the very opposite of death. And therefore, as I see it, if you're quiet you are not living. You've got to be noisy, or at least your thoughts should be noisy and colorful and lively." In contrast, there is a Zen haiku, "Sitting quietly, doing nothing. The spring comes, and the grass grows by itself." So the road to the creative encounter combines the wisdom of Mel Brooks and Zen.

Encounter: Three Tibetan Practices

You already know about the bardo at the moment of death when you go through an out-of-body experience, take dreamy and visionary trips through the transcendent realms, do a life review, and all that (see chapter 8). The problem is to maintain awareness through it all. It is the perfect balance of doing and nondoing that can take you through it to the clear light.

The Tibetans suggest three practices to help the action-dynamic of the doing/nondoing duo in the creative approach to death.[29] These are: the death prayer, which is a practice of devotion; perfect sacrifice, which is a practice of virtue in action; and effortless contemplation, which is the practice of jnana (wisdom/inquiry). Each of these practices is found in many other traditions as well.

---

[29]I had much help from the spiritual teacher Joel Morwood in writing this section.

In the Tibetan version, the death prayer means praying to Amitabha Buddha while thinking of the Land of Bliss, the Buddhist version of Heaven. This is similar to the last rites in the Catholic tradition, when the priest takes you through a final confession and a prayer to Jesus. Of course, if you make the death prayer your practice for death yoga, you can't wait for the priest to be present every time you do the practice. Similarly, Moslems are told to die saying, "No God but Allah, and Muhammad is the messenger." Hindus practice *japa*, meditating internally on a name of God.

When Gandhi was shot, his death prayer was so internalized, he was so ready, that his instant last word was "Ram"—a name of God. The idea of the death prayer is exactly to have this kind of readiness so that the moment of death becomes a true encounter between God and you, your quantum self and you.

How to practice? Create a short mantra for yourself with an archetype of your particular tradition (to which image you are naturally devoted) as the centerpiece of the prayer, and then repeat it at all conscious moments. If it is, "God, I surrender to you," then you are saying that in your mind whenever you are aware. Pain comes. "God, I surrender to you." You doze off. You wake, "God, I surrender to you." Distraction comes. You become aware that you are distracted, "God, I surrender to you." After you do this a while, the prayer will internalize; it will go on by itself as unconscious processing. You have now reached the perfect balance of doing and nondoing. The Hindus call this *ajapa-japa* (japa without japa).

What happens? All traditions claim that this prayer practice enables you to recognize consciousness in its suchness (the clear light of the Tibetan Book of the Dead).

The second practice, perfect sacrifice, is the practice of one of the highest ideals in spiritual traditions. It is based on the intuition that voluntary sacrifice is a highly efficacious way to arrive at the nature of truth. Jesus chose crucifixion to redeem humanity, and in the process he himself arrived at resurrection. Buddhists call this the bodhisattva practice, to sacrifice even one's own liberation until all beings are liberated. The Bhagavad Gita talks about *tyaga*, sacrifice, as the highest practice; it is the theme of the Gita's last chapter, "The Yoga of Liberation."

So, instead of looking at pain and suffering and recoiling from them, we embrace pain and suffering to relieve not my pain but the pain of humanity.

How to do this practice? If you are going through a particular suffering (not uncommon for people who know they are going to die), imagine that you have taken on this suffering for the sake of others. If you are not suffering from anything in particular, you can imagine taking on a particular suffering for the sake of others. Feel the joy of those who would be relieved from this particular suffering. Coordinate your breath: as you breathe in, take on the suffering of all beings; as you breathe out, send the happiness of release to all beings. Again, you cannot do this by striving alone; you will need to arrive at a balance of will and surrender.

Why does this practice work? You can see that it is akin to bhakti yoga with a touch of karma yoga (see chapter 9). Ordinarily, in our ego we are solipsistic—we literally think or behave as if we are the center of the universe and all else is real only to the extent that we relate to it. From this state, it is impossible to sacrifice for anybody unless we "love" them. I love my spouse, my children, my country, so I can sacrifice for these entities. The practice of sacrificing for others leads to the discovery of the otherness of others, which is the discovery of true love—love that is not conditional on the other being related to me or being my extension. The more you find that you can love others, the less is the dominion of your ego over you. If you can truly die to relieve others' suffering and to bring them joy, you have transcended the self-imposed boundaries of the ego and clearly have entitled yourself to see the light of consciousness.

The psychiatrist Stan Grof has inadvertently discovered a wonderful and effective method for this practice—holotropic breathing, breathing that literally leads to more holistic identification. Initially, when Grof first administered this practice to his clients, they were going through what seemed to be pre-natal and perinatal experiences in the birth canal. But as people went deeper, the experiences that came up involved collective pain, the suffering of the whole of humanity. Read, in particular, the experience of the philosopher Christopher Bache with this technique; you will see its power (Grof 1998; Bache 2000).

The jnana path discussed in the last chapter can be used, but this way of developing effortless contemplation is said to be the most difficult—it is to discover consciousness by staying within its nature, within the present moment, without allowing distraction. This is the true meaning of the phrase "conscious dying."

"Of all mindfulness meditations," said the Buddha in the *Parinirvana Sutra*, "that on death is supreme." In practice, however, only people who are already practicing meditators, who can hold attention for prolonged periods of time, can expect to stay with all the pain, all the suffering, all the distraction, all the grubbiness that death usually involves.

On the other hand, there is the following anecdote about a sage named Tukaram in India. A disciple inquired of Tukaram about how his transformation came, how he never got angry, how he was always loving, and so forth; he wanted to know Tukaram's "secret."

"I don't know what I can tell you about my secret," said Tukaram, "but I know your secret."

"And what secret is that?" the disciple asked curiously.

"You are going to die in a week," said Tukaram gravely.

Since Tukaram was a great sage, the disciple took his words seriously. During the next week, he cleaned up his act. He treated his family and friends lovingly. He meditated and prayed. He did everything he could in preparation for his death.

On the seventh day, he lay down on his bed, feeling weak, and sent for Tukaram. "Bless me, sage, I'm dying," he said.

"My blessing is always with you," said the sage, "but tell me how you've been spending the last week? Have you been angry with your family and friends?"

"Of course not. I had only seven days to love them. So that's what I did. I loved them intensely," said the disciple.

"Now you know my secret," exclaimed the sage. "I know that I can die at any time. So I am always loving to all my relationships."

Just so, the special leverage that the dying situation gives you is intensity—the most essential component of concentration.

Effortless contemplation of the nature of reality is not thinking, but paradoxically it is transcending thinking via thinking. Franklin Merrell-Wolff said, "Substantiality is inversely proportional to ponderability." The more substantial your contemplation of reality becomes, the less ponderable it is. And the less ponderable it is, the less effort is required. Finally, a stage comes when you realize that, as Ramana Maharshi often reminded people, "Your effort is the bondage." When effort blends with surrender, everything becomes effortless—*sahaj* in Sanskrit.

When contemplation becomes substantial and imponderable and no effort is needed, you are in the natural flow of consciousness—sahaj samadhi. As Bokar Rinpoche says, "When death finally comes, if the practitioner remains in the nature of the mind [consciousness], he or she will obtain full awakening and become a Buddha at the stage called the absolute body or clear light of the moment of death."

You Don't Have to Wait for Death to Practice Death Yoga

There is a great story in the Upanishads. There was a young boy, Nachiketa, whose father arranged a great *yajna* (Sanskrit word meaning sacrificial ritual) of sacrifice, a give-away orgy, to assure his place in Heaven. But the father was calculating; for example, he kept the best cows for himself, giving away the weak ones. Nachiketa, noticing his father's half-hearted giving, challenged him. "Father, to whom are you giving me?" No answer. But Nachiketa persisted. When he asked the third time, the father angrily replied, "Yama, the death god. I've decided to give you to the death god."

But a promise is a promise, so Nachiketa went to the abode of Yama. Since he was premature, nobody was there to receive him. Nachiketa waited for three nights after which the death god returned. Yama was embarrassed that a guest had been ignored for three nights, and to make up for it, he granted Nachiketa three boons.

The first two boons were trivial, but for the third boon, Nachiketa wanted to know the secret of death—what happens after death? "Some say we die, some say we don't. What really happens?"

Now Yama was in a bind and tried to bribe himself out of giving away the secret of death. But nothing doing. So finally, he taught Nachiketa the truth about existence—consciousness does not die with death. Realizing this truth within oneself, said Yama, one learns the mystery of death.

It happens. Ramana Maharshi was sixteen when one day he had the strange feeling that he was going to die and "a violent fear of death overtook me." He began thinking what to do about death. What does death mean? What is it that is dying? He also began dramatizing the coming of death. He stretched out stiff, as though rigor mortis had set in, imitating a corpse. And he thought to himself, "Now that this body is dead, with the death of this body, am I dead? Is the body I?" The force of his inquiry precipitated an unexpected transformation in being. Later he wrote:

> It flashed through me vividly as living truth that I perceived directly, almost without thought process. "I" was something very real, the only real thing about my present state, and all the conscious activity connected with my body was centered on that "I." From that point onwards the "I" or Self focused attention on Itself by a powerful fascination. Fear of death had vanished. Absorption in the Self continued unbroken from that time on. Whether the body was engaged in talking, reading, or anything else, I was still centered on "I" (Quoted in Osborne 1995).

11.

QUESTIONS AND ANSWERS

I often give lectures and workshops on the insights that quantum theory gives us on the subject of survival after death and reincarnation. The idea of this chapter grew out of the many questions that I am asked at these lectures and workshops, upon seeing how the question-answer format is better suited for a certain kind of personal questions (as opposed to general philosophical or scientific questions). However, as I got going, I couldn't resist making this sort of a summary chapter. Enjoy.

Q: What is the purpose of life?

A: The purpose of the individual life is the same as the cosmic purpose which is to manifest the possible, to engage in the creative play of discovering what is potential in consciousness. Consciousness, thus seeing itself, seems to express itself within certain contexts. There are contexts that a human individual must live fully, must express creatively.

Q: What is the purpose of death?

A: At first glance, it seems that there is no purpose in death. Why isn't the purposiveness of life exhausted in just one long life? But the demand of manifestation is a different one. In the idealist view, life is the battleground of two forces: creativity and entropy. Entropy produces wear and tear in the physical body which is the hardware for creativity to make new programs that we call learning. Eventually, entropy wins this battle and the organism ceases to involve itself with further creativity. This is when consciousness begins to withdraw. This withdrawal terminates in death.

Long ago I read a science-fiction series of stories by the British author Michael Moorcock about an antihero named Jerry Cornelius (available as *The Cornelius Chronicles*) which depicts this struggle between creativity and entropy: Jerry and his friends jump from one reality to another in a multireal London from episode to episode, always searching for that one manifestation where creativity reigns and life wins over death. Of course, Jerry never finds this reality, because he himself carries the germ of entropy.

But why regard this as a failure? What is the necessity of finishing all our creative purpose in one life? So we die, but we come back in another time and place with a clean slate to have another chance at creativity in another incarnation.

Q: Now you are confusing me. If reincarnation gives us clean slates, how could we remember past lives, and why would we? Wouldn't that dirty our slates? And what about karma? How does karma propagate from life to life of the individual without filling up our new slates?

A: The clean slate refers only to the physical body that dies after becoming overwhelmed by classical memory. In contrast, the vital and mental bodies of the quantum monad that survive death carry quantum memory. Quantum memory weights probabilities in favor of past experiences; this creates a predisposition, and it is through this predisposition that karma travels from one physical incarnation to another. And past-life recall of the content of previous lives arises from the nonlocality of quantum processes and consciousness. A nonlocal connection between incarnations is available but is not easy to access.

Quantum memory is written into the mathematical equations that govern the quantum monad. Since it is not coded in manifest form, it does not deteriorate. Of course, predispositions can be a barrier when they are used to avoid collapsing certain contexts. However, the traditions claim that we do not bring all our past predispositions (propensities or karma) into each incarnation, only a selected few (called *prarabdha*).

This idea of predispositions becoming a barrier is also the reason for the admonition to avoid bad karma. And this is where good karma helps us to get on with the job of creatively discovering and learning the contexts that are potential in us.

Q: What does learning entail? Creative discovery of the themes of our lives?

A: Discovery and manifestation in living. Unless we live the theme we discover ("walk" our discovery), the discovered theme does not become a conditioned propensity of the mind. People who don't "walk" their discoveries of the themes of the supramental intellect are called intellectuals as opposed to intelligent. You comprehend?

Q: I think so. Would you repeat how you define good and bad karma?

A: Karma is much misunderstood, especially in the popular mind. Even many East Indians (let alone people in the West) think that if they do good deeds—give to the poor, serve their parents, and such—they accumulate good karma. Not necessarily. The only good karma is dispositional quantum memory, which enables you to creatively discover and express your purposiveness, to live the contexts through which consciousness knows itself. On the other hand, if your deeds produce dispositions toward habits, phobias, and the like that diminish your creativity in the next life, you obviously are accumulating bad karma.

Q: I am still not convinced that we need reincarnation to manifest the purposiveness of the universe. Agreed, one life is limited in scope. But instead of many lives, why not have many people? There is no limit as to how many people we can have, is there?

A: Isn't there? Obviously, the planet can sustain only a limited population. Without reincarnation, we severely abbreviate the opportunity to create good dispositions that nurture the creativity required for the discovery of truly sophisticated contexts that civilization thrives on. Think about the phenomena of savants and child prodigies, about the achievements of people like Einstein and Shankara, who almost certainly were born with propensities toward greatness from past lives.

Q: Ah, I just thought of something. If people understood what you are saying about good karma, they would live ethically, wouldn't they? Because ethics is directly related to creativity. Ethics consists of enhancing your own creativity and that of others and, at the least, of not harming it. In societies where karma is misunderstood or ignored, people become unethical.

A: You are absolutely right. Take India. Karma is believed but misunderstood with very limited and myopic ideas of good and bad. Good, creative dispositions are rarely developed. On the other hand, take the United States, where karma is not believed; good, creative dispositions are developed but along with bad ones.

Q: So what can we do to manifest the purposiveness of our lives besides paying attention to the karma that our actions create?

A: Pay attention to death. Remember the lessons of the Tibetan Book of the Dead and of our model of reincarnation. Conscious death may lead to nonlocal experiences that would be very valuable for the next life.

Q: But that's only if the model is the correct model.

A: Of course. Scientific models are designed for our use. You now have a scientific model; put it to use and you see for yourself whether it is valid. My intuition is that the death experience is potentially very valuable to us.

Q: In the Hindu literature, one finds the concept of burning karma. Can karma be burned?

A: Yes, in a sense. We bring propensities (karma) from past lives to this life to work on a certain learning agenda. When the agenda is fulfilled, there may be no further need for those particular propensities. So one may say that by our creative action of learning new themes of life, we have burned some karma.

Q: What about the number-of-souls question? You know, that so many more people are being born now that there aren't enough old souls to accommodate all of them?

A: Nothing in our model prohibits new souls from coming into being at any time; neither the theme nor the mental and vital bodies are reducible to any countable number. We all use the same mental and vital functions, except that they propagate in different patterns. It is these different patterns that give individuality to our vital and mental being. We know that the propagation has an end (liberation). Why not also a beginning?

There is also another factor working here. Many old quantum monads are now beyond the cycle of rebirth. Spiritual life was easier in ancient times, more supported by the culture. Hindus called that age the *Satya yuga* (golden age). People were liberated within a few births. Now, there are so many material distractions that it is hard to hold attention on learning. (The Hindus don't call the current age *Kali yuga* [age of ignorance] for nothing.) Thus, quantum monads are born into physical bodies many more times before they "see the light." This is also borne out by Helen Wambach's data (see chapter 5). Naturally, there are many more people born now.

But ultimately, this whole issue of number of souls comes up again and again because we fall prey to dualistic thinking— a finite number of eternal souls independent of God (the whole). The quantum view (as is the mystical) is that the soul has no existence apart from God (or consciousness). Soul is a limited identification that consciousness assumes for the purpose of exploration of possibilities. When this job is done, the soul-identification surrenders into the whole.

Q: A recent book documents that death is often a very painful experience devoid of dignity (Nuland 1994). You seem to ignore these aspects of death.

A: From the data on deathbed visions, it seems that, although disease is painful, death itself may not be. In our model, we can see why. There may be pain at the moment of death, but we need not identify with it. If we pay attention, we may catch the timeless beauty of that moment and be liberated.

Any lack of dignity comes from our fear of death. I had a mystic philosopher friend and teacher, Franklin Merrell-Wolff, who died at the age of ninety-eight from pneumonia. He experienced pain from the disease, but there was no lack of dignity. Wolff maintained his sense of humor even while his body parts were gradually losing their proper functioning. He was prepared for death.[30]

Q: To change the subject slightly, as a scientist, how do you feel about subtle bodies, even with the fancy name of quantum monad? Isn't it believing in ghosts?

A: I avoided the idea of "subtle" bodies for a long time for that reason alone. It sounds very dualistic. Of course, the problem with dualism disappears when we realize that the quantum monads have no direct interaction whatever with material bodies; consciousness mediates that interaction.

Q: But how do we see them as ghosts, apparitions?

A: Perhaps when a telepathic communication occurs between an incarnate being and a quantum monad, mediated by nonlocal consciousness, some people react to it by externalizing the experience as that of a being who is trying to communicate with them. The ghost, then, is the seer's own projection. The important point to note is that ghosts and

---

[30]Read Merrell-Wolff 1994 for an idea of the spiritual depth of this man.

apparitions are internal phenomena; they do not appear in shared external reality; therefore, they are fundamentally consistent with the model proposed here.

Q: When I die, what will happen to me? To tell the truth, I am a little afraid of becoming a ghost, or even a noninteracting quantum monad, roaming around not knowing what to do.

A: It depends on your karma and on how aware you are at death. Yes, if there is not much awareness at death, there may be some confusion; you may inadvertently create a hell experience for yourself. But remember, once you die and no longer have any connection to a physical body, you will have no manifest experience, as in ordinary waking awareness. However, possibilities will accumulate, and some of these possibilities you will live retroactively when you are reborn, giving you memories to cope with, so you have to watch it when you die. The possibilities that will arise in your subtle bodies when you are dead and unconscious will depend on the state of your dying consciousness.

Q: How do I make sure I don't go to Hell?

A: One thing is certain. You take all your desires with you, desires you were not able to satisfy during life and could not give up.

A rabbi went to Heaven and after a while found out where his venerable teacher lived. At once he visited him. The venerable rabbi was at his desk working, but, to the visiting rabbi's astonishment, there was a beautiful, naked woman on the teacher's bed, ready for action. The visitor winked at his former teacher, "Rabbi, that must be your reward for all the good deeds you did." To this, his host replied wryly, "No, I am her punishment." This is Hell.

Desires involve events of the mental-vital-physical—all three of our individualized bodies. The intellect or theme body has no mapping in the physical; so it cannot be conditioned, cannot be individualized; what we experience as the discriminating intellect is part of our mind. If we live life completely identified with the brain-mind, with little awareness of our vital/physical body and its quantum modes—prana, if you will—desire arises unconsciously. This predisposition continues from one incarnation to another until we make the unconscious conscious in our lives. When the unconscious becomes conscious and we live that desire fully and consciously, the predisposition then can fall away. When that happens, you no longer need to worry about Hell.

Q: This may sound silly, but where does the quantum monad go exactly? Where is Heaven or all those lokas we hear about in Hindu lore?

A: Good question. In the olden days, people thought dualistically. Hindus would place specific lokas in certain spots in the Himalayas. The Greeks thought that outer space was Heaven. But the spiritual teachers of the world have always known better; Plato or the sages of the Upanishads would answer your question by saying that Heaven is transcendent. One of the great conceptual achievements of quantum physics is the concept of quantum nonlocality, which gives us something to reference when the spiritual traditions use the word "transcendent." But what is nonlocality? It's a connection among potentialities outside space-time that can affect events in space-time. Where is it? It is both everywhere (because every point in space and time can be connected via nonlocality) and nowhere (because we cannot localize it).

Q: Shall I find my dead friends and relatives in the afterworld?

A: You sound like Woody Allen, who wrote, "There is the fear that there is an afterlife but no one will know where it's being held." First of all, when we enter death through that great nonlocal window that lies open to us, many experiences are possible. All we can say about after we die is that there is unconscious processing. States of the vital and mental bodies may go on developing in possibility via some internal dynamics that we have yet to discover. One of these possible pathways will manifest retroactively when the next incarnation takes place. The manifested pathway may contain experiences with your friends, but you created these experiences with your mental body. These are not experiences in the same sense as those of your waking awareness; they are more like dreams (see chapter 5).

Q: When I am ready to rebirth, how will I find my particular incarnation? Do I choose my parents?

A: Nonlocal correlation picks the particular womb at once and without having to go anywhere; remember, there is no space and no time in the nonlocal domain. Do we pick our parents? The nonlocal correlations that bind us to our future incarnations all exist in possibility; thus, choice may be involved. There is some data from hypnotic regression which suggest that we may indeed be able to choose our parents. This choice may be due to past patterns and not free, or it may be free, depending on my identification status at the moment of death.

Q: When I am reborn, will my friends and lovers take rebirth with me?

A: They may, if their lives are karmically correlated with yours. Barbara Young, the biographer of the poet Kahlil Gibran, talks of a time when, while working with the poet, she sat on the floor on cushions instead of in her usual chair and felt a strange sense of familiarity in the position. She said, "I feel as if I've sat like this beside you many times—but I really haven't." To this Gibran replied, "We have done this a thousand years ago, and shall do it a thousand years hence."

Q: Are we always born of the same race, same sex, and same nationality?

A: I had a dentist (white American male) who once practically fell into shock when I asked him if he had ever thought of being reborn as a woman. Unfortunately for him, the quantum monad has no sex, no creed, no race, and no nationality, only habits, tendencies, and contexts to learn. Whatever our birth— male or female, black, white, brown, or yellow, Eastern or Western—it gives us the maximum learning opportunity, which we choose, and always in accordance with our past karma. As the novelist Romain Rolland said, "There is neither East nor West for the naked soul. Such things are merely its trappings. The whole world is its home."

Q: To change the subject again: Can a discarnate quantum monad affect a living person? If so, what are some of the ways?

   A: As I said before, for the concept of quantum monad to be scientifically tenable, we must postulate no direct interaction between it and the material reality. However, consciousness may choose to collapse possibility waves simultaneously in the monad and in an Earthside person; thus, communication is possible, for example, with a medium or a channeler. This could be the explanation of how channelers function, since they often show the disposition of the dead person that they are representing. Other people may interpret such altered states as "possession." There can be other instances of such communication, too, inspired automatic writing, for example. This is also a good question for experimentalists.

Q: Does such communication affect the karmic propensities of the monad?

   A: Yes. This is the reason that mediumships and channelings are not encouraged in the esoteric literature. (Read, for example, Barker 1975.) The exceptions are those angelic beings who have transcended karma altogether. They are available to serve us. If we have purity of intention, they can, and do, help our creativity.

Q: What can you say about suicide?

   A: That depends. Remember what we are learning here. Death does not rid us of our existence. We continue as discarnate quantum monads with quantum memory of our dispositions, habits, conditioning. So we carry the problems that drive us to suicide with us after death. Thus, suicide as denial or avoidance does not solve anything. The English playwright

J. B. Priestley, in one of his plays, expresses this sentiment just about perfectly:

> *Ormund:* If I had any sense I'd use [my revolver to kill myself]. No more questions that can't be answered, twisting like knives in your guts. Sleep, a good sleep, the only good sleep.
>
> *Dr. Goertler:* I am afraid you will be disappointed. . . . The questions will still be there. You cannot blow them to bits with a pistol.
>
> *Ormund:* I suppose you believe that if I take the jump into the dark, I'll find myself back again on the old tread-mill. Well, I don't believe it. I can find peace.
>
> *Dr. Goertler:* You can't. Peace is not somewhere just waiting for you. . . . You have to create it. . . . Life is not easy. It provides no short cuts, no effortless escapes. . . . We each live a fairy tale created by ourselves.
>
> *Ormund:* What—by going around the same damned dreary circle of existence as you believe?
>
> *Dr. Goertler:* We do not go round in a circle. . . . We move along a spiral track. It is not quite the same journey from cradle to grave each time. . . . We must set out each time on the same road, but along that road we have a choice of adventures (Quoted in Cranston and Williams 1994, 387–88).

Q: So you must be against euthanasia, on principle.

A: Should terminally ill patients have the right to terminate their lives when their body is being kept alive artificially or when the pain is unbearable? That is a far more complicated issue.

I rather like the Native American custom. When one feels that the time has come, one just goes to the hilltop and lies down and lets nature take care of it. Of course, you remember the movie *Little Big Man*—sometimes it works, sometimes it doesn't. This is why the Tibetans have developed very sophisticated methods for voluntary dying.

Q: I read about a near-death suicide survivor who had an out-of-body experience in which he saw a boy following his father and saying repeatedly, "I did not know that mom would be affected like this. I wouldn't have done it if I had known." Is this compatible with your scientific model?

A: Yes, the story illustrates what I said about suicide quite well, doesn't it?

Q: But how could one hear in the afterworld?

A: This NDEer was hearing telepathically; remember, he was not dead yet. One may have a correlated possibility wave running in the subtle body that consciousness can collapse as long as there is a connection with the physical body. Then one can hear the message directly, without signals. The image the NDEer saw was perhaps his own projection.

Q: Here's another loaded question. At what point does the quantum monad enter the new incarnate body?

A: The vital body (of the quantum monad) can be mapped immediately in even the single-celled embryo. But the mental body of the quantum monad cannot be mapped until the fetus develops a brain, which takes from fourteen to sixteen weeks. Thus, life as a human can begin only around that time.

Q: Let's change the subject. How about food and sex when we are discarnate?

A: Food and sex serve the physical body in specific roles of metabolism and reproduction. They have no corresponding function for the quantum monad.

Q: I've been wondering how I avoid getting bored during my long after-death hiatus. Even in a dream, I hate to be bored.

A: This calls for another story. A man dies and finds himself in a beautiful place. After a while, the mere enjoyment of the scenery becomes boring, and he begins thinking of food. Instantly, an attendant appears. "How does one get some food here?" he asks. "Oh, you just think the food, and it will appear," he is told. He eats well, but after a while a different kind of desire arises. The attendant appears again and, again, tells him to think what he wants. Accordingly, a most beautiful woman appears. He has sex a few times but soon feels bored again. He summons the attendant once more and complains quite irritably, "I thought that in Heaven one never gets bored. I thought boredom can happen only in Hell." The attendant was surprised. "Where do you think you are?" he asked.

We take our dispositions with us in death. If you are plagued by boredom (which is a major suffering in this information age), then, with all that unconscious processing ahead of you (which is what death is), you are going to create a hell experience of boredom for yourself; and the memory of that is going to bother you when you reincarnate. Work on your dispositions now before it is too late.

Q: When children die, they haven't acquired much conditioning yet. What happens to their quantum monads?

A: Children's death-side experiences can be quite pure and beautiful. Of course, for very young children, the dispositions of the previous life may still dominate the death-side experience.

Q: Tell me more about angels.

A: I thought you would never ask. Those karmically fulfilled quantum monads that are "reborn" in Sambhogakaya form are what we call angels. They are available to help others through channeling, although they may never return to incarnate in a physical body. It may not be exactly like the movie *It's a Wonderful Life*, but it's close.

In Mahayana Buddhism, the highest ideal is not liberation in the clear light in the fourth bardo after death, it is in becoming a bodhisattva (one who waits at the gate to help others until everyone is liberated). I think waiting at the gate refers to rebirth in the discarnate form of the quantum monad in the angelic Sambhogakaya domain.

Q: What happens to those who choose the clear light?

A: They merge their identity with consciousness, with God, if you will; they become, in timeless nonlocality, the witness of the whole play as it unfolds.

Q: Ah, God. That reminds me. I've not always understood the difference between your concepts of God and the quantum self.

A: God and the quantum self are very similar concepts since quantum self, like God, is also universal consciousness. But we use one or the other terminology, depending on the perspective. If the perspective is from this side (the manifest side) of the tangled hierarchy, quantum self is the more appropriate term for the creator because it is taking place in connection with a particular body-mind complex. If, on the other hand, we are conceptualizing about the transcendent side, for example, when we speak of the creator as a whole, the totality of all the quantum self-experiences of all people, God is the appropriate term.

Q: Let's change the subject. Do animals have souls?

A: A prejudice against animals having souls developed in this culture, partly because of the ecclesiastical ruling against the idea and partly because Descartes thought animals were just machines without any mind. It is true that animals are guided by conditioned instincts, but each species has its own theme collective that it fulfills. Thus, at the least, animals have group souls, a monad for the entire species.[31]

Q: Why should a Christian believe in reincarnation? We have some fine Christian concepts about after-death realities. When we die, we go to purgatory, where we wait until the day of Judgment comes. True Christians, on Judgment Day, will be resurrected in physical bodies and become immortal, enjoying eternal life in Heaven—God's abode.

---

[31]The philosopher Arthur Young agrees with me on this. See Young 1976.

A: These are fine concepts, and I do not see any incompatibility of these concepts with the reincarnation scenario. Purgatory is more than waiting in limbo. Saint Catherine of Genoa said, "The soul, so seeing that it cannot, because of the impediment, attain to its end, which is God, and that the impediment cannot be removed from it, except by means of purgatory, swiftly and of its own accord throws itself into it." How close this is to the idea that Easterners and, now, the new science is proposing—we choose our next incarnation according to the needs of our monadic fulfillment. As the philosopher Geddes MacGregor has emphasized, the two notions—purgatory and reincarnation—can be integrated with some necessary adjustments. "When so adapted," says he, "the series of embodiments or chain of rebirths can be seen as functioning so much like a Christian purgatory as to be a perfect expression of the purgatorial pains which, despite the intensity of their anguish, are by no means without joy, for they are the pains of love, which entails both the sharpest of sufferings and the most ecstatic of joys" (MacGregor 1992, 150).

Q: What adjustments are you talking about?
A: The classic goal of reincarnational Eastern religions is liberation and re-identification with consciousness, the ground of being, popularly conceived as merging with God. In the occidental, monotheistic religions (which are also dualistic—God separate from the world), the emphasis is on achieving a heavenly abode and staying with God as perfected beings, but separately.

The adjustments you have to make consist of recognizing that within each of these traditions, the other goal also exists, although not as the preeminent one. In the esoteric traditions, including the mystical branches of the occidental religions, we find the supreme goal of humanity to be realizing that we are that and relinquishing our separate identities—in other words, the great liberation of merging into God. On the other hand, many branches of Eastern traditions emphasize remaining in separation from God, even after perfection is reached. For example, for many Buddhists, the goal is to become bodhisattvas; what are bodhisattvas but perfected beings in Heaven, yet with separate identities? Many Hindus of the Vaishnavite tradition believe that the jiva (quantum monad) never relinquishes identity to the supreme being.

Q: You haven't spoken of resurrection. How do you reconcile that idea with your science?

A: Again, the conventional popular view is what confuses you. In I Corinthians, St. Paul teaches that the resurrected body is different from the perishable physical body; it is *pneumatikos*, a spiritual body—imperishable. It is possible to interpret the spiritual body as a Sambhogakaya body outside the death-rebirth cycle, a discarnate quantum monad whose job on the Earthside is done.

If Jesus was reborn in a spirit or Sambhogakaya body, could the apostles have seen him resurrected? Yes. There is nothing in the story of resurrection that does not fit. The apostles were correlated with the disembodied spirit body of Jesus; thus, they were able to experience Jesus' propensities, memorized in the subtle body. In the purity of their intention, which they shared with Jesus, they might simultaneously have accessed the nonlocal window of Jesus' incarnations. The projections that they saw could have been formed by the same mechanism as apparitions. St. Paul's experience on the way to Damascus, an experience of seeing intense light and hearing the words "Saul, Saul, why are you persecuting me?" also fits this interpretation of resurrection (however, see chapter 12 for a more upbeat view).

Q: So, in your considered opinion, is reincarnation scientific?

A: Resoundingly, yes. Think about it. Reincarnation data gives us definitive evidence that mind is not brain because it survives the death of the physical body. Also, the purpose of science is to bring people's private realizations, experiences, and wisdom to the public arena through developing theories and experiments in which everyone can participate in principle and everyone finds useful. I think that the model we have studied here fulfills that purpose.

Q: Life is complicated enough without having to worry about past and future lives. Why should we bother? Is reincarnational thinking helpful to people, in general, people who do not, for example, have any therapeutic need for it?

A: Definitely. First, reincarnational thinking can be a big help to ordinary people in seeing the value of ethics in their lives. In materialist societies, ethics is regarded as relative; this erodes morality, legality cannot replace the role of morality fast enough, and societies degenerate as we see amply today. But if people know that ethical malpractice in this life leads to karmic repercussions in the next, ethics become important. Second, the idea of reincarnation enables us to see that death is part of a creative journey; this realization can change our entire attitude toward death and minimize our fear of death, and also, by implication, change our attitude toward life. Last but not least, reincarnation theory tells us that we come Earthside in a particular incarnation with some meaningful work to do, some contexts to learn, some bad karma to remove. In other words, we have a destiny to fulfill. People who are aware of their destiny are not haunted by meaning-of-life questions; they *know*.

Q: As the worldview changes from the current materialist one to one based on the primacy of consciousness, which accepts a reincarnational view of life and death, how do you think the human being will change?

A: The focus of materialist societies is pleasure and consumption fueled with newer and newer material gadgets of entertainment. The focus is always either matter or mind in its lowest common denominator—information. Realizing that the object of human life is not pleasure or consumption or entertainment but, instead, is the joy of learning and creativity will bring the focus back to us. How can I better manipulate matter to produce more gadgets of entertainment? Or how can I use mind to process evermore information? These questions will give way to, How can I transform so that I can manifest the creative purposiveness I chose for myself before I was born? It's not that we stop materials and information research but that we also direct ourselves toward transformation, toward real service to humanity. The important focus is always us, our creativity, our happiness (not to be confused with just sensory pleasure).

In the reincarnational context, our relationship with our environment does not end with this life. We become friendly with our environment not just for the sake of our grandchildren but for our own sake. We ourselves in a future incarnation have to deal with the damage we do now to our environment. The people I deal with in this life may have been karmically entangled with me for many lives. How do I untangle this web of past karma?

Q: So people will become more sensitive toward themselves, their relationships, their environment. Any advice as to how to enhance this sensitivity now and get going, get the job done?

A: We must ask: how do I surrender my identification with the current content-centered melodrama and identify with the context-centered traveler that I am and have been through many reincarnations? (Read chapter 9.)

12.

THE PHYSICS OF IMMORTALITY

People fear death, hence their quest for immortality. Books about immortality easily make the best-seller list, which suggests a popular belief that immortality is a possibility. Some scientists subscribe to this belief as well when they direct their research to inventing an immortality drug or some such thing. Formally, materialist science has replaced the quest for personal immortality with the quest for immortal scientific laws. But what science has tried to accomplish formally has not changed people's and scientists' quest for immortality of the physical body.

In terms of atoms, the atoms of our body are practically immortal, and they are being recycled over and over. I sometimes teach basic physics to nonscientists. Textbooks at this level usually go on and on about how we all share a few atoms which once formed the bodies of Cleopatra, Gandhi, and John Lennon. That's the materialist version of reincarnation, I suppose. "Even while you live, and certainly when you die, the atoms and molecules which are at present locked into your shape and appearance are being unlocked and scattered into other shapes and forms of construction," says the philosopher John Bowker. There is no other significance to death than that it is the way the universe operates: atoms get together in structure, dissipate, and form other structures.

Some biologists take the view of the immortality of genes instead of atoms. First, they say, notice that single-celled creatures like the bacteria don't die in the usual sense; they just replicate themselves at times, there is really no individuality of life at all. True, with sexual reproduction, the DNA of one creature mates with that of another, some gene recombinations take place, and individuality enters the scene. But here, too, these biologists say, note that the genes are immortal; they are merely recirculated to form new combinations.

If we regard ourselves as gene machines (Dawkins 1976) ("a person is only a gene's way of making another gene"), as no more than the outer garment of genes, then there is no meaning of our lives after we have produced babies; death then is nothing but a recycling of the raw material for the survival of the next generations of gene machines. But this constricted view allows no significance to the hopes, aspirations, and purposes that we live for until we die and that death seems to terminate. Thus, it is no wonder that the desire for immortality is not satisfied by the knowledge that atoms and genes are virtually immortal. The quest remains.

The quest for immortality is usually discussed in several different contexts:

1. Quest for a death-defying drug that rejuvenates a dead person.

2. Quest for immortality in the physical body, either in the form of an immortality drug or in a search for an ageless body that somehow turns off the aging agents or mechanisms of the body.

3. Immortality as resurrection in the physical body via divine grace or plan as envisioned by many Christians.

4. Immortality outside of time via a spiritual quest for liberation. This is how spiritual philosophers talk about immortality.

People also seek immortality through fame. The idea is that if you are famous enough, you will live on in other people's minds, in history books, in folklore. Examples are

Alexander the Great, Queen Anne, and Robin Hood, who have become immortal in our minds. But we need not speak of this kind of immortality in a scientific context.

Further note that propounders of spiritual immortality maintain that the first three contexts for speaking about immortality are not foolproof. Immortality in the physical body, ageless or resurrected from the dead by drug or grace, is not true immortality; it cannot be, they say, because this kind of immortality is envisioned as occurring within time. With the end of time, this kind of immortality must come to an end. And time, as we know it, does end. Our planet Earth will be destroyed with all its sentient life when the sun becomes a red giant—that's the end of time on Earth. The universe will come to an inglorious heat death when it finally loses its battle with entropy; long before then, conditions for life and sentience will be impossible anywhere in the universe—that's the end of time for all the manifest world.

However, quests for an immortality drug or an ageless body are worth talking about because they are materially based desires that generate a lot of interest. And resurrection, as in Christianity, is worth talking about because, along with reincarnation, this probably is the most intriguing after-death scenario ever intuited by human beings. And in truth, these scenarios have their own answers to the "end of time" argument. Of course, if immortality beyond time is true immortality, it is certainly worth talking about.

Ultimately, it seems that there are only two ways to quest for immortality—one, material, and the other, spiritual. If you think about it, all of the above quests fall into one or the other of these two categories.

But the purpose of this chapter is not only to discuss these two great human quests but also to point out that a third way to define the quest for immortality is gradually emerging that integrates both material and spiritual immortality.

The Quest for Material Immortality

Perhaps the earliest allusion to a drug that can bring one back from the dead occurs in the Summerian myth of Gilgamesh, whose quest for the drug began when his friend died. After a long search, Gilgamesh found a plant that rejuvenates even the dead, but he lost it to a snake through carelessness.

In the Indian epic *Ramayana*, however, the plant *bishalyakarani* is found and brought back by the famous monkey-God Hanuman to rejuvenate Rama (the hero of Ramayana) and his troops who were killed in one episode of their war against the demon-king Ravana to rescue Sita, Rama's wife, who was abducted by Ravana. Rama and his army were rejuvenated, eventually to win the war and rescue Sita, but all the plant was used up in the process and nobody since has ever seen any.

There is also a story in *Mahabharata* in which the great ocean is churned by the combined might of *suras* and *asuras*, gods and demons, for *amrita*—the immortality potion which the gods drank to become immortal. But the demons were surreptitiously prevented from drinking the potion, and thus it is that they can be slain. (Actually this myth has great metaphorical significance. The demons represent negative emotions; since they didn't get the immortality potion, they can be slain. Only gods representing positive emotions can be immortal.)

An immortality potion, of course, is also known in the West, where it is called ambrosia—the food of the gods. It has never been available for human consumption. But there is data suggesting that if we live properly, limiting stress, eating the right foods, and partake of no more than one glass of wine with our meals, we may attain long, healthy lives (Pelletier 1981). (See also Chopra 1993.) If long, healthy life is available, can immortality be far behind? Perhaps we could augment such proper living with an immortality plant—mushrooms, maybe? Don't laugh. The psychedelic-mushroom researcher, Terence McKenna, suggests this quite seriously. He sees taking "heroic dosages" of psychedelic mushrooms as the way to reach immortality at the end of time (McKenna 1991).

Other tracks toward material immortality are also being proposed. In an episode of the TV show *Picket Fences*, the plot evolves around the ethical dilemma created by the technology of freezing a live human—in this case, a boy with terminal cancer—until such time as a cure for the cancer becomes available. Should one go for a small chance that freezing will work and a cure will be found in the future, or let the boy enjoy his last six months?

The idea of prolonging our lives through freezing has been suggested by new-age thinkers Robert Ettinger and Timothy Leary. In Ettinger's freezer program, the idea is to freeze the body so as to suspend all organic decay until genetic engineering or other miracles of science can be used to rejuvenate the body and restore its youth (Ettinger 1964). To this, Leary has added the idea of preserving digitalized memories of the frozen person as insurance.

Why do we die? We die because of the march of entropy, the wear and tear that our body takes in the process of adult living. Life is the battleground of two forces: creativity and conditioning. Conditioning enables our bodies to function within established patterns. Unfortunately, as these patterns go awry as a result of the march of entropy, we get disease.[32] Creativity of the body-mind is needed to establish new pathways of healthy living.

Creativity research has shown that the act of creation involves unconscious processing, which is the processing without awareness, without the experience of subject-object split, of accumulated quantum possibilities in the physical/vital/mental/theme body complex. Unconscious processing leads to sudden insights which are quantum leaps of choice by consciousness from among these possibilities (Goswami 1996). Healing—creativity of the

---

[32]Since subtle bodies do not have micro-macro distinction and their motion is always quantum and never degenerates to classical, even approximately, there is no entropy in the subtle worlds, and no deterioration.

body—involves unconscious quantum processing of emotionally laced mental visualizations of health alternating with striving with the disease leading to quantum leaps of insight; it is being called quantum healing (Chopra 1989).

But even if we are creative about our body, during evolution consciousness chose to impose an ultimate limit on how long we should live. Most of our cells can reproduce only a finite number of times, about fifty. Every time the chromosomes of the cells of our body reproduce, the rate of reproduction goes down just a little. Eventually, no further reproduction happens, and the cells die. This programmed cell death is sometimes called the Hayflick effect; the physician Leonard Hayflick (1965) discovered the effect while experimenting with human cells cultured in the laboratory, but his results are believed to have universal validity.

For humans, what the Hayflick effect translates to is a lifespan of about a hundred years. Why did consciousness choose to limit us in this fashion? Survival is a crucial factor in evolution. In a finite ecosystem, it makes sense to have finite lifespans of all living creatures, and nature seems to ensure that.

When frozen animals are revived, they live only what remains of their normal lifespan, no longer. So freezing does not alter the commands of the Hayflick effect—the chromosomes, remember? But people of the ilk of Ettinger and Leary hope that future science will circumvent the limits of the Hayflick effect.

K. Eric Drexler (1986) envisions cell repair machines based on the technology of the small scale—nanotechnology. He maintains that aging "is no different from any other physical disorder." Aging results because somewhere in the body molecular machines are not functioning properly. Fix the machine with nanotechnology, and you will have unlimited youth, ageless body.

But the specter of the Hayflick effect hangs over the head of all these ideas. Is there any way to bypass the Hayflick effect?

The physician Deepak Chopra knows all about the Hayflick effect, but he does not think its command is invincible (Chopra

1993). Through healthy diet, stress reduction, yoga, meditation, and balancing the body by techniques laid out in the Vedic book of medicine, Ayurveda, Chopra says one may approach an ageless body. After all, ancient yogis in India and Tibet might have been able to slow down their body functions through the above practices so much so that they have lived for hundreds of years.

But admit it, this is still promissory. If we have to depend on promises, why not heed the promises of religious masters— past and present. We can start with Zarathustra, the Iranian founder of the Zoroastrian religion. In Zarathustra's vision, at the end of time, the power of almighty Ahura Mazda will resurrect the bodies of all people, and they will have a ball. "They will have intercourse with their wives, even as they do on Earth today, but no children will be born to them." Immortality with sex for pure amour. What more do you want?

But Zarathustra's ideas are echoed in some interpretations of resurrection in Christianity, and thus they are popular even today. Many Christians (for example, Jehovah's Witnesses) believe that there is going to be an Armageddon after which some people will be restored to their physical bodies by grace to live forever (only the saved ones, of course) in the presence of God. Even a book based on materialist physics tries to uphold this view with a new proposal for the equations of physics (Tipler 1994).

You get the gist of the ideas that are playing in the quest for immortality in a material body. The philosopher Michael Grosso sums it up well when he says, "So we come to full circle with Zoroaster [Zarathustra] who, like Terence McKenna, sees the end of history as a gigantic party—a party to which the entire human family, including the dead, will be invited" (Grosso 1995).[33]

---

[33]I received much help from Grosso 1995 (chapter 11) in researching the material of this section.

The Quest for Spiritual Immortality and the Science of Liberation

It seems fair to argue that true immortality is timeless, that it occurs outside of time. Time brings sorrow, fear and self-torment, difficulties, and evil that keep us from freedom. When we discover this, we become free in life (*jivanmukta*) and arrive at immortality after death. The novelist Hermann Hesse, in *Siddhartha*, captured the timelessness of immortal Being in this conversation between Siddhartha and his friend Govinda:

"Have you also learned [this] secret from the river; that there is no such thing as time? The river is everywhere at the same time, at the source and at the mouth, at the waterfall, at the ferry, at the current, in the ocean and in the mountains, everywhere, and the present only exists for it, not the shadow of the past, nor the shadow of the future?"

"That is it," said Siddhartha, "and when I learned that, I reviewed my life and it was also a river, and Siddhartha the boy, Siddhartha the mature man, and Siddhartha the old man, were only separated by shadows, not through reality. Siddhartha's previous lives were also not in the past, and his death and his return to Brahman are not in the future" (Hesse 1973).

How does one go beyond time? Timeless experiences, called samadhi in Sanskrit, are not that uncommon. For example, in creativity, when we have an ah-ha insight, we momentarily make a discontinuous quantum leap into timelessness. But we act in time where ordinary creative acts in arts, music, and the sciences, acts of outer creativity, are manifested. Even inner creativity, creative insights about our true nature that help to shift our identity beyond the ego, has a goal—transformation. Transformation is change and is therefore time-bound. To realize that Being is beyond time is to go beyond creativity; it is liberation, say the wise (Krishnamurti 1992).

The journey to liberation cannot begin in earnest as long as we are enamored with the mind and its moods. It cannot begin as long as we are in conflict with ethical principles for our actions. It does not begin seriously as long as we are attached to this guna or that—even sattwa, creativity, ultimately does not make us free.

It is "realizing" the truth that sets us free—the truth that I am the whole, I am Brahman. Once the truth is thus known about the reality of Brahman alone, and the epiphenomenal nature of the manifest world reveals itself, then there is no more identifying with a particular body-mind complex except as a functional necessity.

So what happens to the karma that has been running this particular body-mind complex—the prarabdha? The prarabdha karma runs its course behaviorally, say the wise, but the liberated being does not identify with it.

This realizing the truth about the self—that the self is all—is a truly discontinuous jump—a gigantic quantum leap. But there is some debate about the necessity of this quantum leap in the traditions. Some maintain that the journey to liberation is continuous: arriving at the truth need not be a discontinuous leap; instead, it initiates further contemplation on the truth, deepening and purifying one's understanding in meditation.

But ask, Who is the one who contemplates the truth to deepen understanding? There is no individual doer. If it is God's will, the will of the whole, certain body-mind complexes will be drawn to this program of purification.

In this purification program for the body-mind complex, we concentrate on transcending opposites: good and evil, subject and object, the gunas, body and mind. We sacrifice our preferences and arrive at equanimity. Our desires fall away. This is karma yoga; we still act, but the attitude is new. We are not apathetic in our action (it is impossible to act appropriately with apathy), but we bring a degree of what Franklin Merrell-Wolff called "high indifference"—equanimity with compassion (Merrell-Wolff 1994). When we surrender to the will of the One so totally that our will becomes the will of the One and vice versa, then do we quantum leap into complete freedom.

The truth is, for liberation, one has to embrace a subtlety. We have to "see" that we are already liberated, that no transformation is needed, no accomplishment. Surrendering accomplishments catapults our jnana practice into a natural embrace of spiritual joy. Similarly, the practice of love now becomes sweet, the Sanskrit word for which is *madhurang*. Sweet, sweet surrender.

How does one carry this out, this total surrender of will to the will of God? This is the discontinuous transition that cannot be avoided even in this way of thinking.

When one is liberated, there is no more rebirth. So when such a one dies, there is immortality in spirit; the quantum monad will never be born again—it has seen the end of time.

How does such a one live in the world, one who is jivan-mukta—free while living? What happens when the freedom of God is available in an incarnate human body-mind? The answer that accrued karma is now lived out without attachment does not satisfy. Fortunately, another answer is emerging, particularly from the insights of the sage Sri Aurobindo (1955).

It gives me goose bumps to know that what I am talking about is within our potential. One day I was reading one of Sri Aurobindo's books in which he writes about being in the supermind, the supramental plane of existence (Aurobindo 1989). Anybody interested in philosophy can recognize these ideas. But to understand their meaning is another thing altogether. Those of us who are mostly in our minds except for fleeting, occasional forays in the supermind (in moments of creative insights, for example), how can we comprehend supermind? I don't know if I will ever arrive at supramental being, and yet the idea intrigues me as much as it did that day.

My mind became very open, soft and malleable. I was reading a paragraph in which Aurobindo seems to express the idea that people of supermind, having aligned their will to the divine will, now have the ability to explore a new realm of creativity—creativity beyond the laws of science. Suddenly, I began to understand as I read this. Shivers were passing up my spine, and there was a distinct feeling that Aurobindo was right there helping me comprehend the enormity of this idea.

225

I also realized, with help from the invisible guidance I was feeling, that there is a possibility to quest immortality as part of this supramental expression. We will never understand immortality completely until we discover stabilized being in supermind.

In the *Katha Upanishad*, when Nachiketa went to the death god, Yama, to find the key to immortality, all Yama taught him, after being totally satisfied about Nachiketa's qualification to receive the teaching, was the practice of spiritual liberation, timeless immortality. And this for a very good reason: spiritual liberation is a prerequisite for the exploration of supermind.

Long ago, the Chinese founded a tradition called the Religion of the Golden Elixir of Life whose rituals have been published as the Secret of the Golden Flower. It is a manifesto, a workbook, for constructing an immortal spiritual body. By meditation, by controlling breath, and other spiritual disciplines, the idea is not only to die consciously but to retain conscious awareness even after death and not to become unconscious.

Aurobindo has the same idea except that he would say that one has to go beyond the mind, which is governed by the causal laws of the theme body of consciousness, in order to retain conscious awareness beyond death.

Supramental Being and Miracles

What is the evidence of supramental beings beyond the physical, vital, and the mental? The evidence is slowly accumulating.

One type of evidence is that of the truly miraculous happening around such beings—miraculous beyond the causal laws not only of science as we know it but also of science within consciousness. In Christianity, there are stories of stigmata (Padre Pio), survival without food and water (Theresa Neumann), materialization, and many cases of healing. Among the Hindus, there are many stories of beings who materialize things (Sai Baba is a living, famous example), beings who can appear in two places at the same time (Neem Karoli Baba, Ram

Dass's guru who passed away fairly recently), beings who can levitate (Shyamacharan Lahiri of *Autobiography of a Yogi* fame), and many cases of totally miraculous healing. There are many Sufi stories suggesting that there are masters, whose behavior is beyond the comprehension of ordinary reasoning, who dance to different laws beyond the realm of physical laws.[34]

In 1993, I visited the neurophysiologist Jacobo Grinberg-Zylberbaum at the University of Mexico. We were collaborating on the paper about transferred potentials (see chapter 4) at the time. During one of our many discussions, Jacobo mentioned his personal experience with a shamanic physician/surgeon known as Pochita (now deceased). Jacobo witnessed an operation by this shaman/doctor in which she literally took the heart out of a patient's body, fixed it with her hands, and put it back. Jacobo wrote a book (unfortunately for us, it is in Spanish) about this great medicine woman. Carlos Castaneda's Don Juan comes to mind; is it all fiction, or is Castaneda's writing based on a factual character? Once we recognize supramental being as a possibility, no longer do the escapades of Don Juan boggle the mind with incredulousness.

I myself have not been fortunate enough to directly witness supramental beings performing miracles. However, I have directly intuited that being can be stabilized in the supramental, in the theme body, and from that place of intuition, the only interpretation of miracles that makes sense is that the people of miracles have arrived at the supramental level of being where they are able to operate beyond the laws of physics, where they have some control over the theme body of laws; in other words, the people of miracles are in some sense the gods and goddesses of mythology. But the control these people gain is control based on giving up control to God, to consciousness.

Aurobindo has identified four powers of supramental beings: *mahakali* (the power of transforming negative into positive); *mahasaraswati* (the power of creative expression even beyond

---

[34]For a discussion of many documented cases, see Murphy 1992.

the laws of physics); *mahalakshmi* (the power of unconditional love); and *maheswari* (the power of harmony and equanimity).

Accordingly, this level of being is expressed as appropriate action (this is the power of maheswari). Secondly, it is said that whatever they will becomes God's will—this is the power of mahasaraswati. The Indian sage Anandamayi Ma sometimes talked about her *kheyals*, for which the appropriate translation is "whimsy." But her whimsies always came true. Both the performance of miracles and the willing of these people always occur in complete harmony with the cosmic purposiveness. In other words, when Jesus converts water into wine, he knows that this act is in consonance with the divine will.

Resurrection As Supramental Creativity

What happens when people who have achieved the supramental level of being die? In Christianity, one answer is found in the story of the resurrection of Jesus. What does resurrection mean? Normally, it is interpreted as resurrection of a dead person's own previous body: "All shall rise with their own bodies, the bodies that they now bear."

In contrast, in I Corinthians, St. Paul is explicit in maintaining that the resurrected body is different from the physical, perishable body; it is a spiritual body—imperishable. What the apostles saw of Jesus' resurrected body and also St. Paul's vision on the way to Damascus fit the idea of angelic visions, as discussed previously (see chapter 11), but I think this is not a radical enough idea. Perhaps the reality is even more radical than expressed in either of these two views.

The point is that something in the human creative intuition, starting with the myth of Gilgamesh and the teachings of Zarathustra, has always maintained that resurrection consists of rising from death within the shareable public domain in an imperishable body in which experience is possible. Subject-object experience (quantum collapse) is not possible in a spiritual body, nor does a spiritual body belong to a public consensus domain.

If resurrection occurs in an ordinary physical body, old or new, it is not immortality—the physical body within the laws of physics must die. If resurrection is in a spirit (Sambhoga-kaya) body, there is no experience without the aid of some incarnate physical body. How can one resurrect in a physical body and still be immortal? Only by going beyond the laws of physics. Immortality via resurrection is a miracle all the way! It is a supramental act of the first order.

Supramental acts involving the mind (mental creativity) do not violate the laws of science. All the paranormal phenomena that we experiment with today are called para or beyond normal, but that is due only to a lack of understanding. In the new science, we are already making good models for the understanding of the paranormal within more general laws.

But supramental creativity as involved in resurrection, creating at will, from nothing, a physical body for the discarnate quantum monad to correlate with, is beyond all laws of science, any science. Supramental creativity may also be the basis of the phenomenon of *avatara*—people who are born with full wisdom about their grounding in consciousness and who have the special mission of reestablishing in our societies the metaphysics of the causal supremacy of Dharma—consciousness.

You may watch repeats of the television show *Star Trek: The Next Generation*. The show has two ongoing subplots: one is good, but the other is great. The good one involves the struggles of an android (Data) to become human. The writers of these episodes see the problem as one of finding the correct software for emotions. This is way short of what it takes to be conscious, to be self-referent, tangled hierarchy and all.

The great one is the story of Q, a supramental being who goes in and out of physical space-time at will. In these stories there is real imagination, real vision. It is this vision that unfolded in the human condition two-thousand years ago with Jesus' resurrection, and it is still unfolding.

Let's consider one aspect of the story of Jesus' resurrection as told in the Bible. It is said that at one point Jesus cried out aloud and in agony: "God, God, why have you forsaken me?" From an enlightened man, such a cry of anguish is baffling. (There are other translations of the original Aramaic which are less baffling.) But it starts making sense when we realize that even on the cross Jesus may have been engaged in a creative act—supramental creativity; he wanted to demonstrate the falsity of death by the ultimate death-defying act of resurrection. And it happened. Jesus must have been one of the first to demonstrate resurrection. Later masters replicated it to the extent of the science fiction-like Q-beings. They were able to create a material body of manifestation at will (always in harmony with the will of the whole). Thus, such a being can be said to be immortal both in spirit and in the body (as necessary). Read Paramahansa Yogananda's book *Autobiography of a Yogi* for a glimpse at one such being, Yogananda's great-grandguru, Babaji.

The Evolutionary Future of Humanity

As Aurobindo would say, the immortality in discarnate bodhisattva being is still an escape because it stops short of the realization of the full human potential, which includes supramental creativity. Reincarnation, yes. But beyond the birth-death karmic cycle, not only does liberation in the spiritual body of Sambhogakaya wait for us. There is also the invitation to the great exploration of the supermind. Let's heed the words of Sri Aurobindo:

> *This world is in love with its own ignorance,*
> *Its darkness turns away from its savior light,*
> *It gives the cross in payment for the crown.*
> *His work is a trickle of splendor in a long night;*
> *He sees the long march of time, the little won,*
> *A few are saved, the rest strive and fail;*
>
> *An exit is shown, a road of hard escape*
> *From the sorrow and the darkness and the chain;*
> *But how can a few escaped release the world?*
>
> *Escape however high redeems not life,*
> *Life that is left behind on a fallen earth.*
> *Escape cannot uplift the abandoned race*

Or bring to it victory or reign of God.
A greater power must come, a larger light
                              (Aurobindo 1970, bk. 6, canto 2).

For the last few hundred years, nay, the last millennium, with a few isolated exceptions, we have pursued the values of the mind and the mental ego. This has led to increasing separateness, but it has also given us more understanding, a scaffolding for the next quantum leap of our evolution as a species. Perhaps the millennium we just entered is going to be the millennium of the flowering of that "greater power"—supermind. How is this going to come about? We can get a glimpse from Aurobindo's own work seen in the light of quantum physics developed here.

Involution and Evolution

Esotericism has an aspect that two philosophers of recent times, Sri Aurobindo, and following him, Ken Wilber, have emphasized (Aurobindo n.d.; Wilber 1981). This is the idea that descent, or involution of consciousness, must occur before ascent, or evolution, can take place.

Aurobindo and Wilber present a model of involution and evolution of consciousness that is implicit, if not explicit, in the mystical branches of all the great traditions—Christian mysticism, Kashmir Shaivism, a branch of Hinduism, Mahayana Buddhism, Sufism, the Kabbala, and so forth.

According to the spiritual cosmologies that Aurobindo and Wilber adapt, for the sake of play the transcendent Godhead or Brahman consciousness throws itself downward and outward into manifest levels that are grosser and grosser. As consciousness descends, it also forgets itself; thus, each descending level corresponds to one of increasing forgetfulness and decreasing freedom. Also at each level, the previous subtler level is forgotten, delegated to the unconscious. At the lowest level, all is unconscious, all is potential. This is the material level. This is called involution because all the higher levels are potential in matter, ready to unfold.

231

Once involution is complete, evolution begins. But the evolution of matter in this picture is quite different from that of the materialists. Thus, life does not emerge from matter, from material properties and interactions alone—a higher level can never emerge from the interactions and causations of a lower one. Life emerges at a certain level of complexity of matter because it was already potential. Mind emerges, likewise, from a certain complexity of life because it was already potential (fig. 12.1).

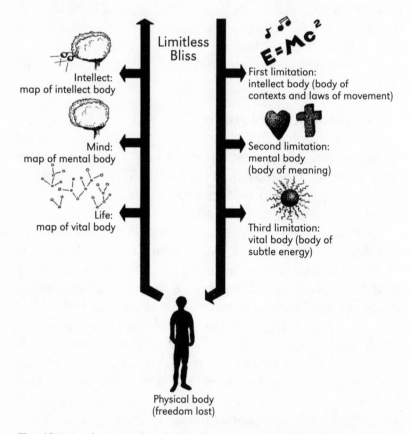

Limitless Bliss

$E=MC^2$

Intellect:
map of intellect body

First limitation:
intellect body (body of
contexts and laws of movement)

Mind:
map of mental body

Second limitation:
mental body
(body of meaning)

Life:
map of vital body

Third limitation:
vital body (body of
subtle energy)

Physical body
(freedom lost)

Fig. 12.1. Involution and evolution of consciousness (following Aurobindo). Consciousness first involutes into greater and greater limitations and forgetfulness. The evolution in this picture is the evolution of representation making of the vital and the mental body in the physical (hardware). Are physical representations of the supramental in our evolutionary future?

Finally, one must not think that all these levels involve any dualism. All this separation in consciousness is illusory, a mere appearance. Consciousness forgets itself for the sake of play—it pretends to forget, so to speak.

This picture is, of course, typical of esoteric traditions. In a certain way, it makes sense and is very satisfying. What it lacks, however, is a description of how what is potential in matter becomes actual. And how does forgetfulness or maya come about?

Idealist science, as already indicated, gives a satisfactory answer to the first question. Manifestation occurs via a tangled hierarchy, causing illusory separateness, which, in turn, causes temporary amnesia. Thus, at the level of the theme body, the theme collective presents laws or contexts of movements of subsequent levels of existence as waves of possibility thus imposing constraints or limits on what consciousness can do, but nothing happens yet. At the subsequent involution of the mental level, the mind's subtle substance presents to consciousness possibility structures that contain the processing of meaning. But consciousness and its mental possibilities still remain an unseparated whole. Similarly, at the level of the vital body, consciousness further limits itself to the exploration of a particular set of vital functions amongst all possibilities, and again there is forgetfulness. However, as explained in chapter 7, no actual collapse or separation takes place until the physical body arrives on the scene.

How does what is potentiality in matter become actuality? At a certain level of complexity of the possibilities existing in physical matter, tangled hierarchy and quantum measurement come into play. Now consciousness can intervene in matter (itself remaining transcendent always) via self-referential collapse of the quantum possibility wave and actual manifestation begins. And consciousness remembers the previous level, the level of life, prana. It employs matter, as we employ a computer, to make software representations, which we call life in the living cell and its conglomerates, of vital functions (notice the similarity here with Sheldrake's idea of morphogenetic fields guiding the development of adult form from an embryo). Evolution and morphogenesis of life now can take place. Eventually, the conglomerate of cells known as the brain evolves so that software representations of the mind can be programmed in the brain hardware.

And here we are—humans, mental beings. From this view, what is the next step of our evolution? It is easy to see. It must be the evolution of the capacity to make representations of the theme body.

I have mentioned being in the theme body before (see chapter 7)—the arupadevas, gods, formless bodhisattvas, angels. They are timeless forms; their existence is limited to possibility waves. In the mental being, our access to these beings requires a quantum leap, and the access is only momentary. Only a great amount of engagement with inner creativity can lift us to stability in supramental being. But when our physical body evolves the capacity of making representations of these beings, every human will have instant access to these beings, as easily as we have access today of the mind through the brain.

Can you imagine what it is to envision the mind for a biological being without a brain? So it is very difficult to envision for mental beings what it would be like when we reach this next step of evolution. But about one thing we can be clear: when we reach this level of being with hardware that can develop supramental software, we would all be gods. This was Aurobindo's great vision. This is what he meant when he contemplated the much misunderstood idea of bringing divinity down to manifestation, to Earth.

The Theosophists have the same vision. The Theosophist-philosopher William Judge expounds:

> Although reincarnation is the law of nature, the complete trinity of Atma-Buddhi-Manas [bliss body—theme body—mental body] triad does not fully incarnate in this [human] race. They use and occupy the body by means of the entrance of Manas, the lowest of the three, and the

other two shine upon it from above, constituting the God in heaven. . . . For that reason man is not yet fully conscious, and reincarnations are needed to at last complete the incarnation of the whole trinity in the body. When that has been accomplished the race will have become as gods (Judge 1973).

Are we destined to become superhuman—gods, in this sense—in the next stage of our evolution? The Sufi poet Rumi wrote:

> I died as a mineral and became a plant
> I died as a plant and rose to animal
> I died as an animal and I became a man.
> Why should I fear?
> When was I less by dying?
> (Quoted in *The Sages Speak about Life and Death*)

When we "die" as mental humans, we will become supramental, superhuman beings. This is the ultimate evolution that awaits us.

13.

UFOLOGY, IMMORTALITY, AND EVOLUTION

What does UFOlogy—the study of unidentified foreign objects—have to do with death, dying, reincarnation, and immortality? Superficially, nothing. In the popular mind, UFOs are crafts, advanced rockets, from outer space piloted by beings who are trying to visit us, and the government is trying its best to suppress the information. The Steven Spielberg movie, *Close Encounters of the Third Kind*, sums up this kind of sentiment.

Some authors believe that such contacts between extra-terrestrials and we humans have been made already (for eons); some of their books become best-sellers, suggesting that there is a lot of sympathy for this kind of notion.

This is the stuff that science fiction thrives on, and I personally have always had a soft spot for science fiction. Years ago, I was writing a book on science fiction, so I researched the subject of rocketry quite thoroughly. The question in my mind was, Can rockets from outer space, from other planets belonging to other star systems, travel to us, considering the vast distances such a rocket has to travel?

Science-fiction writers, in general, are not particularly bothered by this problem because modern physics has enhanced their arsenals. In the 1930s, 1940s, and 1950s, science fiction was getting by with Einstein's theory of relativity. Relativity says time slows down inside a ship that is moving at a high speed comparable to lightspeed, so the passengers age slower than they would on their home planet. Beginning in the 1960s, science fiction has used the concept of hyperspace drive for space travel. You see, relativity limits spaceships to sub-lightspeed, but distances between stars even within our galaxy can be as large as 100,000 light years. You cannot speak about galactic empires with puny sub-lightspeeds for the imperial navy. In hyperspace, the ships can travel faster than light, at "warp-speeds."

Although both ideas make some scientific sense, thanks to Einstein, they are not practical ideas. Consider: Our chemical fuel-burning rockets travel at speeds of tens of kilometers per second; but light travels at the speed of 300,000 kilometers per second. The gap is quite unbridgeable with any physical technology. Rocket scientists have studied them all: plasma rockets, nuclear-fusion rockets, matter-antimatter propulsion (this one is very popular with science fiction), you name it, somebody has cranked out some numbers. All numbers make one thing very clear: no physical rocket can travel at a speed high enough for the relativistic slowing down of aging to help. At realistic speeds, even travel to and from our nearest stars would take such a long time that it is impossible to envision that any living beings with reasonable lifespans could make such trips (although the idea of freezing people for such travel remains popular).

Hyperspace, by the way, is a plausible "fourth" dimension of space, plausible because, according to Einstein's theory, space is curved, which can be interpreted with the concept that we live on the three-dimensional (hyper-)surface of a four-dimensional volume. Some science-fiction writers figure hyperspace to be where the electron goes when it takes a quantum leap. It is a fact that when the electron goes quantum leaping, it does not travel through intervening space; it's here, then it's there. But nobody has ever thought of any macro physical drive to get us to hyperspace, quantum leaping or otherwise.

So the net upshot of my research was this: it is impossible for any extraterrestrials to travel to us. Incidentally, rockets carrying robots are an exception to this rule. It is a mini-mystery why robot-bearing rockets have not reached us yet. As the famous physicist Enrico Fermi used to puzzle, "Where are they?" Many people translate this mystery to mean that there is no extraterrestrial life to launch robots around, that we are quite alone in the universe! I would like to argue in this chapter that we don't have to be that pessimistic.

Of course, people who encounter UFOs and extraterrestrial beings never mention robots; they are meeting with live creatures, mostly ones with by-now-familiar pointed, hollow faces and short bodies. If rockets from outer space are an impossibility, what are these people seeing? Although scientists in general have been very unsympathetic to these people's travails, dismissing their sightings (and even abductions) as hallucinations, psychologists could not entirely disregard the phenomenon; one thing that could not be denied is that the UFO sighters often were traumatized and needed psychological help.

So one idea that gradually became popular with psychologists, beginning with Carl Jung, is that UFOs are altered-state sightings of mental and emotional archetypes. In previous times, people saw these archetypes in their dreams and fantasies as gods and demons. In this scientific-technological age, the archetypes are appearing in this super-space technological form.

While I was working on my book on the physics of science fiction, this idea of UFOs and associated aliens being archetypes of the human consciousness made a lot of sense to me (Goswami 1983). In truth, I myself had already noted the parallel in a slightly different context. The neurophysiologist John Lilly described many of his drug-induced experiences in terms of visitations with aliens (Lilly 1978). But his experiences did not read all that differently from those, for example, of Swami Muktananda, an East Indian spiritual teacher who wrote about his journeys in states of samadhi into the realms of the gods (Muktananda 1994).

As and when I became interested in death and dying and near-death experiences, I came across the work of the psychologist Kenneth Ring (actually, my friend Hugh Harrison brought me one of Ken's books on the subject, *The Omega Project*). I found that Ring has taken the idea that UFO aliens represent archetypes quite a bit further. One of Ring's ideas particularly appealed to me.

Why are there so many UFO sightings these days? Ring, through a research survey that he conducted, found that a large number of UFO abductees later underwent a kind of transformation of their self-identity beyond ego. No longer were they me-centered; instead, they were more loving toward their human and natural environments (Ring 1992). Ring had discovered previously that the same kind of transformation was quite common among near-death experiencers. Bingo! Perhaps both kinds of experiences are a hint that Gaia-consciousness, our earth mother, is trying to warn us (with a two-by-four, to be sure, but we don't listen to anything less) about an impending ecological disaster. There have been many prophesies for such a disaster to occur around this time, as we go into a new millennia (this is another subject of popular books). And, of course, anybody can look at our hedonistic exploitation of the Earth and its environment during the past hundred years and predict a disaster; and that, too, is quite common.

Right about this time, I was traveling and stopped at Portland, Oregon, for the taping of an interview. Robert McGowan is an amateur astronomer who had designed a new poster of the cosmos that includes, along with the big bang and all that, the idea that the universe is self-aware. He was going to interview me about my book, *The Self-Aware Universe*. We got to talking, one thing led to another, and he asked me about the meaning of the UFO sightings and abductions. I told him about the physical impossibility of aliens arriving in rockets, but then I heard myself saying, "I think that the UFO sightings and abductions are suggesting that in some altered state of consciousness, some people are communicating with sentient beings from an extraterrestrial civilization." When Robert pressed me for more details, all I could say was that consciousness is nonlocal and can collapse similar possibilities in two brains correlated by intention, even though they are located at interstellar distances.

Later, I thought more about what I had said to Robert (which surprised me quite a bit) in that interview, and I realized that I was unconsciously processing Ring's thesis and something in it was unsatisfactory. Sure, I can believe that the UFO experience, like the near-death experience, is transformative. But the near-death experience is not just a transformative experience. Many people think, and my own research concurs, that NDEs are also telling us something about the death experience itself. Similarly, suppose that the UFO experience could also be telling us something about extraterrestrials as well. But the problem with asserting that this was nonlocal communication between Earth humans and aliens was, of course, that such communication needs quantum correlation between the subjects.

Meanwhile, Kenneth was coming to Los Angeles for a conference, and Hugh was eager to set up a meeting between us. We met at a midtown L. A. hotel in a conference room reserved for us. There was Hugh, myself, a psychologist named Mike Davidson, Dick Robb, a Theosophist, and, of course, Kenneth Ring.

It took us almost two hours to get warmed up. Sometimes it is so hard to go through the preliminaries. But finally, I asked my question to Ring.

"Ken, whereas I agree that the UFO experience, like the NDE, is transformative, surely you are not ruling out that they may also be telling us something about real extraterrestrial consciousness. Might the UFO abductees really be communicating with aliens from an extraterrestrial civilization through nonlocal consciousness?"

Ken avoided answering me directly, but he didn't voice any disagreement, either. But it was clear that his sympathy lay with the idea he propounded in his book—that there is a catastrophe waiting to happen, geological, environmental, or whatever its nature, and the UFO and the near-death experiences are Gaia's way of warning humankind to transform before the impending disaster. But then things got very interesting. I was sharing with Ken some of the ideas of this book, about disembodied beings, quantum monads, and all that when Ken asked me a question. "Tell me this. Do you think, if a real disaster hit Earth, that we could survive it as disembodied beings? Suppose we transcend the need for a physical body. Could we not carry on our civilization as disembodied beings? Is that our future?"

"We would certainly survive as disembodied beings, just as anybody who dies now does," I answered. "But, Ken, there is one problem. According to my model, you cannot have experience without a physical body. The state of consciousness of a disembodied being is like that of sleep; the possibility wave does not collapse. So as a civilization, we could hardly choose this state of limbo and be satisfied."

Dick Robb voiced agreement with what I said. The Theosophical literature has the same view, he insisted. One needs a human birth in order to further one's karma. This is why the human birth is so precious. I was pleased that he saw it that way.

Ken was a little disappointed, or so it seemed to me. I tried to console him. "Of course, it is quite possible that we can choose disembodied existence en masse to survive Armageddon on Earth, and then, through unconscious processing, find another habitable planet and start taking birth there. What's interstellar distance in nonlocality? Everything is 'near.'"

We went into other issues after that. The meeting broke up after a while, and I returned to where I was staying. And then, suddenly, lightning struck me! Well, I shouldn't really claim that the idea that came had the truth-value of a genuine act of creation, because, in retrospect, I just don't know. But the idea was novel and it sent a shiver up my spine.

What if we reverse what I said to Ken? Suppose the alien abductors connected with the UFO experience are disembodied beings from an extraterrestrial planet who are here because their planet is extinct. They cannot take rebirth on Earth because their species are not quite the same as the human species (so the contexts of the theme body are not the same). But they certainly can communicate with us as disembodied beings communicate with a medium.

This simple idea would explain many strange facets of the UFO experience; for example, how it is possible for a person to experience abduction while his wife, lying in bed beside him, has no idea of what is going on. Read Whitley Strieber's very credible story *Communion* (1988); you will see what I mean.

I am not saying that the alternative, mass hypnosis, is excluded; it is just far less probable. Even less probable is the possibility of the presence of real, physically embodied beings.

Clearly, I take the idea of discarnate alien quantum monads seeking relationship with us seriously, but much study needs to be done before we know if such a theory is useful to explain data or guide further research. The point is this. When we are ready to found our science on the primacy of consciousness, we can take better note of phenomena that we can handle. Lightning was known to human beings from the beginning of civilization. But until the advent of the science of electricity, we never noticed many of the subtleties of this phenomenon. The same thing is happening with death, reincarnation, and maybe even UFOlogy.

And not so surprising to me, there is now some data about this controversial subject that supports my idea. A distant-viewing researcher named Courtney Brown (1999) claims to have found a protocol for carrying out distant-viewing experiments with discarnate alien beings. One of his findings is that there is a discarnate alien race here now on Earth that is trying to find a new abode on Earth, trying to take human birth even if that needs a genetic alteration of the human genome. The methodology of the research seems sound to me. Check it out.

UFOs and Immortality

But what have UFOs got to do with immortality? A couple of years ago, I took part in some very interesting discussions with UFO experts. The discussions took place in one of the most idyllic places that you can imagine: Paradise Island in the

Bahamas. How can UFO experts and a quantum physicist afford Paradise Island? We were hosted by Swami Swaroopananda, director of the Sivananda Yoga Retreat Center at the island.

I came away from these discussions with some new respect for the UFO sightings. Materialists debate this data incessantly and as vehemently as the paranormal data. For many years, I have been able to see that the materialist scientist's view of the paranormal is prejudiced. This is partly because I myself have had paranormal experiences and, secondly, because quantum nonlocality gives us an explanatory framework for the paranormal once you introduce consciousness in the equation (see chapter 2). But somehow I continued to accept some of the materialists' criticism of the UFO sightings without much critical examination, until these discussions that is.

The data on the sightings are quite good and their implication may be much more radical than one ordinarily assumes. How do you frame the data when you hear somebody citing a UFO? You probably, like me (until these discussions), assume that if the claim is true then some alien beings are coming to Earth with a spacecraft and all your judgment about the authenticity of the sightings get mixed up with this implicit assumption that you presuppose. At least, that was my implicit assumption, and I have given you earlier in this chapter all the scientific reasons that exist to convince me that there could not be any alien rocket ship from another star visiting Earth. So intimate discussion with these UFO scientists of good credibility created a conflict in me between two belief systems. One belief is based on my theory that the data make no sense; another belief is that since the data collectors were credible, I, as a scientist, must have an open mind to take their data seriously.

I suffered from this conflict for a while, but eventually a new idea broke through. What if the spaceships that the UFO citers experienced were real, but they did not come from outer space? And they are not human-made either! Can this be? It can if you are able to entertain the idea of materialization and dematerialization. Suppose the UFO citers experience alien beings (not every citer experiences alien beings in connection with the spaceships they see, but some do) that are so advanced in their civilization that they can materialize and dematerialize entire spaceships!

What is an advanced civilization? Again, usually, we think of advancement in terms of material technology, and then physical laws exclude certain possible directions of advancements, such as materialization and dematerialization. But as Aurobindo has envisioned, the next evolution of humanity is going to raise us in the supramental direction.

As I mentioned in the last chapter, beings of the supermind who are established in their command of the theme body can go at will (always in harmony with the divine will and purpose) beyond the conventional laws of physics. So in the UFO data, are we seeing a verification of Aurobindo's idea of supramental beings, beings who have already evolved to that supramental stage of evolution with which we are struggling right now?

The Evolution of the Brain or the Evolution of Matter?

The psychiatrist Uma Goswami, when she teaches Aurobindo's ideas, likes to talk about the layered structure of the brain. The liver is a lobe, the heart is a muscle, the layered structure is nowhere to be found in the body. Then what does it mean that the brain is layered? It must be a signature of the evolution of the brain. While the other parts of the body have not much evolved from their past, the brain has. The oldest and the hindmost brain is the reptilian brain, the middle brain is the mammalian brain, and the foremost brain, the neocortex, is the human brain. The layered structure of the brain speaks of our animal ancestry. Then she quotes Aurobindo. "The animal was the laboratory for the evolution of man; and man must similarly be the laboratory for the creation of superman." And maybe this will happen through the further evolution of the brain—a new layer, a neo-neo cortex (Krishnamurthy 2000)?

This is one way to approach the subject of human evolution. But I can find one flaw with it. All the three brains make representation of the mind. The first two layers, evolutionarily speaking, make representations of emotional thoughts, first the crude emotions, and then finer emotions; the neocortex evolved to make representations of abstract thoughts (for which language is necessary). Can any evolution of the brain make representation of something that is not thought, that is beyond thought?

Aurobindo, and also his associate the Mother, themselves experimented with another idea. They intuited that to map the supramental, to make physical representations of the theme body, matter itself has to evolve, has to become more refined. So Aurobindo and the Mother spent major parts of their lives trying to transform the matter of their bodies. But from all unprejudiced accounts, they did not succeed. When Aurobindo died, many disciples thought that the transformation of the body may show in the fact that it won't decay, as normal corpses do; many even thought that the body should be preserved because, like Jesus, Aurobindo may resurrect. The body was preserved for a while, but it decayed. No evidence of transformation of the physical body or resurrection was found.

Is the idea of transformation of matter to a more refined form scientifically tenable? Wouldn't that old problem of dualism—How does the subtle matter interact with the present variety?—haunt us? I myself never liked the idea of another more refined form of matter because of this reason. It is much easier to ponder the evolution of a new structure of the body beyond the brain—a superbrain, perhaps. The superbrain would make representations of the theme body, integrate the functions of the three brains, and would constitute our new god-like identity!

I've already mentioned Swami Swaroopananda of Paradise Island. Born in Israel and quite knowledgeable of the Kabbala, he became a Vedantin (an expert of the Indian Vedanta) after he studied under the famous flying Swami Vishnudevananda (so called because he liked to fly his own airplane). Swami Swaroopa is what the traditions call a jnana yogi, one who discovers the nature of reality through the wisdom path, quantum leaping from thought. So naturally he and I like to converse together and, in general, he approves of the new science within consciousness.

In one of our discussions on Aurobindo's work, he surprised me. "Aren't you being prematurely prejudiced about another form of matter and how it would interact with regular matter?" said he. "Why can't consciousness mediate their interaction just as it does for matter and the psyche?"

And a veil lifted. Why not indeed? Indeed, dualism should not stymie us from recognizing the validity of Aurobindo and the Mother's pursuit. If so, we should also pay heed to the method of integral yoga that they developed for the purpose of transforming matter.

This is not the time and place for discussing the ideas of integral yoga. Very briefly, the proposal is to bring the integrative thrust of all the known yogas (see chapter 9) to bear on the creativity of first the vital body, and then the physical. The key is to be steadfast in the intention of transforming the body so that it can map the supramental theme body, whichever way it comes, or the development of the superbrain, or the development of supermatter.

I also think that the kundalini phenomenon discussed earlier may be a key. Kundalini rising seems to release the latent power of consciousness for making new representations of the vital onto the physical. There is evidence. People in whom kundalini has risen and been properly integrated undergo extraordinary bodily changes (for example, the development of nodules on the body that has the figure of a serpent). There is a living kundalini master by the name of U. G. Krishnamurthy who lives in Bangalore, India, whose body shows such extraordinary physical signs of kundalini integration that anyone can verify it.

If we intend to use the thrust of the kundalini power creatively to make the superbrain or supermatter, as the case may be, and if we do it collectively, maybe we can hasten the hitherto largely unconscious evolutionary ways of nature. The mystic philosopher Teilhard de Chardin (whose idea of the evolution of the humankind to the omega point is quite similar to Aurobindo's idea of the evolution of supermind) used to talk about harnessing the energy of love. (Read, especially, Teilhard de Chardin 1964.) I now think he was literally talking about harnessing kundalini energy. And what better way to harness it than pave the way for the evolution of humanity to the omega point.

THE NINE LIVES OF THE SOUL

So is there a soul and is there a physics of the soul? You be the judge; I will summarize the ideas of physics that progressively lead to a convincing and fairly complete model of the soul. Just for fun, I will use the metaphor of the nine lives of a cat, but there is a twist. The more lives the cat lives, the closer it gets to eventual death. Here, it is the opposite. As the physics is expanded, as the model of the soul gets better, the soul approaches immortality. And as a bonus, the more are the data that can be accommodated within the model.

1. In the first life, soul is dualistic, meaning that it is conceived as a separate world made up of a nonmaterial substance, and physics is used to negate it. A dualist soul is distinct from matter and the material body and survives the death of the material body. A dualist soul is individual and also separate from God (which can be thought of as a world-soul, or oversoul, *paramatman* in Sanskrit) but is eternal like God. This soul dies because of criticisms based on physics, questions such as, How does the nonmaterial soul interact with the material body without a mediator? or, How can we explain the conservation of energy principle, that the energy of the material world alone is conserved? Wouldn't an interacting soul, interacting with the material world, occasionally take away from or contribute to the material world's energy? Another thorn on the side of this model is, if souls are eternal and the number of souls is conserved, then how can we

explain today's population explosion, that is, where do new souls come from?

2. In the second model of the soul, the soul is material and it is stillborn; it doesn't survive, meaning that it is an epiphenomenon of the material body and dies with it. However, one can take consolation that, although the epiphenomenon, the individual soul, dies, the basic stuff, matter in the form of the atoms and elementary particles, lives on and is recycled. The physics here is conservative and noncontroversial but is not of any use for explaining survival and reincarnation data.

3. In the third incarnation, soul is identical with consciousness, the one and only, which is the ground of being. Matter is an apparent manifestation in this ground and is an epiphenomenon of this ground. Matter is thus ephemeral, coming into apparent being when it is registered in a sentient being's experience and then dissolving into the whole. The material body perishes, but the soul lives on eternally.

    In this life, the individual soul dies because it never is; the soul is always cosmic and has no attribute. The physics of the soul begins here and consists of quantum physics in its idealist interpretation—the idea that nonlocal and unitive consciousness creates actualized reality out of quantum possibilities of matter.

4. In the fourth incarnation, the idea that the cosmic soul has an attribute is posited, and this attribute is recognized as a body of themes. We all belonging to the human species are required to learn these themes—that is the purpose of our lives. Naturally, it takes many incarnations to creatively discover them and learn to live them since some of the themes, such as love, are very subtle. Our various incarnations are correlated through quantum nonlocality across space and time and connected through the theme body as a thread connects flowers of a garland.

This is the reason the theme body can be recognized as what is called the *sutratman* (*sutra* means thread, and *atman* means soul in Sanskrit). But the physics of the soul is still inadequate; the individual soul still does not exist; what survives the death of the physical body is the theme body, which is a universal monad for the entire human species. The good part of the model is that some of the important data of reincarnation, especially past-life recall by children, is explained.

5. In the fifth life of the soul, the cosmic soul is postulated to have additional attributes, a mind for the processing of meaning and a vital body for the blueprints behind the forms that manifest in the evolution of life. The theme body now can be seen to set the context of movement for both mind and the vital body (as well as the physical). In its role of setting the context of meaning, it now can be recognized as what we call the (supramental) intellect—the facility of creativity, unconditional love, moral discrimination, etc.

    The supramental intellect, mind, vital body trio, which together now constitutes the soul or monad, are all non-physical, but because of their quantum nature (which is also the nature of the physical), consciousness mediates their interaction with the physical body. All four bodies are quantum possibilities of consciousness. For its manifest experience, consciousness collapses correlated possibilities of these bodies into actual events of (apparent) subject-object split epiphenomenon.

    Clearly, the physics of the soul thrives in this incarnation, but the soul looked upon as a quantum monad is not mature yet; it still does not have the power to explain the individual soul.

6. In the sixth incarnation of the soul, the physics of the soul matures. With proper acknowledgment of the dynamics of the mind and the vital body, individualization of the soul or monad can be seen to take place. Although, like the supramental

intellect, the mind and the vital bodies are also universal (without individual structure) for all of us to share, the universality is compromised as a result of the accumulation of experience.

As experiences are lived, the probabilities of quantum mental (and vital) possibilities are modified; they develop a bias toward past responses to stimuli, a process that psychologists call conditioning. I call it quantum memory because the memory of this biasing is contained not in the object as in ordinary memory; instead, the memory is contained in the quantum mathematics that the modified possibilities obey.

As a result of conditioning or quantum memory, we all develop an individual (functional) mind and vital body. So when the physical body dies, our history recorded in the physical body (especially the brain) dies with it, but our pattern of habits or propensities survive in the form quantum memory of the probability modified possibility waves of the individual quantum monad.

At long last, the quantum monad becomes a successful model of the surviving and reincarnating soul. When the physics of the quantum monad is integrated with the physics of quantum nonlocality between correlated incarnations producing a more complete model of the soul, many kind of data regarding survival-after-death and reincarnation can be explained, among them, near-death experiences, the phenomenon of child prodigies, unexplainable phobias, and channeling.

All this is good. However, the soul is now solidly established in the wheel of karma (acquired propensities from past lives), repetition of incarnations with no end in sight. The physics of the soul is still inadequate to explain the evolution of the soul toward liberation.

7. In the seventh life of the soul, the physics of the soul recognizes a law of karma on the basis of empirical data that we only bring some of our past propensities to bear in any

particular life. Those are the propensities (*prarabdha*) that would enable us to satisfy the particular learning agenda of a particular incarnation that would contribute to the evolution of our soul toward liberation. To the physics of the soul, we now add the art of remembering our *prarabdha*, an art called *dharma* in Hinduism. Now we actively practice to remember the propensities we bring to this particular incarnation to fulfill the learning agenda, dharma, of this particular life. When we learn according to our purposiveness, our life becomes specially joyful. Our life now becomes saturated with meaning as we fulfill our learning agenda.

Materialist-physics practitioners complain that "the more we comprehend the universe, the more it seems pointless." Behold! By comparison, physics of the soul recovers the lost meaning.

8. In the eighth life of the soul, the soul fulfills its monadic responsibilities of creative discoveries in accordance with its physics and is liberated from the karmic wheel. The soul no longer evolves and has now achieved the first kind of immortality as an angel or spirit guide to help other striving souls, striving to gain liberation.

9. In the ninth incarnation of the soul, a speculative incarnation that goes beyond current physics, the soul's objective is its creative attempt to take on an immortal physical body (resurrection). Further development of the physics of the soul will tell us if this involves a new kind of matter that can make representations of the supramental intellect or a new development in the brain that can do the same.

Thus ends the saga of the soul as explored in this book.

GLOSSARY

Algorithm: a rule-bound procedure to get from step A to step B.

Archetype: a Platonic idea that is the precursor of a material, vital, or mental manifestation; also the Jungian symbol of the instincts and primordial psychic processes of the collective unconscious.

Aspect, Alain: the experimental physicist at the University of Paris-Sud acclaimed for the 1982 experiment named after him that established quantum nonlocality. This experiment is a prime example of experimental metaphysics.

Atman: the Sanskrit word meaning "higher cosmic self beyond ego," the quantum creative self of primary experience.

Aurobindo: visionary philosopher-sage who gave us the idea of the supermind. *See* supermind.

Awareness: subject-object split consciousness.

Bardo: Tibetan word meaning "passageway" or "transition."

Behaviorism: the primary paradigm of psychology in this century, it holds that the explanation of human behavior is to be found in the history of stimulus-response-reinforcement patterns of a person.

Bhakti yoga: the yoga of love or devotion.

Bliss body: consciousness as the ground of being, the source of all bliss.

Bodhisattva: realized people (in Buddhism) who, instead of opting for merging into the clear light of consciousness, instead stand in the doorway helping people until everyone arrives.

Bohr, Niels: a Danish physicist, discoverer of the Bohr atom and of the complementarity principle. During his lifetime, he was the most influential spokesperson for the message of quantum mechanics.

Brahman: Sanskrit word signifying consciousness as the ground of all being; godhead or Tao.

Causal body: consciousness as the ground of being; bliss body.

Causal determinism: *see* Determinism.

Causality: the principle that a cause precedes every effect.

Cerebral cortex: the outermost and most recently evolved segment of the mammalian brain; also called the neocortex.

Chakras: the location of those places of the physical body where the vital body is collapsed along with the correlated physical cellular conglomerate or organ that represents a vital body function. Also, centers of feeling.

Chaos theory: a theory of certain deterministic classical systems (called chaotic systems) whose motion is so sensitive to initial conditions as not to be susceptible to long-term predictability. To materialists, this determined but not predictable character of chaotic systems make them an apt metaphor for subjective phenomena.

Character: the tendencies, patterns, and learned repertoire of contexts that define an individual.

Chi: the Chinese word for the modes of motion of the vital body.

Circularity: *see* self-reference.

Classical mechanics: the system of physics based on Isaac Newton's laws of motion; today it remains only approximately valid for most macroobjects as a special case of quantum mechanics.

Classical physics: *see* classical mechanics.

Collective unconscious: unitive unconscious—that aspect of our consciousness that transcends space, time, and culture, but of which we are not aware. A concept first introduced by Jung.

Complementarity: the characteristic of quantum objects possessing opposite aspects, such as waveness and particleness, only one of which we can see with a given experimental arrangement. The complementary aspects of a quantum object refer to transcendent waves and immanent particles.

Consciousness: the ground of being (original, self-contained, and constitutive of all things) that manifests as the subject that chooses, and experiences what it chooses, as it self-referentially collapses the quantum wave function in the brain or in a living cell or other cellular conglomerates.

Context: the interpretive field consciousness uses to guide the flow of meaning into the world; the causal underpinning behind content.

Correspondence principle: the idea, discovered by Bohr, that under certain limiting conditions (which are satisfied by most macrobodies under ordinary circumstances) quantum mathematics predicts the same motion as Newtonian classical mathematics. A similar correspondence principle is found to hold for idealist science; under conditions of complete conditioning idealist science corresponds to materialist science.

Creativity: the discovery of something new of value in a new context or with new meaning.

Darwin, Charles: the discoverer of the theory of evolution that bears his name.

Decay: the process in which an atomic nucleus emits harmful radiations and transforms to a different state.

Determinism: the philosophy according to which the world is causal and completely determined by Newton's laws of motion and the initial conditions—the initial positions and velocities of the objects of the space-time universe.

Deva: a Sanskrit word meaning "angel."

dharma: the ethical and creative path of discovery of every individual, an individual's creative destiny of life, so to speak.

Dharma: consciousness, the whole, the ground of being. Spelled with a lower case "d," it means duty and creative destiny. Also, in Hinduism, the god of justice.

Dharmakaya: in Buddhism, the body of consciousness, the ground of being.

Death: the withdrawal of conscious supervention—in the form of the collapse of the possibility waves—and conscious identity from the living.

Death yoga: practices designed for conscious death.

Double-slit experiment: the classic experiment for determining characteristics of waves; a beam of light or electrons, for example, is split by passing it through two slits in a screen to make an interference pattern on a photographic plate or a fluorescent screen.

Dualism: the idea that mind and brain belong to two separate realms of reality.

Ego: the identity with the content of an individual's story line in addition to the character.

Einstein, Albert: perhaps the most famous physicist that ever lived, he is the discoverer of the relativity theories. He was a major contributor to quantum theory, including the basic ideas of wave-particle duality and probability.

Epiphenomenon: a secondary phenomenon with no causal efficacy; something that exists contingent on the prior existence of something else.

Free will: freedom of choice undetermined by any necessary cause.

Freud, Sigmund: the founder of psychoanalysis; according to some, of modern psychology.

Gene: components of the DNA molecule that are believed to be the elements that transfer hereditary traits in reproduction; genes are also believed to be selected for or against in biological evolution; according to some biologists, the genes are the fundamental elements of biological being.

God: the creative principle behind the totality of all manifestation.

Gross body: the physical body that manifests in our awareness as external.

Gunas: qualities of consciousness in ancient Indian psychology that correspond to psychological drives in more modern terminology. There are three gunas: *sattwa* (illumination), *rajas* (libido), and *tamas* (conditioned ignorance).

Hayflick effect: the effect discovered by Leonard Hayflick that human cells can reproduce only about fifty times.

Heaven: archetypal realm; also archetypal realm of godly traits.

Heisenberg, Werner: a German physicist and codiscoverer of quantum mechanics. His discovery of quantum mechanics is widely regarded as one of the most creative events in the history of physics.

Hell: archetypal realm of consciousness corresponding to the violent emotions.

Idealism: the philosophy that holds that the fundamental elements of reality must include the mind as well as matter. In this book, we have used idealism as synonymous with monistic idealism. *See* monistic idealism.

Idealist science: science based on the primacy of consciousness; *see also* science within consciousness.

Immanent reality: a monistic idealist's designation of the immanent space-time-matter-motion ordinary world of our experience to distinguish it from a transcendent world of ideas and archetypes; however, note that both transcendent and immanent worlds exist in consciousness, the first as possibility forms (ideas), the second as the result of a conscious observation.

Immanent space-time: *see* immanent reality.

Individual self: the ego-content and character together define the individual self.

Intellect: the supramental body of consciousness that provides the contexts for mental, vital, and mental movement. In ordinary usage today, intellect more refers to the mental ideas of the contexts of the intellect body; *see also* theme body, supramental.

Interference: the interaction of two waves incident in the same region of space that produces a net disturbance equal to the algebraic sum of the individual disturbances of the respective waves.

Interference pattern: the pattern of reinforcement of a wave disturbance in some places and cancellation in others that is produced by the superposition of two (or more) waves.

Jiva: the Sanskrit word for the quantum monad.

Jivanmukta: an individual who has arrived at liberation from the birth-death-rebirth cycle.

Jnana yoga: the yoga based on using the intellect to transcend the intellect.

Jung, Carl G: the psychologist who founded a major force of modern psychology that carries his name; he is famous for his concept of the collective unconscious and for his visionary insight that physics and psychology one day should come together.

Karma: past-life propensities, learnings, and good and bad conditioning that are carried from one incarnation to the next.

Karma yoga: the yoga of action, a yoga in which one acts but surrenders personal interest in the fruit of the action.

Ki: the Japanese word for the modes of movement of the vital body.

Koan: a paradoxical statement or question used in the Zen Buddhist tradition to enable the mind to make a discontinuous (quantum) leap in understanding.

Kundalini: coiled-up vital energy whose rising along a nadi that parallels the spine opens the chakras. *See also* chakras.

Law of conservation of energy: the idea, which has been vindicated in every scientific experiment so far, that the energy of the material universe remains a constant.

Law-like behavior: behavior governed solely by causal laws such as the laws of physics.

Liberation: liberation from birth-death-rebirth cycle.

Life: the ability of subject-object cognition that arises from the self-referential quantum measurement in the living cell and its conglomerates.

Locality: the idea that all interactions or communications among objects occur via fields or signals that propagate through space-time obeying the speed-of-light limit.

Macrobodies: large-scale objects such as a baseball or a table.

Manas: Sanskrit word meaning "mind."

Maslow, Abraham: the founder of transpersonal psychology, which is based on a monistic idealist framework.

Material realism: a philosophy holding that there is only one material reality, that all things are made of matter (and its correlates, energy, and fields), and that consciousness is an epiphenomenon of matter.

Materialist: in this book, we have used the word materialist to mean material realist, one who holds matter to be the ground of all being.

Matter waves: material objects such as electrons and atoms (and even macrobodies) have wavelike properties, according to quantum mechanics. Waves of material objects are called matter waves.

Maya: the apparent separateness of I and the world; also translated as illusion. According to the present theory, maya arises from tangled hierarchy of quantum measurement.

Medium: a person able to communicate with the dead.

Mental body: the body of mind stuff that belongs to a separate world. Mind gives meaning to brain stuff.

Meridian: Chinese concept for the pathway of the flow of chi, vital energy

Mind: *see* mental body.

Moksha: Sanskrit word meaning liberation from birth-death-reincarnation cycle.

Monism: the philosophy that mind and brain belong to the same reality.

Monad: the entity that survives physical death.

Monistic idealism: the philosophy that defines consciousness as the primary reality, as the ground of all being. The objects of a consensus empirical reality are all epiphenomena of consciousness that arise from the modifications of consciousness. There is no self-nature in either the subject or the object of a conscious experience apart from consciousness.

Morphogenesis: the making of biological form.

Morphogenetic fields: the information fields that, according to Rupert Sheldrake, contain the morphogenetic plan of biological beings.

Mystical experience: an experience of consciousness in its primacy beyond ego.

NDE: abbreviation for near-death experience; *see* near-death experience.

Nadi: Sanskrit word meaning channels for the flow of prana, vital energy.

Near-death experience: the experiences that subjects revived from heart failure and other near-death situations report.

Neocortex: *see* cerebral cortex.

Neumann, John von: a mathematician who was the first to postulate that consciousness collapses the quantum wave function; he also did fundamental work in game theory and the theory of modern computers.

Newton, Isaac: the founder of classical mechanics.

Nirvana: Sanskrit word literally meaning the extinction of the flame (of desire). It is conceptual equivalent in Buddhism of the Hindu idea of Moksha.

Nonlocal correlation: a phase relationship that persists even at a distance between two quantum objects which have interacted for a period and then stopped interacting. In the model of this book, the Einstein-Podolsky-Rosen correlation corresponds to a potential nonlocal influence between the objects.

Nonlocality: an instantaneous influence or communication without any exchange of signals through space-time; an unbroken wholeness or nonseparability that transcends space-time; *see also* transcendence.

Nirmanakaya: the manifest body of consciousness, a Buddhist term.

Nucleus: the heavy core of the atom around which electrons revolve.

Ontology: the study of the essence of being or fundamental reality; metaphysics.

Out-of-the-body experience (OBE): experience of people that they are out of their body in which state they report seeing things beyond their local vision, such as surgery being performed on their own bodies.

Paradigm shift: a fundamental change in the supertheory or umbrella world view that governs scientific work at a given time.

Phase relationship: a relationship between the phases (conditions) of motion of objects, especially waves.

Photon: a quantum of light.

Plato: one of the original monistic idealists in the West.

Possibility wave: a multifaceted quantum state with phase relations among its different facets (or possibilities). For example, an electron going through a double slit becomes a wave of two possible states, one state corresponding to its passing through slit 1 and another state corresponding to its passing through slit 2.

Potentia: the transcendent domain of the possibility waves of quantum physics.

Prana: Sanskrit word that means "vital energy" (and also means breath and life).

Program-like behavior: behavior not only governed by cause but also by purpose, as in computer programs.

Psychokinesis: psychic ability to move things.

Psychophysical parallelism: the idea that mind and body belong to two separate, noninteracting realities in which things happen in parallel. In other words, to every state of the brain, there is a corresponding mental state.

Punctuated equilibrium: a theory of evolution that says that there are punctuation marks—periods and commas, periods of rapid evolution—within the otherwise continuous text of Darwinian evolution.

Quantum: a discrete bundle of energy; the lowest denomination of energy or other physical quantities that can be exchanged.

Quantum leap: a discontinuous transition of an electron from one atomic orbit to another without going through the intervening space between orbits.

Quantum measurement theory: the theory of how a multifaceted quantum possibility wave reduces or collapses to a single facet upon measurement. According to this author, measurement is accomplished only with conscious observation by an observer with awareness.

Quantum mechanics: a physical theory based on the idea of the quantum (a discrete amount) and quantum jumps (a discontinuous transition), first discovered in connection with atomic objects.

Quantum memory: memory based on the modification of the probability calculus of nonlinear quantum equations that govern the quantum dynamics of the brain, mind, and the vital body. As a result of this memory, the probability of recall of learned responses is enhanced.

Quantum monad: a monad that transmigrates lived propensities and learned contexts from one incarnation to another via quantum memory of its mental and vital body.

Quantum self: the primary subject modality of the self beyond ego where resides real freedom, creativity, and nonlocality of the human experience.

Radioactivity: the property of certain chemical elements to spontaneously emit harmful radiation while their atomic nuclei undergo decay. Radioactive decay is governed by quantum probability rules.

Rajas: the Sanskrit word for the tendency towards activeness, akin to libido—a psychological drive of Freudian vintage.

Realism: the philosophy that propounds the existence of an empirical reality independent of observers or subjects. *See also* material realism.

Reality: all that is the case, including both local and nonlocal, immanent and transcendent; in contrast, the universe of space-time refers to the local immanent aspect of reality.

Reductionism: the philosophy that all phenomena can be reduced to matter at some microlevel.

Reincarnation: the idea that there is survival after death and rebirth; that there is a continuity of some essence of us that transmigrates from one birth to the next.

Relativity: the theory of special relativity discovered by Einstein in 1905 that changed our concept of time from the Newtonian absolute time to a time existing and changing in relation to motion.

Resurrection: the rising from the dead; a Christian term.

Rupa: a Sanskrit word meaning "form."

Samadhi: the experience of the quantum self that transcends the egoic identity. In this experience, the observer and the observed tend to merge.

Sambhogakaya: the archetypal body of consciousness, a Buddhist term.

Sambhogakaya body: a karmically fulfilled discarnate quantum monad that has transcended rebirth in the manifest world.

Satori: the Zen term for samadhi—the experience of the quantum self.

Sattwa: the Sanskrit word for creativity, one of the psychological drives according to Hindu psychology.

Schrödinger, Erwin: an Austrian physicist, co-discoverer with Heisenberg of quantum mechanics, he was opposed to the probability interpretation for quite some time. Later in life, he embraced some elements of the philosophy of monistic idealism.

Science within consciousness: a science based on the idea that consciousness is the ground of all being. *See also* idealist science.

Self: the subject of consciousness. *See also* individual self and quantum self.

Self-reference: the logical loop of referring to itself; *also see* circularity.

Semantics: the study of meaning.

Sheldrake, Rupert: the biologist who gave one of the first idealist theories of science, the theory of biological morphogenesis.

Solipsism: the philosophy that only one's own self can be proved to exist.

Soul: the entity that survives the death of the physical body; the quantum monad.

Speed of light: the speed at which light travels, 300,000 km/s; it is also the highest speed in space-time that nature permits.

State of consciousness: conditions within consciousness of varying degrees of awareness; examples are waking state, deep sleep, dream sleep, hypnosis, meditative states, and so forth.

Stevenson, Ian: the most celebrated researcher of reincarnational anecdotes of children.

Subtle body: the mental, vital, theme body conglomerate that is normally experienced only internally, as private.

Supermind: activities when one has "control" over the causal body of being, including the laws of physics.

Supramental: the body of consciousness beyond the mind that governs the movement of mental, vital, and physical bodies. *See also* theme body, intellect.

Synchronicity: acausal but meaningful coincidences, a term employed by Jung.

Tamas: a Sanskrit term meaning the tendency toward conditioned action in Hindu psychology.

Tangled hierarchy: a loop between levels of categories; a hierarchy that cannot be causally traced without encountering a discontinuity. An example is the liar's paradox "I am a liar."

Theme body: the supramental body of themes or contexts for the movement of mental, vital, and physical bodies. *See also* supramental, intellect.

Theosophy: the doctrines of a modern movement that started in 1875 in the U.S. by Helena Blavatsky based on Eastern mystical ideas about evolution and reincarnation.

Transcendental domain: pertaining to a realm of reality that is paradoxically both in and outside of physical space-time. According to this book, the transcendent realm is to be interpreted as being nonlocal—it can influence events in space-time by making possible connections without exchange of signals through space-time. *See also* nonlocality and potentia.

Transcendental experience: a direct experience of consciousness beyond ego.

Transpersonal psychology: the school of psychology based on the idea that our consciousness extends beyond the conditioned individual ego to include a unitive and transcendent aspect.

Uncertainty principle: the principle that such complementary quantities as momentum and position of a quantum object cannot be measured simultaneously with complete accuracy.

Unconscious: in this book, the reality of which there is consciousness, but no subject-object split awareness; *see also* collective unconscious.

Unconscious perception: perception without awareness of it; in this book, perception for which there is no collapse of the quantum brain state.

Unconscious processing: processing by consciousness without the presence of awareness (that is, without the collapse of possibility waves).

Vedanta: the end or final message of the Hindu Vedas, which appeared in the Upanishads, that propounds the philosophy of monistic idealism.

Vital body: the body of life-processes made of life-substance (prana or chi or ki) as opposed to physical and mental processes; this is a body separate from and independent of the physical and the mental body. It is the carrier of morphogenetic fields.

Vital energy: the modes of movement of the vital body; also called prana, chi, or ki.

Wave function: a mathematical function that represents the wave amplitude of quantum possibility waves; it is obtained as a solution of the Schrödinger equation.

Wilber, Ken: transpersonal philosopher whose voluminous work has been instrumental in bringing Eastern wisdom to the Western psyche.

BIBLIOGRAPHY

Abhedananda, Swami. 1944. *Life Beyond Death*. Hollywood, Calif.: Vedanta Press.

Almeder, Robert F. 1992. *Death and Personal Survival: The Evidence for Life after Death*. Lanham, Md.: Rowman & Littlefield.

Andrews, C. S. 1990. "Promoting Health and Well-Being through a Sense of Connectedness." *Frontiers Perspective* 1:18–20.

———. 1994. "Promoting Global Health and Well-Being by Individually Developing a Sense of Connectedness." *Journal of Exceptional Human Experience*.

Aspect, Alain, Jean Dalibard, and Gérard Roger. 1982. "Experimental Test of Bell's Inequalities Using Time-Varying Analyzers." *Physical Review Letters* 49:1804–06.

Aurobindo, Sri. 1955. *The Synthesis of Yoga*. Pondicherry, India: Sri Aurobindo Ashram.

———. n.d. *The Life Divine*. Pondicherry, India: Sri Aurobindo Ashram.

———. 1970. *Savitri*. Pondicherry, India: Sri Aurobindo Ashram.

———. 1989. *The Riddle of the World*. Pondicherry, India: Sri Aurobindo Ashram.

Ayala, F. J. 1972. "The Autonomy of Biology as a Natural Science." In *Biology, History, and Natural Philosophy*, edited by A. Breck and W. Yourgrau. New York: Plenum Press.

Bache, Christopher M. 1991. *Lifecycles: Reincarnation and the Web of Life*. NewYork: Paragon House.

———. 2000. *Dark Night, Early Dawn: Steps to a Deep Ecology of Mind*. Albany: State University of New York Press.

Banerji, Ranan B. 1994. *Beyond Words*. Preprint. Philadelphia: St. Joseph's University.

Barker, A. Trevor. 1975. *The Mahatma Letters to A. P. Sinnett*. Pasadena, Calif.: Theosophical University Press.

Bass, L. 1971. "The Mind of Wigner's Friend." *Harmathena* 112. Dublin: Dublin University Press.

———. 1975. "A Quantum Mechanical Mind-Body Interaction." *Foundations of Physics* 5:155–72.

Becker, Carl B. 1993. *Paranormal Experience and Survival of Death*. Albany: State University of New York Press.

Blavatsky, Helena P. 1968. *The Secret Doctrine: The Synthesis of Science, Religion, and Philosophy*. Los Angeles: Theosophy Co.

Blood, Casey. 1993. *On the Relation of the Mathematics of Quantum Mechanics to the Perceived Physical Universe and Free Will*. Preprint. Camden, N.J.: Rutgers University.

Bly, Robert. 1977. *The Kabir Book: Forty-four of the Ecstatic Poems of Kabir*. Boston: Beacon Press.

Bohm, David. 1951. *Quantum Theory*. New York: Prentice-Hall.

Brown, Courtney. 1999. *Cosmic Explorers: Scientific Remote Viewing, Extraterrestrials, and a Message for Mankind*. New York: Dutton.

Cairns, J., J. Overbaugh, and J. H. Miller. 1988. "The Origin of Mutants." *Nature* 335:141–45.

Chopra, Deepak. 1989. *Quantum Healing: Exploring the Frontiers of Mind/Body Medicine*. New York: Bantam Books.

———. 1993. *Ageless Body, Timeless Mind: The Quantum Alternative to Growing Old*. New York: Harmony Books.

Cranston, Sylvia L., and Carey Williams. 1984. *Reincarnation* 2 vols. Pasadena, Calif.: Theosophical University Press.

Davies, Paul. 1989. *The Cosmic Blueprint: New Discoveries in Nature's Creative Ability to Order the Universe*. New York: Simon & Schuster.

Dawkins, Richard. 1976. *The Selfish Gene*. New York: Oxford University Press.

Descartes, René. 1972. *Tractatus de Homine*. Cambridge: Harvard University Press.

Dossey, Larry. 1989. *Recovering the Soul: A Scientific and Spiritual Search*. New York: Bantam Books.

Drexler, K. Eric. 1986. *Engines of Creation: The Coming Era of Nanotechnology*. Garden City, N.Y.: Anchor Press/ Doubleday.

Eccles, John C. 1994. *How the Self Controls Its Brain*. New York: Springer-Verlag.

Edelman, Gerald M. 1992. *Bright Air, Brilliant Fire: On the Matter of the Mind*. New York: BasicBooks.

Eldredge, N., and S. J. Gould. 1972. "Punctuated Equilibria: An Alternative to Phyletic Gradualism." In *Models in Paleontology*, edited by T. J. M. Schopf. San Francisco: Freeman, Cooper.

Ettinger, Robert C. W. 1964. *The Prospect of Immortality*. Garden City, N.Y.: Doubleday.

Evans-Wentz, W. Y., ed. 1960. Tibetan Book of the Dead. Oxford: Oxford University Press.

Fenrick, Peter. 1999. Private communication.

Feynman, Richard P. 1981. "Simulating Physics with Computers." *International Journal of Theoretical Physics* 21:467–88.

Fischer, John Martin, ed. 1993. *The Metaphysics of Death*. Stanford, Calif.: Stanford University Press.

Frawley, David. 1989. *Ayurvedic Healing: A Comprehensive Guide*. Salt Lake City, Utah: Passage Press.

Gallup, George. 1982. *Adventures in Immortality*. New York: McGraw-Hill.

Gauld, Alan. 1982. *Mediumship and Survival: A Century of Investigations*. London: Heinemann.

Goldberg, Bruce. 1982. *Past Lives, Future Lives: Accounts of Regression and Progression through Hypnosis*. North Hollywood, Calif.: Newcastle Publishing.

———. 1996. *Soul Healing*. St. Paul, Minn.: Llewellyn Publications.

Goswami, Amit. 1983. *The Cosmic Dancers: Exploring the Physics of Science Fiction*. New York: Harper & Row.

————. 1989. "The Idealistic Interpretation of Quantum Mechanics." *Physics Essays* 2:385–400.

————. 1990. "Consciousness in Quantum Mechanics and the Mind-Body Problem." *Journal of Mind and Behavior* 11:75–92.

————. 1993. *The Self-Aware Universe: How Consciousness Creates the Material World*. New York: Tarcher/Putnam.

————. 1994. "Science within Consciousness." Research Report. Sausalito, Calif.: Institute of Noetic Sciences.

————. 1995. "Monistic Idealism May Provide Better Ontology for Cognitive Science: A Reply to Dyer." *Journal of Mind and Behavior* 16:135–50.

————. 1996. "Creativity and the Quantum: A Unified Theory of Creativity." *Creativity Research Journal* 9:47–61.

————. 1997. "Consciousness and Biological Order: Toward a Quantum Theory of Life and Its Evolution." *Integrative Physiological and Behavioral Science* 32:86–100.

————. 1999. *Quantum Creativity*. Cresskill, N.J.: Hampton Press.

————. 2000. *The Visionary Window: A Quantum Physicist's Guide to Enlightenment*. Wheaton, Ill.: Quest Books.

————. In press. *The Physicists' View of Nature, vol. II: The Quantum Revolution*. New York: Kluwer Academic/ Plenum.

Goswami, Uma. 2000. *Yoga and Mental Health*. Unpublished manuscript.

Greenwell, B. 1995. *Energies of Transformation*. Saratoga, Calif.: Shakti River Press.

Grinberg-Zylberbaum, Jacobo, M. Delaflor, L. Attie, and A. Goswami. 1994. "Einstein-Podolsky-Rosen Paradox in the Human Brain: The Transferred Potential." *Physics Essays* 7:422–28.

Grof, Stanislav. 1992. *The Holotropic Mind: The Three Levels of Human Consciousness and How They Shape Our Lives*. San Francisco: HarperSanFrancisco.

————. 1994. *Books of the Dead: Manuals for Living and Dying*. London: Thames and Hudson.

————. 1998. *The Cosmic Game: Explorations of the Frontiers of Human Consciousness*. Albany: State University of New York Press.

Grosso, Michael. 1992. *Frontiers of the Soul: Exploring Psychic Evolution*. Wheaton, Ill.: Theosophical Publishing House.

————. 1994. "The Status of Survival Research." *Noetic Sciences Review* 32:12–20.

————. 1995. *The Millennium Myth: Love and Death at the End of Time*. Wheaton, Ill.: Theosophical Publishing House.

Guirdham, A. 1978. *The Psyche in Medicine*. Jersey, U.K.: Neville Spearman.

Harrison, Peter, and Mary Peterson. 1983. *Life before Birth*.

Hayflick, L. 1965. "The Relative in Vitro Lifetime of Human Diploid Cell Strains." *Exp. Cell Res.* 37:614–36.

Hearn, Lafcadio. 1897. *Gleanings in Buddha Fields*. Boston: Houghton, Mifflin.

Hellmuth, T., A. G. Zajonc, and H. Walther. 1986. In *New Techniques and Ideas in Quantum Measurement Theory*, edited by Daniel M. Greenberger. New York: New York Academy of Sciences.

Herbert, Nick. 1993. *Elemental Mind: Human Consciousness and the New Physics*. New York: Dutton.

Hesse, Hermann. 1973. *Siddhartha*. London: Pan Books.

Hobson, J. A. 1990. "Dream and the Brain." In *Dreamtime and Dreamwork*, edited by Stanley Krippner. New York: St. Martin's Press.

Hofstadter, Douglas R. 1979. *Gödel, Escher, Bach: An Eternal Golden Braid*. New York: BasicBooks.

Imara, M. 1975. In *Death: the Final Stage of Growth*, edited by E. Kübler-Ross. Englewood Cliffs, N. J.: Prentice-Hall.

Jahn, R. 1982. "The Persistent Paradox of Psychic Phenomena: An Engineering Perspective." *Proceedings of the IEEE* 70:135–70.

Joy, W. Brugh. 1978. *Joy's Way: A Map for the Transformational Journey*. Los Angeles: J. P. Tarcher.

Judge, William Quan. 1973. *The Ocean of Theosophy*. Pasadena, Calif.: Theosophical University Press.

Jung, Carl G., and W. Pauli. 1955. *The Interpretation of Nature and the Psyche*. New York: Pantheon.

————. 1971. *The Portable Jung*. Edited by Joseph Campbell. Translated by R. F. C. Hull. New York: Viking.

Kak, S. 1995. "Quantum Neural Computing." In *Advances in Imaging and Electron Physics*. Forthcoming.

Kason, Y. 1994. *A Farthest Shore*. Toronto, Canada: Harper Collins.

Kornfield, J. 1990. *Buddhist Meditation and Consciousness Research*. Sausalito, Calif.: Institute of Noetic Sciences.

Krippner, Stanley, ed. 1990. *Dreamtime and Dreamwork: Decoding the Language of the Night*. New York: St. Martin's Press.

Krishnamurti, Jiddu. 1992. *On Living and Dying*. San Francisco: HarperSanFrancisco.

Kübler-Ross, Elisabeth, ed. 1975. *Death: The Final Stage of Growth*. Englewood Cliffs, NJ: Prentice-Hall.

Levine, Stephen. 1982. *Who Dies? An Investigation of Conscious Living and Conscious Dying*. Garden City, N.Y.: Anchor Press/Doubleday.

Libet, Benjamin E., E. Wright, B. Feinstein, and D. Pearl. 1979. "Subjective Referral of the Timing of a Cognitive Sensory Experience." *Brain* 102:193.

Libet, Benjamin. 1985. "Unconscious Cerebral Initiative and the Role of Conscious Will in Voluntary Action." *The Behavioral and Brain Sciences* 8:529–66.

Lilly, John C. 1978. *The Scientist*. Los Angeles: J. P. Tarcher.

Lucas, Winafred Blake. 1993. *Regression Therapy: A Handbook for Professionals*. Crest Park, Calif.: Deep Forest Press.

MacGregor, Geddes. 1978. *Reincarnation in Christianity: A New Vision of the Role of Rebirth in Christian Thought*. Wheaton, Ill.: Theosophical Publishing House.

Mailer, Norman. 1973. *Marilyn, A Biography*. New York: Gosset & Dunlap.

May, Rollo. 1975. *The Courage to Create*. New York: Norton.

McKenna, Terence K. 1991. *The Archaic Revival*. San Francisco: HarperSanFrancisco.

Meek, George W. 1987. *After We Die, What Then?* Columbus, Ohio: Ariel Press.

Merrell-Wolff, Franklin. 1994. *Franklin Merrell-Wolff's Experience and Philosophy*. Albany: State University of New York Press.

Mishlove, Jeffrey. 1993. *The Roots of Consciousness*. Tulsa, Okla.: Council Oaks Books.

Mitchell, Mark, and Amit Goswami. 1992. "Quantum Mechanics for Observer Systems." *Physics Essays* 5:525–29.

Moody, Raymond A. 1976. *Life after Life: The Investigation of a Phenomenon—Survival of Bodily Death*. New York: Bantam.

Motoyama, Hiroshi. 1981. *Theories of the Chakras: Bridge to Higher Consciousness*. Wheaton, Ill.: Theosophical Publishing House.

———. 1992. *Karma and Reincarnation*. Edited and translated by Rande Brown Ouchi. New York: Avon.

Moura, G., and N. Don. 1996. "Spirit Possession, Ayahuasca Users, and UFO Experiences: Three Different Patterns of States of Consciousness in Brazil." Abstracts of Talks at the 15th International Transpersonal Association Conference, Manaus, Brazil. Mill Valley, Calif.: International Transpersonal Association.

Moyers, Bill. 1993. *Healing and the Mind*. New York: Doubleday.

Muktananda, Swami. 1994. *Play of Consciousness*. South Fallsburg, N.Y.: SYDA Foundation.

Murphy, Michael. 1992. *The Future of the Body: Explorations into the Further Evolution of Human Nature*. Los Angeles: J. P. Tarcher.

Nagendra, H. R., ed. 1993. *New Horizons in Modern Medicine*. Bangalore, India: Vivekananda Kendra Yoga Research Foundation.

Netherton, Morris, and Nancy Shiffrin. 1978. *Past Lives Therapy*. New York: Morrow.

Neumann, John von. 1955. *Mathematical Foundations of Quantum Mechanics*. Translated from the German by Robert T. Beyer. Princeton: Princeton University Press.

Nikhilananda, Swami, trans. 1964. *The Upanishads*. New York: Harper & Row.

Nuland, Sherwin B. 1994. *How We Die: Reflections on Life's Final Chapter*. New York: A. A. Knopf.

Osborne, A. 1995. "The Great Change." In *The Sages Speak about Life and Death*. Piercy, Calif.: Chinmaya Publications.

Osis, Karlis, and Erlendur Haraldsson. 1977. *At the Hour of Death*. New York: Avon.

Parente, A. 1984. *Send Me Your Guardian Angel*. San Giovani Rotondo: Our Lady of Grace Capuchin Friary.

Parisen,, Maria. 1990. *Angels and Mortals: Their Co-Creative Power*. Wheaton, Ill.: Quest.

Pasricha, Satwant. 1990. *Claims of Reincarnation: An Empirical Study of Cases in India*. New Delhi, India: Harman Publishing House.

Pelletier, Kenneth. 1981. *Longevity: Fulfilling Our Biological Potential*. New York: Delacorte Press.

Piaget, Jean. 1977. *The Development of Thought: Equilibration of Cognitive Structures*. New York: Viking Press.

Popper, Karl R., and John C. Eccles. 1976. *The Self and Its Brain*. London: Springer-Verlag.

Posner, Michael I., and Marcus E. Raichle. 1994. *Images of Mind*. New York: Scientific American Library.

Remen, Rachel Naomi. 1996. *Kitchen Table Wisdom: Stories that Heal*. New York: Riverhead Books.

Ring, Kenneth. 1980. *Life at Death: A Scientific Investigation of the Near-Death Experience*. New York: Quill.

———. 1992. *The Omega Project: Near-Death Experiences, UFO Encounters, and Mind at Large*. New York: William Morrow.

Ring, Kenneth, and S. Cooper. 1995. "Can the Blind Ever See? A Study of Apparent Vision during Near-Death and Out-of-Body Experiences." Preprint. Storrs, Connecticut: University of Connecticut.

Rinpoche, Sogyal. 1993. *The Tibetan Book of Living and Dying*. San Francisco: HarperSanFrancisco.

Roberts, Jane. 1975. *Adventures in Consciousness: An Introduction to Aspect Psychology.* Englewood Cliffs, N.J.: Prentice-Hall.

Sabom, Michael B. 1982. *Recollections of Death: A Medical Investigation.* New York: Harper & Row.

Sagan, Carl, ed. 1973. *Communication with Extraterrestrial Intelligence (CETI).* Cambridge, Mass.: MIT Press.

Saltmarsh, Herbert Francis. 1938. *Evidence of Personal Survival from Cross Correspondences.* New York: Bell and Sons.

Sancier, K. M. 1991. "Medical Applications of Qigong and Emitted Qi on Humans, Animals, Cell Cultures, and Plants: Review of Selected Scientific Research." *American Journal of Acupuncture* 19:367–77.

Schmidt, Helmut. 1976. "PK Effect on Prerecorded Targets." *Journal of the American Society of Psychical Research* 70:267–91.

———. 1993. "Observation of a Psychokinetic Effect under Highly Controlled Conditions." *Journal of Parapsychology* 57:351–72.

Searle, John R. 1987. "Minds and Brains without Programs." In *Mind Waves*, edited by C. Blackmore and S. Greenfield. Oxford: Basil Blackwell.

———. 1992. *The Rediscovery of the Mind.* Cambridge, Mass.: MIT Press.

Seymour, C. R. F. 1990. "The Old Gods." In *Angels and Mortals*, edited by Maria Parisen. Wheaton, Ill.: Quest.

Sheldrake, Rupert. 1981. *A New Science of Life: The Hypothesis of Formative Causation.* Los Angeles: J. P. Tarcher.

Smith, Norman Kemp, trans. 1958. *Descartes Philosophical Writings.* New York: Modern Library

Sperry, Roger. 1983. *Science and Moral Priority: Merging Mind, Brain, and Human Values.* New York: Columbia University Press.

Stapp, Henry P. 1982. "Mind, Matter, and Quantum Mechanics." *Foundations of Physics* 12:363–98.

———. 1993. *Mind, Matter, and Quantum Mechanics.* New York: Springer-Verlag.

————. 1996. *A Report on the Gaudiya Vaishnave Vedanta*. San Francisco: Bhaktivedanta Institute.

Stevenson, Ian. 1961. "The Evidence for Survival from Claimed Memories of Former Reincarnations." The winning essay of the context in honor of William James. Privately published.

————. 1974. *Twenty Cases Suggestive of Reincarnation*. Charlottesville: University Press of Virginia.

————. 1977. "Research into the Evidence of Man's Survival after Death." *Journal of Nervous and Mental Disease* 165:153–83.

————. 1987. *Children Who Remember Previous Lives: A Question of Reincarnation*. Charlottesville: University Press of Virginia.

Strieber, Whitley. 1988. *Communion: A True Story*. New York: Avon.

Stuart, C. I. J. M., Y. Takahashy, and M. Umezwa. 1978. "Mixed System Brain Dynamics." *Foundations of Physics* 9:301–29.

Sugrue, Thomas. 1961. *There Is a River: The Story of Edgar Cayce*. New York: Dell.

Tart, Charles T. 1990. "Who Survives? Implications of Modern Consciousness Research." In *What Survives?* edited by Gary Doore. Los Angeles: J. P. Tarcher.

Teilhard de Chardin, Pierre. 1964. *The Future of Man*. Translated from the French by Norman Denny. New York: Harper & Row.

Tipler, Frank J. 1994. *The Physics of Immortality: Modern Cosmology, God, and the Resurrection of the Dead*. New York: Doubleday.

Varela, Francisco J., Evan Thompson, and Eleanor Rosch. 1991. *The Embodied Mind: Cognitive Science and Human Experience*. Cambridge, Mass.: MIT Press.

Viney, Geoff. 1993. *Surviving Death*. New York: St. Martin's Press.

Walker, E. H. 1970. "The Nature of Consciousness." *Mathematical Biosciences* 7:131–78.

Wambach, Helen. 1978. *Reliving Past Lives: The Evidence Under Hypnosis*. New York: Harper & Row.

———. 1979. *Life before Life*. New York: Bantam.

Watts, Alan W. 1962. *The Joyous Cosmology*. New York: Pantheon Books.

Wheeler, John A. 1983. "Law without Law." In *Quantum Theory and Measurement*, edited by J. Wheeler and W. Zurek. Princeton, N.J.: Princeton University Press.

Whitman, Walt. 1969. *Leaves of Grass*. New York: Arco Press Co.

Wickramsekera. I., S. Krippner, J. Wickramsekera, and I. Wickramsekera, II. 1997. On the Psychophysiology of Ramtha's School of Enlightenment. Preprint.

Wilber, Ken. 1980. *The Atman Project: A Transpersonal View of Human Development*. Wheaton, Ill.: Theosophical Publishing House.

———. 1981. *Up from Eden: A Transpersonal View of Human Evolution*. Garden City, N.Y.: Anchor Press/Doubleday.

———. 1990. "Death, Rebirth, and Meditation." In *What Survives?* edited by Gary Doore. Los Angeles: J. P. Tarcher.

———. 1993. "The Great Chain of Being." *Journal of Humanistic Psychology* 33:52–55.

Wolf, Fred Alan. 1984. *Star Wave: Mind, Consciousness, and Quantum Physics*. New York: Macmillan.

———. 1986. *The Body Quantum: The New Physics of Body, Mind, and Health*. New York: Macmillan.

Woolger, Roger. 1988. *Other Lives, Other Selves*. New York: Doubleday.

Young, Arthur M. 1976. *The Reflexive Universe: Evolution of Consciousness*. New York: Delacorte Press.

INDEX

ABOUT THE AUTHOR

Amit Goswami, Ph.D., is a teacher, lecturer, researcher, and the resident quantum physicist at the Institute of Noetic Sciences. His father was a Hindu guru in India, and in his work Dr. Goswami brings knowledge of mystical traditions together with his love for scientific exploration. He is the author of numerous books including *The Visionary Window* (Quest Books, 2000), *Quantum Mechanics* (McGraw-Hill, 1996), and *The Self-Aware Universe* (J. P. Tarcher, 1995). He lives in Eugene, Oregon.

Hampton Roads Publishing Company

... for the evolving human spirit

Hampton Roads Publishing Company
publishes books on a variety of subjects,
including metaphysics, health, integrative medicine,
visionary fiction, and other related topics.

For a copy of our latest catalog, call toll-free
(800) 766-8009, or send your name and address to:

Hampton Roads Publishing Company, Inc.
1125 Stoney Ridge Road
Charlottesville, VA 22902

e-mail: hrpc@hrpub.com
www.hrpub.com